D1547332

Bourgeois consumption

Manchester University Press

Bourgeois consumption

Food, space and identity in London and Paris, 1850–1914

Rachel Rich

Manchester University Press

Manchester and New York

distributed in the United States exclusively

by Palgrave Macmillan

Published by Manchester University Press
Oxford Road, Manchester M13 9NR, UK
and Room 400, 175 Fifth Avenue, New York, NY 10010, USA
www.manchesteruniversitypress.co.uk

Distributed in the United States exclusively by
Palgrave Macmillan, 175 Fifth Avenue, New York,
NY 10010, USA

Distributed in Canada exclusively by
UBC Press, University of British Columbia, 2029 West Mall,
Vancouver, BC, Canada V6T 1Z2

British Library Cataloguing-in-Publication Data
A catalogue record for this book is available from the British Library

Library of Congress Cataloging-in-Publication Data applied for

ISBN   978 0 7190 8112 5   hardback

First published 2011

Typeset 10/12pt Plantin
by Graphicraft Limited, Hong Kong
Printed in Great Britain
by the MPG Books Group, UK

Contents

List of figures and tables   vii

Acknowledgements   viii

Abbreviations   ix

Introduction   1

1   Eating by the rules: prescriptive literature and the dissemination of knowledge   24

2   Family dinners: timekeeping, privacy and women's knowledge   61

3   Dinner parties: ideal versus experience   96

4   Respectable restaurants and the commercialisation of dinner   135

5   Members and subscribers only: clubs and banquets   172

Conclusion   207

Bibliography   214

Index   235

List of figures and tables

Figures

1 Siège de Paris (1870–71). Menu de Noël 1870.
Crédit photographique © Roger-Viollet.   5
2 Allenbury's Food, 1904. Courtesy of The History of
Advertising Trust Archive.   42
3 'Many Happy Returns of the Day', 1856 by Frith,
William Powell (1819–1909). Harrogate Museums and
Arts, North Yorkshire, UK © Harrogate Museums and
Arts/The Bridgeman Art Library.   65
4 'Diner de famille Roger'. Octobre 1898. Crédit
photographique © Roger-Viollet.   66
5 Affaire Dreyfus. 'Un dîner en famille' (1899),
par Caran d'Ache (1858–1909). RV-937899.
Crédit photographique © Roger-Viollet.   110
6 Queen's Hotel, Leicester Square, 1890. Courtesy of
City of London, London Metropolitan Archives.   140
7 Queen's Hotel, Leicester Square, 1890. Courtesy of
City of London, London, Metropolitan Archives.   141
8 Les serveuses d'un 'Bouillon Duval', restaurant
économique ouvert à Paris par le boucher Duval
(1811–70). Gravure d'après Norbert Goeneutte (1891).
BNF, collection Blondel. Crédit photographique
© Roger-Viollet.   153

Tables

1 Numbers of restaurants in London.   146
2 Numbers of restaurants in Paris.   146

Acknowledgements

This book has been the outcome of many years of work, through which I have been very fortunate in receiving advice and support from a number of people. I would like to thank Erika Rappaport and Anna Davin for their advice on London archives, and Natasha Cocquerie, Lisa Tiersten and Marie Chessel for helping me navigate researching in Paris and for pointing me in directions I had not considered. Many thanks must go to Leonore Davidoff, Pam Cox, Simon Gunn, Rebecca Spang, and Brenda Assael for their insights on the subject matter and all their helpful comments. Many people have been very generous in reading and commenting on draft chapters and I would like to thank them all for their time and help: Lisa Smith, Leif Jerram, Johanna Helgadottir, Kara Colton, Sylvia Rich, and Ethel Saltzman. Above all else, I want to thank Geoffrey Crossick who has been an amazing supervisor, mentor and friend and has always come up with the ideas and advice I have needed. Though all these people have made invaluable contributions, all the shortcomings are entirely my own.

I owe great thanks to the various bodies who have helped fund this research: the Social Science and Humanities Research Council of Canada, the *Fonds pour la Formation de Chercheurs et l'Aide à la Recherche du Québec*, the Royal Historical Society, the Overseas Research Student Award and the University of Essex, for both the University Studentship and the Sir Eric Berthaud Travel Grant. I also want to extend my thanks to the various librarians and archivists who have helped me find my way through their amazing collections.

My family have been generous beyond what anyone should expect, and have always believed in me, even though I have not always believed in myself. This book is lovingly dedicated to Graeme and Henry, who make life exciting and who make me laugh every single day.

Abbreviations

AN	Archives Nationales de France
A de P	Archives de Paris
BHVP	Bibliotèque Historique de la Ville de Paris
BN	Bibliotèque Nationale de France
CLRO	Corporation of London Record Office
LMA	London Metropolitan Archive
BL	British Library

Introduction

The Ritz Hotel, in Paris's Place Vendome, opened its doors on 5 June 1898. It was a joint venture of Cesar Ritz and his head chef Auguste Escoffier, who had worked together since 1884. The renowned pair had worked in several countries, but their work at London's elegant Savoy Hotel was the source of their fame. Their style of hotel and restaurant management was part of a broader trend which saw London, Paris and other Western cities develop an eating out culture that was detached from local tradition and became part of a shared, transnational bourgeois way of life. Cesar Ritz was elegant, energetic and ambitious. He understood the hotel business, and knew how to attract the cream of European society.[1] At his side was Auguste Escoffier, the most celebrated of celebrity chefs, credited with creating the French haute cuisine of his age. He too understood the needs of his elegant clientele, and no detail was too small to receive his personal attention. While Ritz was flamboyant and fast paced, Escoffier was calm, diligent and, by appearance, not what one would have expected of a celebrity chef.[2] Together they personified the competing tendencies of their day: the bourgeoisies of Europe were torn between tendencies of moderation and gluttony, towards economy and conspicuous consumption, towards conservatism and radicalism.

From 1850 to the end of the century, restaurants in London and Paris diversified and played an ever growing part in shaping both eating habits and leisure pursuits. Escoffier's and Ritz's ventures were at the top of an industry that encompassed working-class cafés in Paris, businessmen's lunch rooms in London and everything in between. And everyone, it seemed, had an opinion on restaurants, which represented the movement of the private act of eating into the public sphere. This was a central feature of what David Harvey has described as the 'the culture of governance and pacification by spectacle'.[3] Restaurants might appear to some a wonderful innovation, a way to enjoy new tastes and sights, and to buy the privilege of being waited on hand and foot, which were formerly the preserve of the aristocracy, or the very rich. Yet for others, the possibility that almost everyone could afford to eat out seemed to threaten the very fabric of society. Perhaps it was hypocrisy on the part of two brothers known to dine regularly in the best restaurants of Paris, but in the Goncourts' diary in 1860, Edmond wrote: 'I can see women, children, whole families in the café. The home is dying. Life is threatening to become public. The club for the upper classes, the café for the lower – this is what society and common people are coming to.'[4]

The Goncourts' anxiety may have led them to exaggerate the extent to which people were eating out, but it was the most visible, and the most public, change to eating habits in the second half of the nineteenth century. This commercialisation of mealtimes was part of a wider trend both of the commercialisation of leisure, and the transformation of shopping into a leisure activity. In *Au Bonheur de Dames*, Emile Zola's department store owner Octave Mouret's capitalism triumphed over women's senses and decency.[5] The new way of stimulating desire exemplified by Mouret was met with mixed emotions, and liberals and conservatives united in their fear of the corrupting effects of rampant consumerism on formerly respectable women. The Ritz-Escoffier partnership created very successful restaurants in both London and Paris, which all followed the same principles: luxury, elegance, attention to detail and all the modern conveniences that money could buy. The food they served was French, but the appeal was international; and what worked in Paris worked equally well in London. Partly this was due to the super-rich, international clientele they brought together. But more than this, the Ritz group drew on decades of development in the catering trade and changes in how respectable people dined.

This book looks at a four key locations – the home, restaurants, clubs and banquets – where middle-class people cooked, ate and socialised. These four were not the only places where people ate: notable omissions include schools, the outdoors, boats and trains. But the sites looked at here allow us to observe the middle classes in a range of environments to which many people had access and which expose the changes, continuities and tensions that shaped

eating and manners in this period. As well as locations, the book considers the various discourses surrounding these activities, arguing
that imagined meals are as revealing as actual meals to our understanding of the ways in which food shaped the experience and
identity of the wide range of people who can be considered as
forming the bourgeoisie. Obviously, people need to eat to survive,
but the conventions of how and what people have eaten have
changed over time. In particular, from 1850 to 1914, changes
occurred in the availability of meals in public venues, of which the
Ritz is only one small example. By accepting that eating could form
a leisure activity in the increasingly commercialised public sphere,
middle-class diners were making a statement about themselves, their
bodies and their wealth. Change also occurred in private meals, once
the responsibility of men, but increasingly taken over by women as
the domestic sphere became feminised. But change is not the only
subject of this book, which also looks into the private lives of the
well off and the more modest middle classes, to find that at home,
meals represented stability and continuity, a time for families and
communities to come together and hold on to something familiar
in a period of rapid social change.

Periodisation in the history of food and eating is difficult to pin
down. Changes in the way people eat are influenced by historical
events, but cannot generally be neatly mapped onto the standard
accepted periods of history. Diets may change slowly, but cata-
clysmic events such as the Franco-Prussian war and the siege of
Paris also had both short and long-term effects on eating habits.
In a period of both continuity and change in eating habits, Paris
experienced a dramatic transition during the winter of 1870–71.
During the five-month siege of Paris, its rich and poor inhabitants
learned to acquire new tastes, as everything from the animals in the
zoo to the rodents in the streets became possible bases for new
recipes. The daily newspaper *L'Illustration* carried on publishing
during the siege, keeping Parisians updated on general matters
as well as on the local food situation. The newspaper maintained
a lively and humorous tone when reporting on matters such as
rising food prices, the imposition of a 10 o'clock closing time for all
cafés, and eventually the introduction of rationing. While the newspaper made its contribution to the upkeep of morale, shortages,
particularly of meat, led first to horsemeat and then to other animals'
flesh being introduced into the Parisian diet. On 15 October,

donkey was reported to have been added, as horse meat was in very short supply.[6] On 22 October, one writer claimed that 'we still have abundance, just not in all things', going on to explain that food was being replaced by lively and animated discussion.[7]

Both Escoffier and Ritz were already working in the catering trade in the 1870s. Ritz worked in Paris, at the Restaurant Voisin, cooking the animals from the zoo, including ragout of elephant trunk sauce chasseur. Meanwhile, Escoffier was drafted to Metz on 25 August 1870, where he served as *chef de cuisine* to the second section of the General Staff. Later, during the ten-week siege of Metz, he cooked from a secret stock of live animals he had had the foresight to amass, and only later had recourse to horse meat, which he made palatable by blanching it before cooking. Ritz and Escoffier, along with the rest of the French population, were willing to lower their standards in response to shortages, but only to the extent of including lower quality foods. What they would not stoop to, though, was dropping the ideals of haute cuisine that was so central to both French cuisine and French identity. Thus menus continued to appear in the traditional style, such as this one (figure 1) from Christmas 1870, in which standard French dishes are listed with alternative ingredients. Hors d'oevres included stuffed donkey's head, which was followed by elephant consommé and main courses including roast camel, cats with rats and antelope terrine.

Of longer-term and greater significance to changes in eating habits was industrialisation. The Industrial Revolution enabled food to be transported more quickly (across greater distances) and the possibility of preserving food by refrigeration. Taken together, these meant that greater numbers of people could make a choice about what to eat, and season and region were largely taken out of dietary consideration. According to food historian Jean-Paul Aron, whose work echoes that of historians such as Carolyn Merchant who argue that the modern, bourgeois drive has been towards the domination of man over nature, the ambivalence of the French towards nature, which they feared but where fascinated by, explains their delight in 'technical discoveries which can modify the calendar and override the rhythm of nature'.[8] Linked to the impact of industrialisation was the effect of modernity, in speeding up the pace at which people experienced their lives, and therefore introducing the continual desire for novelty. This is most clearly highlighted in discussions about food, which took place around the time of the

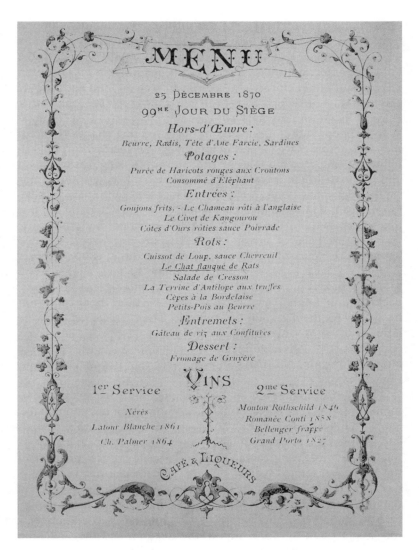

Figure 1 Siège de Paris (1870–71). Menu de Noël 1870.

Great Exhibition of 1851, and the subsequent exhibitions hosted by London and Paris. These prompted commentators to discuss ways of speeding up and modernising meal service as well as the influence of foreign foods. These discussions suggest links between a European eating culture and recent research on food and Empire and the ways in which European felt they were imbibing other cultures by consuming their cuisines.[9]

In London, author Ursula Bloom believed that changes in commercial catering played a part in improving the standards of English home cooking. She felt that, in 1900, home cooking was less good and less varied than it would later become, and she attributed this to 'American magazines, better restaurants with continental cuisine, more travel, and all that sort of thing'.[10] But in France in the late nineteenth century, there were those who worried that modernity, and the fast pace of urban life, was destroying people's eating habits. As a kind of mission statement in June 1890, culinary journal *La Salle à Manger* stated that life had so altered as to require a new code, or set of rules. To men they declared: 'Come back to your homes, give yourselves a few more hours for your meals and for the digestion that follows.' Their female readers were accused of murdering their delicate flesh in the pursuit of beauty, and enjoined to 'give more care to your dining rooms, pay more attention to your menus and, between each new novel, reread your cookery books'.[11]

The comparative study of London and Paris has a long tradition. From Dickens's *Tale of Two Cities* onward, it has come to feel almost natural to link these two great nineteenth-century capitals and see their histories as somehow intertwined. Political historians might point to their geographical position at the western end of the European range of great powers, while social historians look to their economic might, the rise of industry and the emergence of the middle and working classes, whose conflictual relations can be seen to characterise this period. Those interested in cultural history might point to modernity, to the freedom and the alienation experienced in equal parts by the urban dwellers of the two cities. Books about each city tend to draw comparisons with the other in order to make sense of key developments such as population growth, political ideologies, urban sprawl and fashion. For a historian of food and eating, these reasons and more inform the choice of comparison, as on each side of the Channel commentators compared their own cuisine to that of their neighbour, often characterised as a rival. As Amy Trubek has argued, France was, and is, the capital of haute cuisine.[12] Like Stephen Mennell before her, she sees Britain as the obvious choice of country to compare with France. While Mennell looks at the differences in culinary tradition in terms of taste rather than 'better' and 'worse' food, Trubek uses the example of Britain to show that French haute cuisine became *the* cuisine of the international bourgeoisie and elite, particularly when it came to public and commercial dining.

This book is not so concerned with comparing the actual cuisines of Paris and London as with comparing the eating habits. For this reason, Paris and London are situated as capitals of consumption, rather than as locations for particular culinary traditions. Particularly in their public guises in restaurants, clubs and banquets, the meals of Paris and London can be seen as part of a broader culture of the consumption of goods and leisure. There is a historical geography to this commercial sphere, which can help us to situate the middle classes and their movements. In Paris, fashionable consumers wanted to be seen on the Champs-Elysées and the grand boulevards, as well as in the Bois de Boulogne. The grandest restaurants were on the Champs-Elysées, among them the famous Tortoni. The parks and gardens on the outskirts of Paris were used for public eating of a different kind, in the picnics taking place on summer weekends. In London, the West End was where fashionable shopping and eating took place, and also where the most elite clubs were located, along St James's and Pall Mall. The almost continual rise in the number of restaurants throughout this period represented the spread of public eating away from centres of consumerism and into residential neighbourhoods, perhaps signalling the fact that restaurant dining was becoming more 'normal' and quotidian, and not much different from eating in or hosting a dinner party.

Through its common attitudes and practices, the bourgeoisie was clearly a transnational class. They read, consumed and travelled extensively enough as a class to be aware of what was going on in other areas. Their aspirations, too, made them look beyond parochial identifications and towards 'good taste' from wherever it might come. Londoners looked to Paris for trends in food and fashion. To Parisians, Londoners could appear the arbiters of good taste in domestic arrangements, and the British Royal family were role models for many fashionable Parisians. London and Paris were the largest cities in the world in this period, and continued to grow through the nineteenth century.

Drawing on J. T. Coppock's figures, Geoffrey Best suggests that from 1841 to 1881 Inner London's population rose from 1,949,000 to 3,830,000 representing 14.1 per cent and 18.4 per cent, respectively, of the total population of England and Wales.[13] According to B. R. Mitchell, London's population in 1851 was 2,685,000, rising to 7,256,000 by 1911, while the population of England and Wales went from 17,928,000 to 36,070,000. Patrice Higgonet argues that, demographically, London and Paris were 'likewise at once alike and different', with roughly the same population size (400,000–450,000) in 1700, but with London's commercial and industrial growth causing it to outstrip Paris in the course of the eighteenth century.[14] According to B. R. Mitchell, Paris's population rose from 1,053,000 in 1851 to 2,888,000 in 1911, while the population of France as a whole increased from 35,783,000 to 39,192,000.[15] Though Paris may have been smaller than London, it is clear from these figures that each city enjoyed steady growth through the period, and also that each, because of the proportion of the population it contained, could dominate the country of which it was capital in cultural as well as in political and economic terms.

Historians of nineteenth-century Paris have, like David Harvey, looked at urbanisation and at the alterations to the landscape imposed by Napoleon III and his Prefect, the Baron Hausmann. Harvey argues that Paris was 'a capital city being shaped by bourgeois power into a city of capital'.[16] Taking Harvey's lead, we can see Paris as a template for some of the worse ways in which modernity and capitalism have been imposed on human interactions, in particular, by implementing structures to facilitate mutual surveillance and prioritising the flow of commercial goods over and above human interaction. Yet, following Higgonnet, we can be tempted to look at Paris in a more poetic light, as the capital of the world because of the variety of artistic and spectacular events which shaped the world view of inhabitants and visitors alike.[17] Food historians like Jean-Paul Aron, Rebecca Spang and Amy Trubek follow the tone set by contemporary culinary writers when they argue for the centrality of cuisine in the cultural history of Paris and Parisians.

London's history has been written about in different ways to that of Paris, partly, perhaps, because while Paris struggled with the aftermath of the Revolution of 1789 and endured (or enjoyed) subsequent revolutionary upheavals through the century, London enjoyed greater stability and prosperity. London's position as capital of the world's most powerful empire also influenced its history, and this had an influence on shaping both diet and identity in the British capital. Where food and eating have been written about extensively in relation to the French capital, cultural historians of Britain have been fewer, perhaps because, as Stephen Mennell argues, unlike France, Britain did not develop its own tradition of haute cuisine – an argument taken up by Amy Trubek, who uses the British example to argue for the global influence of French food and language in elite cuisine.

Mennell and Trubek each compare, in different ways, French and English cuisine.[18] Higgonet argues that it is nearly impossible to discuss Paris in the nineteenth century without offering some comparison with London, arguing that 'the modernization of the two capital cities often involved a kind of simbiosis'.[19] And this simbiosis, brought about, Higgonet continues, by inhabitants of each city looking to the other for ideas of urban planning, in good and bad ways, is also very evident in their cultural practices, such as the ways in which they organised and consumed meals, which forms the subject of this book. Yet most historians have been reluctant to use comparison, sticking closely to national paradigms and assuming, sometimes without any basis, that each national experience is unique and particular.

Much has and can be made of the different foods eaten in London and Paris. There are, of course, many clear differences in the cuisine of the French and the English, such as the emphasis on sauces versus condiments, or of complex recipes versus joints of roasted meat. And people care deeply about the foods which are familiar to them, and can attach their distrust of strangers to disgust at what those strangers eat. Paris has always been held up as the culinary capital of Europe. Both within and without its borders, historians have emphasised the importance of gastronomy in French culture and identity. Within Paris, gastronomy was a much written about topic but though food was of central importance to French national identity, commentators often remarked on declining standards. It was when comparing Paris, and France, to the rest of the world that the French found most to say in favour of their own cuisine. Similarly, in England there was a good deal of ambivalence, with

French generally being the language of haute cuisine, and much criticism then, as now, of the plainness of English food. Yet it was this very plainness which was often exulted as its principal virtue, being taken by some to stand for the straightforwardness and honesty of the English national character. It is all the more surprising, then, that in setting out to contrast lacklustre English cuisine as a result of English indifference to matters of the table, with French gastronomic genius emanating from a culture that places food and eating at the forefront of everyday life, what has resulted is a book which argues that when it came to eating habits, there were more similarities than differences in the Parisian and London middle classes.

The emergence and ascendance of the bourgeoisie in Europe has formed the subject of several studies.[20] The cliché of the 'rise' of the middle class has been replaced by a greater understanding of its long-term origins and the historical factors which brought this class to the powerful position it held during the nineteenth century.[21] While historians continue to argue about the timescale of this development, they have seen it as marking the emergence of new ways of feeling: privacy, childhood and affectionate families are associated with bourgeois values and morality.[22] Historians of gender have looked to the bourgeoisie as evolving new definitions of masculinity and femininity, as well as new divisions between the sexes based on the separation of home and public life.[23] Davidoff and Hall's influential argument that middle-class women were increasingly relegated to the domestic sphere while men inhabited the public sphere of work and politics has more recently been critiqued and revised. Both the domestic lives of women in the eighteenth century, and the role of nineteenth-century middle-class women in public life have called into question the separate sphere theory, but gender continues to be an essential analytic category for our understanding of bourgeois culture.[24] In this book, I argue that gender is one of the axes that shapes ideas about behaviour and eating habits. In particular, men and women are shown to have been encouraged to enjoy different types of food, and to take different attitudes towards their appetites and bodies. As with sexual appetites, the desire for food and drink was acceptable in men, but could elicit anxious and critical responses when exhibited by women.

As historians have moved beyond determining who comprised the bourgeoisie and how their lives were organised, other aspects of bourgeois life have come under scrutiny. Of particular relevance is research on consumption and how material life shaped bourgeois identity.[25] Work on leisure has increasingly revealed that the bourgeoisie was constituted as much through the performance of identity in the public sphere as through its relation to the means of production.[26] Similarly, research on clothing and fashion has expanded our understanding of the extent to which identity was performed through its physical representation.[27] Michel de Certeau's assertion that consumers are also producers, as meaning is created through choices about how to use spaces and objects veer away from the original intentions of producers, is borne out by findings about how clothes are worn, homes furnished and city streets inhabited. Finally, research on etiquette and manners has increasingly shown that how people think they should behave is an indication of their moral standards, their ideology and their shared aspirations.[28] This book builds on several of these strands of research, by placing eating in the context of public and private divisions, material culture, and manners and the performance of identity.

Exactly who can be defined as part of the bourgeoisie, and where the boundaries of a class can be drawn, is an issue which is much debated but is unlikely ever to be resolved. Occupation, wealth and the ability of a man to maintain his wife and children at leisure are all defining characteristics of the bourgeoisie, as is participation in a shared culture of respectability. Jurgen Kocka argues that in spite of the difficulty of defining the bourgeoisie in nineteenth-century Europe, there is enough evidence of common values and cultural practices to make the bourgeoisie a meaningful category of analysis. He notes the different terminologies used in France (*bourgeoisie*) and Britain (middle class), but argues that the two terms are used in ways that suggest similarities as well as differences. While the English refer to the middle social strata in the term 'middle class' the French term '*bourgeoisie*' refers to the urban origins of this population. More significantly, it must be noted that 'middle class' was often used as a term of approbation in England, taking into consideration this class's perceived sobriety, work-ethic and moderation in personal habits. In contrast, in French 'bourgeois' was often used as a term of derision, as was the case in Molière's play *Le Bourgeois Gentilhomme* of 1670. Yet Adeline Daumard argues that the huge part played by the bourgeoise in France over the past two centuries make the history of this class central to the history of French identity. And in spite of the ambivalence felt about the term 'bourgeois' as applied to French people, Alexis de Tocqueville argued that France in the nineteenth century was a bourgeois nation, as opposed to England, which, he argued, had an aristocratic spirit and also as opposed to the society of orders which persisted in Prussia.[29]

This book works with a broad definition in order to analyse the cultural experience of being bourgeois, and to include in the study people who were solidly part of the bourgeoisie, people who aspired to become part of it but could only afford to participate in its cultural practices to a limited extent, and finally those who could belong, but balked at the perceived mediocrity of being bourgeois.[30] Though broad, this grouping of people is not arbitrary. The range of people who appear in this study, either indirectly as consumers of various literatures and experiences, or directly through their diaries, memoirs and letters, all have in common the ability to make choices about what to eat. This is, for many culinary historians, what distinguishes the middle from the working class. Michel de Certeau argues that poor people have no cuisine and it is therefore only possible to study the history of a cuisine where there are choices being made.[31] This, I believe, is an overstatement. However, there is a greater connection between eating and identity where a wider range of options are possible, as the choices made are more relevant and based on a wider range of options. For the working classes, necessity determined food consumption, with choice operating on a very limited basis. In contrast, the bourgeoisie could afford, to greater and lesser degrees, to choose what to eat and how to participate in the culture of the mealtime sociability which surrounded them, and it is the motivations for these choices that are the subject of this study.

By the second half of the nineteenth century, bourgeois culture was dominant in the cities of western Europe.[32] Their influence on the economy and politics was widely felt, though there was no uniform response to the desire to emulate aristocratic practices, including the choice to transform commercial or industrial wealth into landed estates. Though broadly defined, the bourgeoisie which forms the subject of this book participated in a variety of shared cultural practices. As Leora Auslander has argued, a class can be defined by its shared knowledge and taste.[33] The prescriptive literature popular in this period provided those who wanted it with a shared body of knowledge on how to behave and how to demonstrate their good taste. The Victorians have been identified as prudish, as well as obsessed with timekeeping and order. While frugality was an ideological cornerstone of the middle classes, conspicuous consumption was the order of the day, as has been exposed in work on consumption and the rise of the department store.[34] The tensions between ideals and practices among bourgeois men and women can be characterised as the struggle between gluttony and moderation. In their eating habits, the bourgeoisie lived out these opposing tensions, which at their most extreme could be seen through the emergence of an obsession with digestive disorders, and the discovery of anorexia nervosa.[35] The eating habits of the bourgeoisie are, therefore, a useful path for discovering the tensions around which bourgeois identity and experience were continually renegotiated.

Knowing how people ate provides the historian with a window into their society and into their private lives. Historians of food have looked at particular products, or the introduction of new ingredients, recipes or objects (forks, teacups) in order to uncover changes in what people ate. Yet anthropologists have known for much longer that what is central to a culture is not so much *what* is eaten as *by whom*.[36] Cultures are organised around sets of morals, regulations about how bodies must be restrained and rules about hierarchy, and by whom, how and when spaces can be inhabited. In the rules and taboos a culture creates, and then transgresses, food and eating always play a large part. Sociologists, and more recently historians, have taken notice of the importance of food and its associated rituals.[37] From the politics of hunger[38] and food riots[39] to the part of luxury food items in creating global markets, food has come to play a key role in many historical enquiries.[40]

But histories of food can be frustrating for historians of society and culture, since they do not generally succeed in explaining why food – ingredients, recipes, ways of cooking – are relevant to an understanding of how people experienced life in the past. Books such as M. Toussaint-Samat's *History of Food* promise to cover such a vast subject area that they are bound to disappoint. Sections such as 'The symbolism of the apple' are general and superficial, and add little to our understanding of the way that human society interacts with food and eating.[41] Knowing that a certain ingredient or recipe reached England at a specific date does not expand our understanding of English history.

Where historians of food have moved beyond studying ingredients they have done so in several ways. Demographic historians have quantified the impact of food availability on whole populations.[42] When class and wealth have been taken into account, these studies have enhanced our understanding of the importance of nutrition in social change.[43] But the cultural significance of specific foods, and the link between food and its eaters, is largely ignored. The link between food and identity is made by cultural historians[44] in works ranging from micro-histories of specific regions,[45] social groups or families and the choices they make about what to eat, to thematic studies of the use of food in film, art or literature.[46] Cultural historians have linked food to religious or moral systems, arguing that what and how people ate can be understood as a physical reflection of their broader system of beliefs. It has, however, proved easier to make general observations about the connection between beliefs, symbolism and food, than to find evidence of behaviour and experience on a smaller scale, to illustrate how these connections operate.[47] Equally difficult to pin down in studies of food and diet has been the bodies of the eaters, yet it is impossible to ignore that food and eating is integrally linked with bodies and corporeal experience,[48] and various studies of medieval fasting girls and modern anorexics have made the link between diet, self-control and the body.[49] Important work has also been done in the social history of medicine on diet, nutrition and experiences of healthy and sick bodies.[50]

This book moves away from food history, concentrating instead on the history of eaters and eating, focusing on a particular social group, the bourgeoisie, in order to understand class in terms of shared cultural practices and norms.[51] Food and eating are central to this research, yet at the same time, are simply a means of entering the debate about how culture and identity interact, and how the bourgeoisie was constituted through its daily practices. By extending the study of the history of food to include the history of eating, it becomes possible to analyse the wider significance of food and its role in cultural history. In line with the recent growth of the field of consumption history, this study aims to integrate food and eating into an analysis of the growth of consumption, commercialisation and a public sphere of leisure. Food is considered as an aspect of material culture. Choices about what to eat are considered as markers of taste and distinction, as well as being analysed through the categories of class and gender. Menus and recipes are useful sources in a variety of ways: they offer the opportunity to compare the costs and complexity of foods served by different people and on different occasions; they allow an analysis of the amount of resources and effort considered necessary to expend on different meals; they reveal cultural assumptions and priorities through a hierarchy of different foods and dishes; and they offer the possibility of drawing comparisons between the role of food in Paris and London. Looking at the behaviours surrounding food consumption, this research reveals ways in which the most mundane activities are actually a daily reflection of culture. Eating habits change slowly, and this study reveals that continuity can be more important than change when analysing eating habits. Through a cultural analysis of eating, it is possible to see how ideas about men and women, about politeness and distinction and about taste and the display of cultural knowledge were slow to change in a period of rapid social change.

This book argues that eating is a complex activity shaped by social and cultural factors as much as by physical ones. It is structured around the distinction between the ideal and the real which can be found by comparing prescriptive sources, such as etiquette and medical advice books, with first-hand accounts such as diaries and letters. Prescriptive literature is interpreted as a set of ideological discourses, taken here to be the set of values and mores and regulations articulated in advice books, and which form an overall impression of what it meant to be part of the middle class as a culturally defined category. By contrasting practice with ideology, I argue that we can gain a clearer understanding both of how ideology was incorporated into daily experience, but also how is was used as a starting point for creating more individual sets of practices found within specific social networks and specific locations and situations. Prescriptive texts of all sorts and first-hand accounts form the bulk of the sources for this research, but this study also looks at the periodic press, architectural plans and drawings, French after-death inventories, club archives and the archives of civic banquets held in London and Paris and a range of newspapers in order to gain a broader understanding of how food was situated, discussed, chosen and eaten in a range of everyday situations and special occasions.

The chapters in this book highlight a series of locations in which food was consumed, in order to argue that an overall bourgeois approach to eating can be subdivided into specific sets of behaviour linked to time and space. The first chapter sets out a series of idealised visions of bourgeois meals as found in the pages of advice literature. From etiquette manuals to cook books, to advice on medicine and architecture, the reading public could absorb ideologically prescriptive rules on how to behave and what to consume. Chapter 2 moves inside the bourgeois home, in order to begin to explore how the lived experience of family life compares to the ideals of advice-giving 'experts'. Much of what took place within the home was punctuated by the daily schedule of meals, and the corresponding buying and preparing of food. Through this daily work, carried out by women and their servants, bonds were forged between family members, and between a family and its community. The imagined good behaviour of Chapter 1 contrasts with the complex reality of housework and sociability in Chapter 2.

Chapters 3 to 5 highlight a series of locations in which sociable meals took place. These range from the domestic dinner party, to the restaurants, clubs and public and private banquets. In looking at the domestic dinner party, the rules of etiquette are once again examined in order to argue that dinner parties were central to middle-class experience on both the imagined and the experienced planes. The first was a world in which the bourgeoisie could aspire to emulate aristocratic forms of sociability: graceful manners, full staffs of servants, and fashionable and exquisite food. The second was daily life, which placed a great premium on mealtime sociability and in which people showed themselves willing to take a flexible attitude towards timekeeping, formality and even the appearance of unexpected guests. It is around the tensions between the ideal and the real that individual members of the middle class forged their self-image and public reputation.

Chapters 4 and 5, in which public meals in restaurants, clubs and at banquets form the subject, the analysis turns towards looking at the impact of urbanisation, modernisation and the commercialisation of leisure on middle-class mores and manners. The main difference between restaurants on the one hand and clubs and banquets on the other lay in the issue of who could attend. In the first, it was anyone who could afford the bill, while in other two there were rules and rituals surrounding membership which made them exclusive in more complex ways. In both cases, taking eating out of the home created new challenges to respectability and to the ordering of class and gender, and allowed women to extend their access to commercial spaces, while – more surprisingly – forcing men to become more knowledgeable about food preparation and presentation.

By analysing the various ways that food was written about, in both prescriptive and descriptive sources, I will argue that eating was a central element in the construction of both class and gender identities. These identities were never fixed, but were instead continually negotiated and interpreted in a range of locations and situations which shaped and punctuated daily life. Each chapter presents a series of comparisons: London and Paris, men and women, the everyday and special occasions, the home and the public sphere and, finally, ideal and experience. These comparisons highlight the complexities of eating arrangements, as well as suggesting that bourgeois habits and rituals were based on notions of modesty and respectability, which were shared by members of that class in London and Paris, England and France, and perhaps Europe as a whole.

Notes

1 According to Roger Dixon and Stefan Muthesius, from the 1880s to the early 1900 all the best London hotels were dominated by Ritz. *Victorian Architecture* (London: Thames & Hudson, 1978).

2 T. Shaw, *The World of Escoffier* (London: Zwemmer, 1994) p. 11.

3 D. Harvey, *Paris: Capital of Modernity* (London: Routledge, 2006) p. 223.

4 Cited in Harvey, *Paris: Capital of Modernity*, pp. 222–3.

5 L. Tiersten, *Marianne in the Market: Envisioning Consumer Society in Fin-de-Siècle France*. (Berkeley: University of California Press, 2001) p. 16.

6 'Courier de Paris', *L'Illustration* (15 Oct. 1870).

7 'Courier de Paris', *L'Illustration* (22 Oct. 1870).

8 J.-P. Aron, *The Art of Eating in France: Manners and Menus in the Nineteenth Century*, trans. N. Roote (London: Owen, 1975) p. 105. Also C. Merchant, *The Death of Nature: Women, Ecology and the Scientific Revolution* (New York: HarperCollins, 1980).

9 See for example T. Bickham, 'Eating the Empire: Intersections of Food, Cookery and Imperialism in Eighteenth-Century Britain', *Past & Present* 198:1 (2008) 71–109; T. Döring et al., *Eating Culture: The Poetics and Politics of Food* (Heidelberg: C. Winter, 2003).

10 U. Bloom, *Sixty Years of Home* (London: Hurst & Blackett, 1960) p. 49.

11 Athénius, *La Salle à Manger* (June, 1890). All translations from the French are my own, unless otherwise indicated.

12 A. B. Trubek, *Haute Cuisine: How the French Invented the Culinary Profession* (Philadelphia: University of Pennsylvania Press, 2000). Also S. Mennell, *All Manners of Food: Eating and Taste in England and France from the Middle Ages to the present* (Oxford: Blackwell, 1985).

13 G. Best, *Mid-Victorian Britain, 1851–75* (London: Fontana Press, 1979) p. 25.

14 P. Higonnet, *Paris: Capital of the World*, trans. A Goldhammer, London: Harvard University Press, 2002) p. 239.

15 B. R. Mitchell, *European Historical Statistics, 1750–1975* (London: Macmillan, 1981) pp. 35, 79. France's overall population declined after 1871 when Alsace and Lorrain became part of Germany.

16 Harvey, *Paris: Capital of Modernity* (London: Routledge, 2006) p. 24.

17 Higonnet, *Paris: Capital of the World*, p. 231.

18 Mennell, *All Manners of Food: Eating and Taste in England and France from the Middle Ages to the present*; Trubek, *Haute Cuisine: How the French Invented the Culinary Profession*.

19 Higonnet, *Paris: Capital of the World*, p. 236.

20 See for example: J. Kocka and A. Mitchell (eds), *Bourgeois Society in Nineteenth Century Europe* (Oxford: Berg, 1993); P. Pilbeam, *The Middle Classes in Europe 1789–1914: France, Germany, Italy, Russia* (Basingstoke: Macmillan, 1990); D. Blackbourn and R. J. Evans (eds), *The German Bourgeoisie* (London: Routledge, 1991); A. Daumard, *La Bourgeoisie Parisienne de 1815 à 1848* (Paris: SEVPEN, 1963); P. N. Stearns, 'The Middle Class: Towards a Precise Definition', *Comparative Studies in Society and History*, 21:3 (Jul. 1979), 377–96; J. Kocka, 'The Middle Classes in Europe', *The Journal of Modern History*, 67:4 (Dec., 1995) 783–806.

21 See for example: S. Hindle, 'The Growth of Social Stability in Restoration England', *European Legacy*, 5:4 (2000) 563–76; M. R. Hunt, *The Middling Sort: Commerce, Gender, and the Family in England, 1680–1780* (Berkeley: University of California Press, 1996); J. Barry and C. Brooks (eds), *The Middling Sort of People: Culture, Society and Politics in England, 1500–1800* (Basingstoke: Macmillan, 1994).

22 P. Ariès and G. Duby (eds), *A History of Private Life. Vol. 4: From The Fires of Revolution to the Great War* (London: Belknap Press, 1990); P. Ariès, *Centuries of Childhood*, trans. R. Baldrick (London: Cape, 1962); P. Gay, *The Bourgeois Experience: Victoria to Freud, Vol. II The Tender Passion* (Oxford: Oxford University Press, 1986).

23 L. Davidoff and C. Hall, *Family Fortunes: Men and Women of the English Middle Class, 1780–1850* (London: Hutchinson, 1988); C. Hall, *White, Male and Middle Class: Explorations in Feminism and History* (Cambridge:

Routledge, 1992); B. Smith. *Ladies of the Leisure Class: The Bourgeoises of Northern France in the Nineteenth Century* (Princeton: Princeton University Press, 1981); J. Tosh, *A Man's Place: Masculinity And The Middle-Class Home In Victorian England* (London: Yale University Press, 1999); C. E. Harrison, *The Bourgeois Citizen in Nineteenth-Century France: Gender, Sociability and the Uses of Emulation* (Oxford: Oxford University Press, 1999).

24 See for example: A. Vickery, 'Golden Age to Separate Spheres? A review of the categories and chronology of English women's history', *Historical Journal* 36:2 (1993) 383–414; M. Donald, 'Tranquil Havens? Critiquing the idea of home as the middle-class sanctuary', in I. Bryden and J. Floyd (eds), *Domestic Space: Reading the Nineteenth-Century Interior* (Manchester: Manchester University Press, 1999).

25 See for example: J. Brewer and R. Porter (eds), *Consumption and the World of Goods* (London: Routledge, 1993); J. Benson, *The Rise of Consumer Society in Britain, 1880–1980* (London: Longman, 1994); R. Bowlby, *Carried Away. The Invention of Modern Shopping* (New York: Columbia University Press, 2001); V. de Grazia, and E. Furlough (eds), *The Sex of Things: Gender and Consumption in Historical Perspective* (London: University of California Press, 1996); M. Finn, 'Sex in the City: Metropolitan Modernities in English History', *Victorian Studies* 44:1 (2001) 26–32; E. Rappaport, *Shopping for Pleasure: Women in the Making of London's West End* (Oxford: Princeton University Press, 2000); L. Tiersten, *Marianne in the Market: Envisioning Consumer Society in Fin-de-Siècle France* (Berkeley: University of California Press, 2001); G. Crossick and S. Jaumain (eds), *Cathedrals of Consumption: the European Department Store, 1850–1939* (Aldershot: Ashgate, 1998).

26 See for example: Harrison, *The Bourgeois Citizen in Nineteenth-Century France*; S. Gunn, *The Public Culture of the Victorian Middle Class* (Manchester: Manchester University Press, 2000); R. Spang, *The Invention of the Restaurant: Paris and Modern Gastronomic Culture* (London: Harvard University Press, 2000); F. Trentmann, 'Gentleman and Players: The Leisure of British Modernity', *Contemporary Record* 7:3 (1993) 685–92; R. Koshar (ed.), *History of Leisure* (Oxford: Berg, 2002).

27 P. Perrot, *Fashioning The Bourgeoisie: A History Of Clothing in the Nineteenth Century* (Princeton: Princeton University Press, 1994); C. Breward, *The Hidden Consumer: Masculinities, Fashion And City Life 1860–1914* (Manchester: Manchester University Press, 1999); D. Kuchta, *The Three-Piece Suit And Modern Masculinity: England, 1550–1850* (London: University of California Press, 2002).

28 Norbert Elias's seminal work *The History of Manners* (Oxford: Blackwell, 1994) (originally published in German in 1939) can still be considered

the most important work in this field. However, there are several other works which treat similar subjects. See for example: L. Davidoff, *The Best Circles* (London: Croom Helm, 1973); A. St George, *The Descent of Manners: Etiquette, Rules and the Victorians* (London: Random House, 1993); M. Curtin, 'A Question of Manners: Status and Gender in Etiquette and Courtesy', *Journal of Modern History* 57 (1985) 61–81; N. Armstrong and L. Tennenhouse (eds), *The Ideology of Conduct: Essays in Literature and the History of Sexuality* (London: Methuen, 1987); C. D. Hemphill, *Bowing to Necessities: A History of Manners in America, 1620–1860* (Oxford: Oxford University Press, 1999); A. Bryson, *From Courtesy to Civility: Changing Codes of Conduct in Early Modern England* (Oxford: Oxford University Press, 1998); C. Kelly, *Refining Russia: Advice Literature, Polite Culture, and Gender from Catherine to Yeltsin* (Oxford: Oxford University Press, 2001).

29 A. Daumard, *Les Bourgeois et la bourgeoisie en France depuis 1815* (Paris: Flammarion, 1991) p. 8.

30 For a fuller account of the boundaries between polite and artistic society in Paris see J. Siegel, *Bohemian Paris: Culture, Politics and the Boundaries of Bourgeois Life, 1830–1930* (London: Johns Hopkins University Press, 1986).

31 M. de Certeau, de, L. Giard and P. Mayol, *The Practice of Everyday Life Vol. II: Living and Cooking*, trans. T. J. Tomasik (London: University of California Press, 1988) p. 115. See also R. Tannahill, *Food in History* (New York: Three Rivers Press, 1988) p. 295.

32 An excellent argument about the cultural hegemony of the bourgeoisie, and the reasons for its success, can be found in J. Frykman and O. Löfgren, *Culture Builders: A Historical Anthropology of Middle-Class Life*, trans. A. Crozier (London: Rutgers University Press, 1987).

33 L. Auslander, *Taste and Power: Furnishing modern France* (Berkeley: University of California Press, 1996).

34 For an overview of research on consumption in the modern period see L. Tiersten, 'Redefining Consumer Culture: Recent Literature on Consumption and the Bourgeoisie in Western Europe', *Radical History Review* 57 (1993) 116–59.

35 On the identification of *anorexia* as a disease see: L.-V. Marcé, 'Note on a form of hypochondriacal delusion consecutive to the dyspepsias and principally characterized by the refusal of food', trans. A. Blewett and A. Bottéro Originally published 1860, reprinted in *History of Psychiatry* 5 (1994) 273–83; E. C. Lasègue, 'De l'anorexie hystérique', *Archives générales de médecine* 1(1873), See also: J. J. Brumberg, *Fasting Girls: The Emergence of Anorexia Nervosa as a Modern Disease* (London: Harvard University Press, 1988).

36 See for example: J. Goody, *Cooking, Cuisine and Class* (Cambridge: Cambridge University Press, 1982); M. Visser, *The Rituals of Dinner:*

The Origins, Evolution, Eccentricities and the Meaning of Table Manners (London: Penguin, 1992); M. Douglas, 'Deciphering a Meal', *Daedalus* 101 (1972), 61–81; H. MacBeth (ed.), *Food Preferences and Tastes: Continuity and Change* (Oxford: Barghahn Books, 1997); P. Wiessner and W. Schiffenhövel (eds), *Food and the Status Quest* (Oxford: Berghahn Books, 1996).

37 See for example: S. Mennell, *All Manners of Food: Eating and Taste in England and France from the Middle Ages to the Present* (Oxford: Blackwell, 1985); J. Finklestein, *Dining Out: A Sociology of Modern Manners* (Cambridge: Polity Press, 1989); A. Beardsworth and T. Keil, *Sociology on the Menu: An Invitation to the Study of Food and Society* (London: Routledge, 1997); A. Warde and L. Martens, *Eating Out: Social Differentiation, Consumption and Pleasure* (Cambridge: Cambridge University Press, 2000).

38 J. Vernon, *Hunger: A Modern History* (London: Harvard University Press).

39 See for example: J. Walter and R. Schofield (eds), *Famine, Disease and the Social Order in Early Modern Society* (Cambridge: Cambridge University Press, 1989); C. A. Bouton, *The Flour War: Gender, Class and Community in Late Ancien Régime French Society* (Pennsylvania: Pennsylvania State University Press, 1993).

40 In the past few years, several such studies have emerged. See for example: S. W. Mintz, *Tasting Food, Tasting Freedom: Excursions into Eating, Culture and the Past* (Boston: Beacon Press, 1996); M. Montanari, *The Culture of Food* (Oxford: Blackwell, 1996); J. Coveney, *Food, Morals and Meaning: The Pleasure and Anxiety of Eating* (London: Routledge, 2000); J. Evans Braziel and K. LeBesco (eds), *Bodies out of Bounds: Fatness and Transgression* (Berkeley: University of California Press, 2001); K. Albala, *Eating Right in the Renaissance* (Berkeley: University of California Press, 2002); T. Döring, T. M. Heide and S. Mühleisenet (eds), *Eating Culture: The Poetics and Politics of Food* (Heidelberg: C. Winter, 2003).

41 M. Toussaint-Samat, *History of Food*, trans. Anthea Bell (Oxford: Blackwell, 1992) pp. 621–4.

42 See for example: R. I. Rotberg and T. K. Rabb (eds), *Hunger and History: The Impact of Changing Food Production and Consumption Patterns on Society* (Cambridge: Cambridge University Press, 1985).

43 A good example of this kind of analysis is M. Nelson, 'Social-Class Trends in British Diet, 1860–1980', in C. Geisser and D. Oddy (eds), *Food, Diet and Economic Change Past and Present* (Leicester: Leicester University Press, 1993). Using household budgets, records of expenditure on food and amounts purchased or consumed, Nelson looks at specific differences in both diet composition and nutritional intake according to class or income.

44 See in particular P. Scholliers (ed.), *Food, Drink and Identity: Cooking, Eating and Drinking in Europe since the Middle Ages* (Oxford: Berg, 2001).

45 For example: M. Glants and J. Toomre, *Food in Russian History and Culture* (Bloomington: Indiana University Press, 1997).

46 See for example: M. Lane, *Jane Austen and Food* (London: Hambledon Press, 1995); G.-P. Biasin, *The Flavours of Modernity: Food and the Novel* (Princeton: Princeton University Press 1991); J.-F. Revel, *Un Festin en paroles: histoire littéraire de la sensibilité gastronomique* (Paris: Pauvert, 1979); J. W. Brown, *Fictional Meals and their Function in the French Novel, 1789–1845* (London: University of Toronto Press, 1984).

47 de Certeau et al., *The Practice of Everyday Life Vol. II*; C. Guy, *La Vie quotidienne de la société gourmande au XIXe siècle* (Paris: Hachette, 1971); L. Moulin, *Les Liturges de la table: une histoire culturelle du manger et du boire* (Anvers: Fonds Mercator, 1989); Montanari, *The Culture of Food*; Tannahill, *Food in History*.

48 On food and bodies see for example: R. Diprose, *The Bodies of Women: Ethics, Embodiement and Sexual Difference* (London: Routledge, 1994); K. Chernin, *Womansize: The Tyranny of Slenderness* (London: Women's Press, 1983); M. Featherstone, M. Hepworth and B. S. Turner (eds) *The Body: Social Processes and Cultural Theory* (London: Sage, 1991); C. M. Counihan, *The Anthropology of Food and Body: Gender, Meaning and Power* (London: Routledge, 1999).

49 See for example: R. M. Bell, *Holy Anorexia* (Chicago: Chicago University Press, 1985); C. Walker Bynum, *Holy Feast and Holy Fast: The Religious Significance of Food to Medieval Women* (London: University of California Press, 1987); I. Loudon, 'The Disease called Chlorosis', *Psychological Medicine*, 14 (1984) 27–66; H. King, 'Green Sickness: Hippocrates, Galen and the Origin of the "Disease of Virgins"', *International Journal of the Classical Tradition*, 2 (1996) 372–87; Brumberg, *Fasting Girls*.

50 The literature on the social history of medicine is too vast to attempt to summarise it here. However, of particular significance to this study are H. Kamminga and A. Cunningham (eds), *The Science and Culture of Nutrition, 1840–1940* (Amsterdam: Rodopi, 1995); and B. S. Turner, 'The Government of the Body: Medical Regimens and the Rationalization of Diet', *British Journal of Sociology* 33 (1982) 254–69, on the interaction of culture and science in the creation of knowledge about food and eating. There are several works on successful books of medical advice literature, such as: Roy Porter, *Doctor of Society: Thomas Beddoes and the Sick Trade in Late Enlightenment England* (London: Routledge, 1992); G. J. Barker-Benfield, *The Culture of Sensibility: Sex and Society in Eighteenth-Century Britain* (London: University of Chicago

Press, 1992); C. J. Lawrence, 'William Buchan: Medicine Laid Open', *Medical History* 19 (1975) 20–35; C. E. Rosenberg, 'Medical Texts and Social Contexts: Explaining William Buchan's *Domestic Medicine*', *Bulletin of the History of Medicine* 57 (1983) 22–42.

51 Tosh, *A Man's Place*; J. R. Gillis, 'Ritualization of Middle-Class Family Life in Nineteenth-Century Britain', *International Journal of Politics, Culture, and Society* 3:2 (1989) 213–35; Frykman and Löfgren, *Culture Builders*; Tiersten, *Marianne in the Market*; Harrison, *The Bourgeois Citizen in Nineteenth-Century France*; Gunn, *The Public Culture of the Victorian Middle Class*; R. J. Morris, *Class, Sect and Party: the Making of the British Middle Class* (Manchester: Manchester University Press, 1990); A. Kidd and D. Nicholls, *Gender, Civic Culture and Consumerism: Middle-Class Identity in Britain 1800–1940* (Manchester: Manchester University Press, 1999).

1

Eating by the rules: prescriptive literature and the dissemination of knowledge

> It not infrequently happens that gentlemen of superior talents and abilities, and ladies of amiable dispositions and first-rate accomplishments, appear lost in society, simply for not having sufficient acquaintance with the somewhat complicated rules and regulations of fashionable life.[1]

So wrote an English author in 1849, giving his reasons for writing a book on the subject of etiquette. His was one of a vast number of etiquette books published, often in multiple editions, throughout the nineteenth century. French and English publishers alike found a market among the aspiring middle classes for books on how to behave, and books which allowed readers a glimpse of what they believed were the habits and customs of their social superiors. According to Dena Attar, in Britain, millions of copies of household management books – one of the many genres of advice literature on offer – were purchased during the course of the nineteenth century.[2] The best way to learn good manners may have been at the family dinner table, but for the many men and women who moved in different circles to those in which they had been raised, some form of instruction was needed. Beyond their didactic role, etiquette books could also provide a form of escapism, a way of catching a glimpse of an elegant, if unobtainable, way of living for the majority of middle-class women who had to meet family obligations within a constrained budget. And etiquette manuals were only one among the great many genres of advice literature which proliferated: books on cooking, staying healthy, buying and decorating a home – could all be found and all found an audience. While advice changed slightly from book to book, there is an over-arching sense of stability in both British and French sources that suggests a mostly uniform bourgeois approach to food and eating, which could be learned by all.[3]

Eating, which offered the greatest potential pitfalls for any would-be social climber, was a favourite topic of advice writers, and the nature of the advice given reveals key areas of tension that developed in the period. Medical and etiquette advice writers struggled with the duelling tendencies towards gluttony and abstemiousness, which threatened the health and social standing of many a middle-class eater. At the same time, architectural and decorating manuals reflected the increasing need for houses that put into physical form the middle-class desire for separation of functions. Homes became increasingly compartmentalised, with each room in the house having a specific function or set of activities ascribed to it.

Advice literature of various kinds has been attracting scholarly attention for some years now. Historians wishing to look at normative models of behaviour have been drawn to looking at conduct and etiquette books, since, as Anna Bryson argues: 'There can be no coherent approach to practice without an understanding of ideals and norms.'[4] Similarly for medical history, there have been some, albeit more limited, attempts to come to terms with the relationship between medical advice and bodily experience, though it has been more common to study this advice as an indication of how ideas are transmitted from professionals to lay consumers. In architectural history, inroads have been made in linking advice to practice as a way of enhancing our understanding of the relationship between space and culture or between people and the built environment.[5] No one has yet systematically studied advice literature as a genre, as opposed to the subdivisions within it, as a way of looking at how rules and prescriptions reflect the societies which produce them. In her study of behaviour manuals in Russia, Catriona Kelly makes similar connections between the types of advice literature argued for here, but her analysis does not extend to medical and architectural advice.[6] Taken together, the prescriptive sources that inform this chapter demonstrate the ways in which middle-class ideals tended towards organisation and compartmentalisation, as well as towards modesty and moderation. It is only by looking at the various kind of advice books as a whole that we can begin to gain greater clarity about the ideals of the cultures that produced them. This chapter examines all the various genres of advice literature as being in a sense equal, in that they represent the shared ideals of the people who identified themselves or wished to be identified as middle class.

In comparing the prescriptive literature published in London and Paris, the similarities are more striking than the differences. Historians who have studied conduct books have pointed to the repetitive nature of the advice, with authors plagiarising one another and books coming out in several editions over many years. As Dallett Hempill argues, this is one of the reasons they are a useful source, as the sameness of the advice indicates a single dominant discourse on manners.[7] The sameness of the advice available in London and Paris gives credence to recent studies suggesting a transnational bourgeois culture in this period.[8] Professionalisation and the importance placed on expertise gave credibility to advice writers. The values, behaviours and sets of rules they presented, when taken as a whole, reveal to us an English middle class and a Parisian bourgeoisie each preoccupied with maintaining the appearance of respectability, living within one's means, maintaining healthy homes and bodies, all the while creating an impression of elegance and comfort. This chapter highlights the differences between London and Paris where relevant, but the overall approach is to argue for the existence of a class-based ideology that transcended national boundaries.

The need for rules

> To be acquainted with every detail of the etiquette pertaining to . . . [the dinner table] is of the highest importance to every gentlewoman . . . How to eat soup and what to do with a cherry-stone are weighty considerations when taken as the index of social status; and it is not too much to say, that a young woman who elected to take claret with her fish, or ate peas with her knife, would justly risk the punishment of being banished from good society.[9]

Being middle class and respectable in nineteenth-century London and Paris meant keeping a tight control over all physical impulses. Norbert Elias has measured the history of civilisation through the progressive repression of bodily noises and fluids.[10] According to this measure, the nineteenth century was the apex of civilisation and Andrew St George argues that the Victorians, more than any society before or since, constructed and adhered to strict rules and patterns of behaviour.[11] In the late eighteenth and early nineteenth centuries, advice books were unrelenting in their advocacy of moderate eating habits. They warned especially against feminine overeating, since women were expected to be more refined than men. John Tussler, in 1791, informed male readers:

> As eating a great deal is deemed indelicate in a lady; (for her character should be rather divine than sensual,) it will be ill manners to help her to a large slice of meat at once, or fill her plate too full.[12]

Injunctions against overeating continued to appear in advice books – both etiquette and medical – up to the end of nineteenth century. For advice writers, overeating was a clear sign of both loose morals and a reckless disregard for the health of the body.

Leonore Davidoff argues that nineteenth-century advice books were at once an aid for those aspiring to greater levels of ease and respectability, and a conservative force in a period of rapid social mobility.[13] Writing in 1849, one anonymous author described the rules of etiquette as: 'the barrier which society draws around itself as a protection against offences the "law" cannot touch'.[14] Acting as a guide for the socially mobile, they made the rules of good behaviour explicit, so that people who had not learned them at home could appear in the know. At the same time, etiquette books had a timeless quality. As a genre, advice literature was extremely resistant to change, with books appearing in many editions over a number of years without any acknowledgement of the dramatic changes occurring in the outside world. Changes in the rules of good behaviour were subtle, making it easy to spot interlopers. Good behaviour could vary between social circles, but the idea of 'good behaviour' existed everywhere and acted as a filter to slow down and control social mobility.[15] Advice literature served a dual purpose as both promoter and restrainer of the outward signs of social ascent. While these may seem inherently contradictory, they served to mutually reinforce the impression of a stable middle-class identity in a rapidly changing world. Social mobility was neither created nor repressed through the acquisition of good manners. But the huge volume of advice books published in this period suggests that the superficial sense of stability created by good manners served a purpose for those who aspired to cultural capital as well as for those who already possessed it.

Though advice manuals were published in large quantities, little is known of the identities of their authors. Writers of domestic advice manuals were usually housewives barely less anonymous than the mass of middle-class women who were their intended audiences, while many etiquette writers preserved their anonymity through the use of pseudonyms. More easily apprehended is the nature of the intended audience. Like the conduct books of the eighteenth century, advice manuals were directed to both men and women. In early modern conduct books, an emphasis on good behaviour went hand-in-hand with a desire to instil morality as the source of politeness. Philip Carter has argued that conduct books provoked fears that too much politeness would feminise Englishmen.[16] By the late nineteenth century, etiquette books, whose focus was more firmly on the appearance of goodness than on goodness itself, were directed more clearly at women, while men were left to learn about diet and nutrition in medical advice books, and about good living in advice books aimed specifically at promoting the pleasures of the table. Books on domestic management and economy, as well as books on domestic architecture and decorating, were generally addressed to female readers since, as Annamarie Adams has argued, the home was so clearly women's domain that it was they who were in league with doctors and architects intent on making houses healthier to live in.[17] It was only in medical advice that men and women were addressed in similar proportions, even if the advice each received was still highly gendered. What united all these sub-genres of advice literature, however, was their broadly middle-class audience, who would all have recognised their own vision of respectability and a well lived life in the pages of these quite varied books.

The success of advice literature throughout this period can, in part, be attributed to the perception that social mobility was difficult to achieve, and that wealth alone could not elevate one's social status. In order to enter a new social class, cultural capital and the appearance of respectability had to be acquired, which was what the rules of etiquette claimed to provide. Likely consumers of this literature were lower-middle-class women aspiring to acceptance in more elevated social circles, or perhaps wishing to impress their own acquaintances, or even simply to daydream about the lifestyles of the rich and famous. French etiquette books were often penned by authors with aristocratic titles, implying that they could teach emulation of the highest social echelons, though what they actually offered was advice to the lower middle classes on how to imitate the upper. Aristocratic titles could hide the real identity of the author, such as the very successful writer of the *Code du cérémonial*, who was born Thérèse Anaïs Rigo, and whose married name was Mme Lebrun, but who enjoyed success as a novelist, journalist and etiquette writer under the pseudonym Comtesse de Bassanville. Medical and architectural advice writers did not need to claim aristocratic lineage to establish their authority: they were 'experts' in their given fields, and their readership included anyone with an interest in that field. Doctors were themselves, of course, very much part of the respectable and educated middle classes. In the advice they offered we can detect that their expert knowledge easily became enmeshed with their own class-based notions of modesty and self-control. Through this blurring of personal and professional knowledge, medical advice came to resemble etiquette books in some rather striking ways.

Historical approaches to advice literature have been varied. The seminal study of courtesy literature was written by Norbert Elias in 1939. It was through a survey of early modern French and German conduct books that he made the argument that the history of civilisation could be traced through the increasing repression of bodily functions.[18] Elias is sometimes criticised for taking a simple linear approach to the evolution of manners and civilisation. Nonetheless, his work has influenced several generations of sociologists and historians who have looked to advice literature as a way of understanding the ideals of various western societies. According to Elias's model, the appearance of a rule in the books of a period indicate the existence of contrary behaviours that were still in practice. For example, if all conduct books from a given period contain a rule that says that everyone should eat with a fork, this should be taken as an indication that the intended readers of those books were not eating with forks. Though this is a good rule in principle, it is difficult to apply, since etiquette books often copy one another, and do not necessarily keep up to date with changes in practice, a point illustrated by a comment in *The Caterer* in 1882:

> A new work on etiquette conveys the startling information that 'soup should be eaten with a spoon.' Those who are in the habit of eating it with a fork or carving-knife will be slow to adopt such a new fangled idea.[19]

A more recent approach to the uses of advice literature as historical sources is to see them as indicators of ideology. While acknowledging that advice literature tells us little or nothing about practice, this approach argues that the genre's popularity, as indicated by the large numbers of publications, often in many editions, indicates that advice literature is an important sources for understanding the values of the societies that produced it. Historians such as Anna Bryson take conduct books as indications of the ideals of a society, arguing that: 'there can be no coherent approach to practice without an understanding of ideals and norms'.[20] The very repetitive nature of the advice found in the books published in any given period has been taken as an indication that there is only one discourse on manners or, at the very least, that there is one discourse so dominant as to drown out any alternative discourses.[21] The advice literatures of Victorian London and Paris reveal such a dominant discourse, and show an idealised set of rules to which all those aspiring to middle-class status should attempt to adhere.

All the various types of advice literature considered in this chapter can be seen as rule books. They lay out sets of rules about how to behave within the specific situations treated, but also more generally, rules for how to lead a good life. Historians looking at advice literature have generally focused on manners and etiquette. Manners are seen to serve a purpose in society, and are more than just superficial manifestations of individual behaviour.[22] Anthropologist Margaret Visser argues that table manners are present in every human society, no matter how primitive.[23] While the rules may have had a practical purpose, they cannot be read as straightforward sets of instructions, since they were highly embedded in the cultures that produced them. In order to understand the meaning of the rules, contemporaries needed to understand the culture. Thus for historians, reading backward from the rules gives an insight into the cultural assumptions of the original readers.

Medical and architectural advice manuals have not yet attracted a great deal of attention from historians. Some, working on the history of architecture and design, have looked at these sources, though not as indicators of culture or values.[24] Similarly, medical historians have touched on advice literature as indicators of the ways in which medical knowledge was transmitted to lay people rather than as a set of ideologically motivated rules and regulations.[25] The social aspects of nutrition from a medical perspective have been touched on only briefly, and popular medical advice on diet is a field still waiting to be explored.[26]

Gluttony and moderation

Jean-Paul Aron described the nineteenth century as the age of gluttony.[27] Yet gluttony was, at least in theory, anathema to the middle classes, whose very essence was 'middleness', or moderation. The tension between gluttony and moderation pre-dates the rise of the bourgeoisie, being at the heart of European attitudes towards food. While gluttony was a sin in the Judaeo-Christian tradition, Germanic tribes considered hearty eating a sign of virility and strength.[28] For the middle classes, luxurious eating was also associated with the aristocracy. This complicated matters, as the extent to which members of the middle classes strove to emulate aristocratic ways varied greatly. In France the tendency towards emulation was more overt. For one thing, the very concept of emulation, as Carol E. Harrison has argued, was considered a positive action.[29]

While it is impossible to generalise a unified bourgeois attitude towards aristocracy, there was certainly a great appetite for etiquette books penned by countesses, and furniture styles named after historic monarchs. In England, Martin Wiener has argued that the desire for aristocratic emulation led to the decline of the industrial spirit in the second half of the nineteenth century,[30] while Martin Daunton argues that an amalgamated landed elite and upper middle class adhered to a gentlemanly capitalism and Bill Rubenstein has found that the British elite was largely recruited from the middle classes.[31] While the English middle class only gradually loosened the traditional elite's hold on economic and political power, their values of modesty and respectability influenced aristocratic practice. But while self-control may have been an ideal and an imperative, causing dinner menus to become shorter and shorter, people's tendency towards overindulgence and obesity remained a matter of general concern.

The tensions surrounding gluttonous eating revealed by doctors and etiquette writers was an outcome of the abundance of food available to the modern eater. Living beyond the margins of survival, middle-class men and women had crucial choices to make about their diets. To enjoy good food, and benefit from a reputation for good taste, were appealing possibilities. But there loomed the danger of going too far, becoming obese and unhealthy, and losing face in society. The gluttony of the middle classes was revealed most clearly through their obsession with digestion and digestive disorders. Arnold Bennett often referred to his digestion in his letters.[32] According to Ursula Bloom, the author of a memoir about growing up in a respectable London home around the turn of the century, overeating and suffering the consequences of it were a normal part of life.[33] The extent to which advice from doctors focused on digestion and food suggests that the first-hand accounts were representative of middle-class experiences more generally.[34] A medical advice book from the 1890s went so far as to assert: 'Indigestion is the prevailing and fashionable malady of civilised life. The doctor is more frequently consulted about disorder of digestion . . . than about any others.'[35] A French doctor in the same decade complained that everyone ate too much. He argued that while people believed that overeating was merely pointless, it was in fact detrimental to their health, leading to indigestion and eventually dyspepsia.[36] The English Dr Crichton-Brown echoed this belief, arguing in 1910 that too much meat was particularly harmful to the diets of well-to-do people in Europe and America.[37] Dr Alexander Haig was even more critical, stating:

> Diet, as at present used, is often the product of a vast amount of ignorance; it is the cause of a hideous waste of time and money; it produces mental and moral obliquities, destroys health and shortens life, and generally quite fails to fulfil its proper purpose.[38]

Some saw the problem of bad diet as a result of the fast pace of modern life,[39] while others simply attributed it to a tendency towards extreme behaviours.[40]

Gluttony among the affluent classes could be seen as a social problem in parallel with the problem of hunger among the poor. Thus, for Crichton-Brown, the key to good nutrition and preventative medicine lay in redistribution. He argued that, 'Could we but secure adequate supplies . . . restricting gluttony on the one hand and abolishing starvation on the other, we should vastly lighten the task of the sanitary and of the social reformer, and witness a gratifying drop in the death-rate.'[41] At the same time, the possibility for many people to eat adequate quantities of food was a positive outcome of industrialisation and modernisation, and could be linked to the idea of human progress. Thus to one French journalist in 1860 it seemed logical to conclude that 'We eat a lot nowadays because we work a lot; we produce a lot, because we eat a lot.'[42] At the same time as plentiful food was an outcome and necessity of modern living, the anxieties of this new fast pace of life could lead to a loss of appetite. While anorexia nervosa emerged in this period as a diagnosis for self-starvation among affluent young women, the general term 'anorexia' was used to refer to any loss of appetite. In *The Family Physician: A Manual of Domestic Medicine*, published in London in the 1890s, anorexia was attributed to anxiety over money, too much alcohol or tobacco, too little outdoor exercise and irregular mealtimes, and was believed to be more common in London than anywhere else.[43] Thus both over- and undereating were concerns of the middle classes, and health was only part of the cause of this concern.

Gluttony was seen as a problem with both physical and moral consequences. It was discussed equally by etiquette and medical advice writers. Like doctors, etiquette writers emphasised the painful consequences of overeating.[44] While doctors used the language of science, and the threat of ill-health, to discourage bad behaviour, etiquette writers played on people's fear of social ostracism.[45] Good etiquette meant moderation, especially at dinner parties, where each guest would be making judgements about his fellows. In spite of St George's assertion of the extent to which the Victorians adhered to their own social rules, these were far too extensive to imagine that anyone actually did every single thing 'by the book', and there is ample evidence that at all levels of the middle class people were happy to be flexible in many circumstances.[46] But the basic rules were moderation in appetite and control over the body. The guidelines for moderation and good manners changed little throughout the period and included the importance of punctuality;[47] that men should look after the women seated next to them, while the women should never themselves ask for anything;[48] that hosts ought always to serve the best food they could afford, never be stingy but likewise avoid extravagance;[49] that hosts should never press guests to eat particular items, but guests should always accept the plate they were given;[50] that neither hosts nor guests were to comment on the quality of the dishes served;[51] that no one was to comment on their likes or dislikes, but this particularly so for women; that if someone was given food they disliked, they should not comment on this, but simply leave the food on their plate;[52] that making noise or doing anything 'disgusting' while at the table was not acceptable[53] and neither was touching food with one's fingers[54] or lifting one's knife to one's mouth.[55] Overall, the emphasis was on the importance of appearing, in public, to have the characteristics of bourgeois respectability, meaning having total control over oneself while eating, when moving about the house and when engaging others in conversation.

The threat of social ostracism enforced advice against overeating. Cautionary tales abounded concerning the risks of being seen as either a social parasite – who tried to get every meal at someone else's expense – or a greedy eater. One anonymous author stated: 'Never overload the plate of a guest or any person you would serve. It is not a delicate compliment.'[56] Mrs. Beeton, probably the best known English advice writer of the period, warned: 'It is generally established as a rule, not to ask for soup or fish twice.' Anyone who did so might be keeping fellow diners waiting for their second course, 'when, perhaps, a little revenge is taken by looking at the awkward consumer of a second portion'.[57] Drawing attention to oneself, and being stared at while eating, were very much contrary to the basic rules of good eating and the so-called 'awkward consumer' would be marked out as lacking in restraint and self-control.

Although meals were generally large, bodies were always expected to stay small. There is no consensus as to when the fashion for thin bodies first emerged, but it was well established by the eighteenth century, when the romantic cult of sensibility dictated that thin, ethereal bodies were the outward sign of a sensitive soul.[58] Lord Byron, possibly one of the key authors of this trend, had famously stated, 'A woman should never be seen eating or drinking, unless it be lobster salad and champagne, the only true feminine and becoming of viands.'[59] The nineteenth-century middle classes, preoccupied as they were with appearances, also read bodies as external indicators of inner worth. Both male and female bodies were judged, with obesity as an indicator of gluttony, lack of self-restraint, or even immorality. Thinness could be interpreted in a variety of ways, depending on the perspective of the observer: as an indication of sensibility, a sign of self-control,[60] or, in extreme cases, a blatant disregard for health.

In the eighteenth century, George Cheyne achieved fame by advising wealthy patients to abstain from meat. Having once weighed over four hundred pounds, he determined that avoiding obesity was the key to both health and happiness.[61] Corpulence continued to be seen as a worrying problem by nineteenth-century doctors. Even writers in the catering trade press, whose business in life was to promote fine dining, were fervent in their condemnation of gluttony and obesity. In 1893, *La Salle à Manger* contained an argument that *embonpoint* caused so many inconveniences that it deserved to be referred to as an illness, whose cure was good hygiene, and especially good diet.[62]

Thinness, in contrast, could be seen as an indicator of various positive attributes, including genius. An English catering trade writer in 1880 suggested:

> Our greatest writers have been little, attenuated men, stomachless, meagre, lean, and lath-like beings who have half-spiritualised themselves by keeping matter in due subordination to mind . . . obesity is a deadly foe to genius.[63]

For the French etiquette writer Eugene Chapus, a developed stomach indicated an egotistical and sensual person. 'Material life takes precedence for him.'[64] He argued that the more the stomach functioned, the less the brain did, and therefore overeating was 'in essence incompatible with elegance'.[65] French advice writers expressed greater concern about obesity than did their English counterparts. One reason for this may have been due to the fact that excess weight was a less serious problem in late-nineteenth-century London than Paris. In 1910, Dr Crichton-Brown argued that, unlike earlier in the nineteenth century, by the beginning of the twentieth weight was not a matter of great concern for the English:

> With us extreme obesity is not, perhaps, as common as it was fifty years ago, before the Banting era. There is a general recognition of its inconveniences and risks . . . The weight-book in any West End Club shows by its frequent and punctual entries and marginal and explanatory notes how jealously middle-aged men regard even a trifling tendency to corpulency, and the advertisements of anti-fat remedies of one kind and another indicate how anxiously women watch their waist-bands.[66]

Like George Cheyne, William Banting came to produce his dietary advice out of his own struggles with obesity. Not himself a doctor, he credited his successful diet to his 'medical adviser', Mr William Harvey of Soho Square. Banting's *Letter on Corpulency*, published in 1864, is probably the best known of the nineteenth-century diet fads, though there were many others in circulation. To Banting, obesity was an illness, cured through a diet high in meat and low in carbohydrates.[67] By the time Crichton-Brown wrote his dietary advice in 1910, the fashion for slenderness pioneered by the likes of Cheyne and Banting had become firmly entrenched, while the French had fewer diet fads. Yet obesity on both sides of the Channel was recognised as a widespread and serious problem. The dislike of fat men, by the French and the English, was exceeded only by the disgust felt towards overweight women.

Chapus reasoned that men generally preferred slender women to large-waisted ones: 'We [men] like to embrace the things we like. The more delicate, carved, agile a woman's body is, the more easily we can wrap our arms around it.'[68] And though he did not articulate it as such, there was inherent in his thinking the notion that the delicate bodies of women who never needed to work were status symbols for the men who 'owned' them: 'It seems that what we hold in this way belongs to us better: it is the symbol of possession.'[69] And it was not enough for women to be slender, they also had to be young and docile: 'Notice also that the more a woman advances in life, the more her character is formed, that she becomes emancipated, she escapes our influence, our authority, and her waist thickens. We govern a woman at twenty, she has a delicate waist; at forty-five she often resists . . . and her waist is fat. God is punishing her.'[70]

Eugène Boursin, self-proclaimed expert on women, described various types of women, and the various ailments that might afflict them. He argued that though the women of the provinces were healthier than Parisian women, they were less graceful and fresh, the implication being that they were less feminine. The reason for this was that there was nothing to do but eat and sleep in the provinces, and so these provincial women found it difficult to keep off excess matter.[71] Thus women who ate more, and weighed more, were found to be healthier but less appealing than thin, graceful Parisians. He argued that *goût* (taste) could have a salutary effect on the health of nervous women, but that:

> One must not deliver oneself to it with too much sensuality, for that would lead to egotism and terrible illnesses. Its influence on beauty is very great. Look at WOMEN after a meal, study their physiognomy, and you will understand the important role of the table on physical beauty.[72]

Obesity was a terrible thing in women, according to Boursin. It caused them to lose their grace and beauty and could lead to sterility and shorter life. He wrote: 'The Spartans viewed obese WOMEN as culpable, they were caned daily and submitted to friction treatments.'[73] Boursin's own advice for how a woman could lose weight without adversely affecting her health was to: 'Live in a warm place, on a mountain; daily exercise in the open air and sun . . . very active life in both body and mind; only six or seven hours in bed.'[74] Alongside this he advocated a diet of small amounts of salted or spiced meats, accompanied with lemonade, white wine or cider.[75] But Boursin's ideal woman had to tread carefully, as he also condemned *maigreur* (skinniness), a condition which he blamed on a range of causes, such as bad digestion, liver and lung disorders, diarrhoea, staying up too late, living in a hot climate, eating spicy foods, or enjoying excessive pleasures. Negative emotions such as ambition, jealousy, hatred, excessive love, melancholy, and all sad passions could also lead to skinniness.[76] For Boursin, the wrong body weight was both symptom and illness and to cure skinniness, a woman needed to keep in check her passions and emotions.[77]

The middle classes distrusted extremes in abstinence as much as in indulgence. While the dangers of overeating were more widely discussed, undereating was an increasingly recognised disorder. The debate over anorexia is far from over, as experts disagree over the extent to which this is a social, psychological or physical illness. Medieval historians have linked the presence of holy fasting women to modern anorexics, while medical historians look at greensickness, an early modern illness in which young women lost their appetite or had strange cravings.[78] Yet the argument that modern anorexia is the same as these earlier forms of self-starvation is weakened when one considers the different causes for the loss of appetite. Key to the modern illness is the crippling fear of fat, perhaps brought on by the onset of puberty and the need to retain control of a rapidly changing body. In his modern history of hunger, James Vernon explores changing ideas about hunger.[79] While he does not specifically discuss anorexia, the changes Vernon traces make it clear that self-starvation was a powerful tool for women to use in the period when new agricultural practices and new technologies were making it seem, for the first time in British history, that there might be enough food to finally eradicate hunger at all levels of society. Similarly, Joan Jacob Brumberg sees anorexia as a way for virtually powerless middle-class girls to gain a voice in a family structure which placed everyone's needs above theirs.[80]

In 1860, French 'alienist' Louis-Victor Marcé published his findings on what he described as 'a form of hypochondriacal delusion, consecutive to the dyspepsias, and principally characterised by the refusal of food'.[81] This text included two case studies, each of adolescent girls who refused food and whose conditions only improved when they were isolated from their families. Yet two doctors, each publishing findings in 1873, are credited with the 'invention' of modern anorexia. William Gull in England and Charles Lasègue in France each independently reported similar findings of young women refusing food, and who could be treated by removing them from their families and force feeding them. For Marcé, Gull and Lasègue, refusal to eat was a mental disorder but with moral overtones, and treatment included being surrounded by people with moral authority over the starving girl.

A distinction between gluttony and abstinence lay in the fact that extreme undereating was considered a disease in itself, while overeating could lead to a range of illnesses. Extremes were abhorred, but for several reasons, gluttony was more acceptable in respectable society. For one thing, the line between gourmandise and gluttony was difficult to draw, but gourmandise – the indulgence of a love of fine foods – was a respectable pastime for men of means. At the same time, much of the eating discussed in this book, that is eating which took place in social settings, was part of an elaborate ritual of showing off, which made indulgence in the finer things almost a necessity. In contrast, to risk starvation when surrounded by plenty was, at best, self-indulgent and, at worst, a sign of mental illness. Very recently, studies have emerged, which suggest that young men, as well as young women suffer from anorexia nervosa. Whether that was true in the 1860s and 1870s is impossible to know. Anorexia nervosa was initially described as an illness exclusively affecting young women, the same young women whom advice writers were at pains to warn against the danger of greed, and the same young women whose mothers brought them to endless dinner parties in hopes of catching the eyes of suitable young men to marry.

Age, class, gender and the science of nutrition

Dr Monin believed that 'man is only what he eats, or rather what he digests',[82] his version of a commonly held belief that people were – morally as well as physically – built from the food they ingested. Gender was one of the factors that determined appropriate diet. Medical advice in this matter echoed the beliefs of the society in which doctors participated. According to Ursula Bloom: 'There lingered the extraordinary belief that young ladies were entirely different from young gentlemen, particularly in the matter of conduct in the home, or food and drink and good manners.'[83] And from their knowledge of food and good manners flowed assumptions about their moral being: 'A girl was pure as the driven snow and knew nothing of the facts of life . . . but young gentlemen knew everything, and all of them were rogues.'[84] Early in the nineteenth century, nutritional advice continued to be dominated by custom and tradition, but as the century progressed, medicine became increasingly scientific, and so did ideas about diet and regimen. The neutral object of medical advice was the middle-aged, middle-class man, while other people existed in relation to this 'normal' person assumed by the author. By 1900, doctors such as Edward Foote argued that men, women, children and the elderly each had particular nutritional needs arising from their size and digestive capability.[85] Similarly, by end of the nineteenth century, many argued that people of different nationalities were physiologically distinct and could therefore be expected to need different quantities and qualities of nutrients. Social status, in particular stemming from occupation, was likewise believed to have an impact on dietary needs.

While each individual's needs were unique, it was also widely accepted that food intake could alter a person, not just physically but also morally and in their character. The belief that eating the right food was essential to morality was a hangover from the humoral system in which things which people saw, ate or smelled could affect the whole of their being mentally, morally and physically.[86] Many elements of this system, prevalent throughout early modern Europe, continued to influence medical advice writers up to the end of the nineteenth century. According to humoral theory, the body was made up of fluids, each of which had its own moral properties, and the boundaries of the body were far from solid. Medical science had abandoned the humoral system by the mid-nineteenth century, but the importance of a unique balance tailored to the individual continued to inform ideas about nutrition and diet. Yet alongside these traditional beliefs there emerged a more modern urge to rationalise and standardise, treating bodies as generally knowable.

Writing in 1911, J. Alan Murray described what he termed the 'standard diet for simple maintenance.'[87]

3 oz.	(85 grams) protein,	giving	350 kal.
3 "	(" ") fat,	"	790"
14 ½ "	(405 ") carbohydrates,	"	1,660"

Total Fuel value   2,800"[88]

This was the diet of the average middle-class adult man. The appropriate intakes for various other categories of people were measured in relation to this average:

> To ascertain the requirements of a family, those of working men may be taken as 1.3 times, and of women 0.85 times, the standard diet; the factors for children are 0.25 under five years of age; 0.5 from five to ten years; and 0.75 from ten to fifteen years.[89]

The 'fact' that women needed to eat less than men grew out of scientific reasoning coupled with cultural assumption. Bernard Macfadden, an influential proponent of physical culture, insisted that a woman should eat little enough to always leave the table hungry.[90] Women's smaller bodies were seen to require less food than men's larger ones. Though to some extent true, this belief failed to take into account factors such as pregnancy, nursing, or women's need for iron during menstruation. Rosalyn Diprose argues that patriarchal social relations rely on the implicit valorisation of male bodies above female ones.[91] Historians of working-class family life have been more sensitive to the symbolic and strategic way in which food was apportioned to men and women. Strategies for acquiring food, and for distributing it among family members with different roles to play in the household economy, were central to the daily life of many poor London families. As Ellen Ross argues, the father, who was often absent throughout the week, used his position at the head of table, carving the Sunday roast, to symbolically enforce his position of authority.[92] Middle-class men did not do hard physical labour, and could afford enough food for all household members to eat as much as they needed, but the symbolic role of food as a marker of position within the family hierarchy was still powerful.

The bulk of published advice was for the young, as they started out in life, but Sir Henry Thompson wrote explicitly about the dietary needs of elderly men. He argued that longevity would only be achieved through a diminution of diet. Specifically, he claimed that in their youth, men learned to partake of whatever pleasures their peers urged them to, including copious amounts of food and drink. As a man aged, he tried to maintain these habits, but his system was no longer able to cope with them.[93] Thompson wrote within the discourse of gluttony and moderation, but tailored his claims to apply specifically to elderly men. Old women were not considered as having specific nutritional needs based on their age, presumably because the only meaningful transition in a woman's life within the structure of the nineteenth-century middle-class family was that from girlhood to womanhood, as demarcated by the rite of marriage. Thus old age, though distinct from adulthood, was rarely considered as a separate nutritional category.

When it came to feeding children, advice writers were expansive, though in France the distinction ended with infancy, while in England children's diet continued to be distinct from adults' for several years.[94] Children were not generally included as dinner party guests, and English children often ate in their own nursery. French homes rarely contained nurseries, which meant that French children ate in the dining room, though some writers were critical of this practice. Infants clearly could not eat solid foods and therefore could not be fed alongside the older members of a family. Wet nursing was still widely practised in the early nineteenth century, but references to it are scarce for the second half of the century.[95] For the bourgeoisie, who idealised woman's natural ability to nurture her children, breastfeeding was prized,[96] and where doctors mentioned the issue they considered it as the best source of infant nutrition.[97]

Though women's nutritional needs were rarely singled out in a positive way by medical writers, by the end of the century, French women were being advised in articles such as 'L'Alimentation des nourrices' in Le Pot-au-Feu, in 1901, of the importance of a mother's diet for producing healthy milk for her babies.[98] There may, too, have been strong economic incentives for eschewing the wet nurse among the stable but not excessively wealthy middle classes. As the century progressed, another alternative to breastfeeding, more accessible to the average middle-class mother, emerged in the form of manufactured milk products – formula – which were advertised as a healthy alternative.[99] Advertisments, like the one for Allenbury's Foods from 1904 (figure 2) emphasised the maternal instinct and

Figure 2 Allenbury's Food, 1904.

the mother's natural role in feeding her child, by depicting a mother looking lovingly at her well-fed child, seemingly entirely oblivious to the outside world. This depiction created the impression that feeding a child formula was just as nurturing as breastfeeding, and did not loosen the mother–child bond, while the text aligned the product with the healthful qualities of breastmilk, stating: 'They are as easy of digestion as maternal milk, and provide a perfect diet for the formation of firm flesh and strong bones.'

Moving into adulthood, occupation was seen as one of the factors determining an individual's nutritional needs. J. A. Murray suggested that 'working men' needed 1.3 times the 'standard' man's diet.[100] The question of diet in relation to occupation, especially where it intersected with the delicate definition of middle-class masculinity, was an ongoing source of tension. Working men, it was argued, needed more food and, in particular, more of the types of foods believed to provide strength and energy, of which red meat was the principal one. As red meat was associated with strength and virility, it was considered a particularly suitable food for men, and English men in particular wrote about steak and roast beef, in a way that reveals them as identity-reinforcing foods.[101] However, middle-class men were not supposed to be involved with physical labour, and so to eat the types of energising foods associated with such labour could threaten the boundary between the middle and working classes. Various doctors explained that people involved in sedentary pursuits could not digest the same quantity of food as those involved in vigorous activity.[102] Other writers chose to reinforce the positive image of the man of genius as someone for whom earthly pleasures like food and drink held little appeal.[103]

An advertisement for Leibig's extract of meat, which appeared in the *Hotel Review* in 1886, used these preoccupations to advantage:

> It is a remarkable fact and a very satisfactory one, that as civilization progresses and intellectual work increases, making increased calls upon the human frame in order to respond to these new requirements, cookery should have made immense progress, and by its efficient assistance to digestion, should have enabled humanity to find physical power enough to carry out the immense intellectual labour to be performed in the present day . . . Leibig Company's Extract of Meat is one of the most efficient means to attain that object.[104]

Because in both France and England there were different foods associated with manual and cerebral work, eating the right foods in social situations could reinforce a person's social standing.

Medical advice appeared to be different from advice about etiquette, because it is presented as rational, scientific discourse. Yet what nineteenth-century doctors provided were a set of ideals acceptable to middle-class notions of respectability, very much allied with the rules for good living to be found in every other form of behaviour book. Doctors were trained professional and, thus, were themselves members of the middle class to whom they addressed much of their advice. The medical discourse contained in advice books incorporated bourgeois values and cultural practices with nutritional advice. To many doctors, the nutritional needs of the body went hand in hand with the social necessity of mealtime sociability.[105] Hubert Mayo, in 1851, explained:

> The pleasures of the table . . . when used in moderation, admit of some defence: they promote social intercourse. Man, unlike animals, is in best humour when he is feeding, and more disposed then than at other times to cultivate those amicable relations by which the bonds of society are strengthened.[106]

And in 1881 the French Dr Fonssagrives echoed this sentiment, stating that as long as one maintained self-control, 'diner en ville' would not be harmful to general health.[107]

By the nineteenth century the humoral system had all but disappeared, as medicine engaged with changing scientific ideas. However, nutrition continued to be made up of a combination of scientific knowledge and traditional customs and beliefs. *Dr Foote's Home Cyclopedia of Popular Medical, Social and Sexual Science*, published in 1908, argued that bad digestion could lead to selfishness and chronic mental disorder, which suggests that ideas about the moral properties of foods were slow to disappear.[108] Manuscript cookbooks – repositories of women's traditional knowledge handed down through the generations – included both recipes and remedies. Like medical advice on the moral properties of food, this combination of cookery and healing reveals the continuity with to an earlier period in which medicines were generally concocted in the kitchen. Taking up the practice of combining the housewife's role as nourisher and healer, many published cookbooks included sections on cooking for the sick, because it was the duty of the mistress of the house to be knowledgeable about all aspects of nutrition, both for daily use and as curative and preventative medicine. Medical advice writers reinforced this ideal of the housewife as home healer, by combining advice on general good health and nutrition with advice on cures for specific illnesses. By using the nurturing housewife as the imagined reader, medical advice writers could offer suggestions for how to stay healthy and in control of the body, without challenging existing – traditional – knowledge or food preferences.

Different theories about how the body worked and how best to nourish it coexisted in early modern Europe. The humoral theory, of Aristotelian descent, had long prevailed, but Bryan Turner argues that the image of the body politic also influenced ideas about regimen, while Lisa Smith has found that, in France, agricultural imagery was used to describe the interior workings of bodies.[109] From the eighteenth century, the image of the body as machine, the origins of which Turner finds in Descartes' mind–body dichotomy, had gained sway and by the 1870s it was by far the most agreed upon theory, even if there was never perfect agreement about how best to 'fuel' the 'machine'.[110] In 1870, an article in French weekly *L'Illustration* set out the current theory of digestion: that the human body worked in the same way as a steam engine, foods were combustibles and that 'everything could be reduced to the production of a certain quantity of force'.[111] Two decades later, Louis Bourdeau argued that nourishment was the most pressing of all needs for human life, because every activity of a living being required the spending of force which was equivalent to the transformation of matter, which then needed to be replaced. He explained: 'Life has often been compared to a chamber in which combustibles are burned and which would quickly be extinguished if it was not regularly maintained.'[112] In 1908, Dr Foote referred to 'the delicate and exquisite machinery which we call life'. As industrialisation increasingly shaped people's understanding of the world, the body-as-machine theory came to be widely accepted as the model for understanding digestion. Along with this, the rational organisation which underpinned modern modes of production also influenced visions of domestic comfort.

Divisions of the home

Categorising and compartmentalising every aspect of daily routine was an ideal espoused by nineteenth-century bourgeois all across

Europe.[113] It was considered a mark of good taste as well as morality to organise your home according to established rules.[114] According to Roger Dixon and Stefan Muthesius, Victorian houses were a reflection both of the social position of their occupiers and of the social position they aspired to.[115] Margaret Ponsonby argues that by the early nineteenth century, middle-class living rooms were no longer expected to be used for multiple purposes as had generally been the case in the eighteenth century.[116] Bernard Denvir argues that by mid-century it had become widely accepted that each area of a house should be separate, and be ascribed certain functions, and advice books as well as periodical articles proliferated on all aspects of interior decor.[117] By 1880, in offering advice on how to choose or design the perfect entirely segregated according to function:

> The Plan must give *Isolation* to the several parts. With our present habits we could not live in those old palaces, in which the only communication for a suite of twenty rooms, is by passing through each in succession . . . This is especially characteristic of modern planning in England as compared with France, where ordinary and regular entrance to one room is through another, a mere backway or *dégagement* by a dark narrow passage being provided for service. With us, from our love of seclusion and retirement, each room must be isolated . . . The dining-room must be capable of being shut off from the rest of the house, communicating during dinner only with the kitchen. The dinner should not have to be carried past the drawing-room door, or through the hall and public passages, and the kitchen must be so placed that smells and noise do not invade the house.[118]

Stevenson raised most of the important points concerning domestic architecture as it pertained to middle-class ideology and dining practices: the importance of privacy, the need for backstage areas for moving through the house, and the importance of dining room and kitchen being placed in such a way that food did not have to be brought through areas of the house where it did not belong. Erving Goffman's concept of the centrality of performance to everyday life was already present in contemporary descriptions of the dining room.[119] According to Chatillon-Plessis: 'The dining-room is a theatre wherein the kitchen serves as the wings and the table as the stage.'[120] Thus we may see the house as divided between front and backstage areas.

Stevenson was mistaken in asserting that the English cared more about privacy than did the French. What was true was that London and Paris had very different styles of middle-class dwellings.[121] While Stevenson made it clear that he considered the English style far preferable to the French, an article in L'*Illustrateur* in June 1895 represented the opposite position:

> It has become an axiom that the English have resolved the problem of the perfect home by each living in their own separate house . . . Perfection is not of this world, but nothing is farther from it than the English private house which is the object of our unthinking envy . . . No need to lift the cover of your neighbour's pot to know what he puts in it . . . the kitchen below ground opening onto a gully bordering the sidewalk, every passer-by sees what is roasting for dinner. Due to the long distances and the complication of service caused by the ladder-style house, cooks in London do not go to the market. Everything is brought to the house. If you have curious neighbours . . . nothing which you consume at home will be unknown to them.[122]

Privacy within the home was as important in Paris as in London. However, in each place there were different notions of how this privacy could be achieved.

All architectural advice literature provided guidelines on how to organise dining space within the home. The first step in creating a respectable dining environment was to have a home in which food production and consumption were clearly separated. Keeping food and cooking smells from infiltrating all areas of the house, including the dining room, was a matter of primary importance. Various similar solutions were offered as to how cooking smells could be kept away from the home's front stage areas.[123] For Gervase Wheeler, writing in 1872, the key was for 'the principal staircase [to] be separated by a lobby with enclosing doors from the back stairway and kitchen passages; and this should have, if possible, an external window upon the upper level'.[124] This system, which was fairly typical, would, he argued 'go far to prevent escape of odours from the kitchen into the hall, and their permeation of the staircase'.[125]

Mrs Beeton asserted that the kitchen should be far from the dining room, so that 'members, visitors or guests of the family, may not perceive the odour incident to cooking, or hear the noise of culinary operations'.[126] Mme D'Alq similarly advised that 'the kitchen, office and all its adjuncts must be kept at a distance and out of sight. The former, in particular, which is revealed by its smell, is placed as far as possible from the masters' quarters and the dining room.'[127] This concern with smell was partly related to the nineteenth-century belief that diseases could be spread through inhaling bad odours, referred to as miasmic contagion.[128] The kitchen–dining room dichotomy also divided private and public, dirt and cleanliness, darkness and light (especially where the kitchen was tucked away in the basement of the house), impurity and purity. The dining room was the pristine space in which guests were received, and the house was designed to protect backstage areas from public scrutiny, while at the same time protecting the public from all the unpleasant tasks and odours of private life.

Conceding that not all middle-class families could reserve their dining room exclusively for eating, Mrs Loftie gave advice on how best to arrange a room under such conditions:

> Its feeding uses ought to be kept as much as possible in the background . . . There should, however, be some arrangement to have a good, large, steady table independent of that on which dinner is served, for it is most unpleasant to be disturbed in the middle of a drawing or some writing by a servant coming in to lay the cloth.[129]

Similar advice appeared in various sources, such as the periodical *The Lady*: 'I never like a sofa in a dining room . . . as a concession to comfort, and to those people who use this room as a sitting room during the morning, I would have an easy chair on each side of the fireplace.'[130] Architect and advice writer Robert Kerr advised that in a room used as both dining and sitting room, attention should be given to furnishing the room in such a way that 'feminine attributes may be, according to circumstance, duly represented'.[131] In this he alluded to the gendering of the furniture itself and of the dining room (masculine) and drawing room (feminine).[132]

In keeping with the nineteenth-century insistence on gender as a guiding principle in categorisations of human behaviour, even the rooms within a private home took on a gender identity. From as early as 1816, according to Ponsonby's evidence, it is clear that living rooms in English homes were a feminine and feminised space.[133] Dining room furniture, it was generally agreed, had to be solid and masculine. In the dining room, the master of the house ruled, and this was reflected in the choice of furniture. Wheeler described the drawing room as an area of the house devoted to the use of the ladies, and insisted for this reason that any woodwork in the drawing room should not be treated as woodwork, since 'there always seems an incongruity and rudeness about grained doors or polished maple'.[134] Likewise, Kerr insisted that: 'The whole aspect of the [dining] room ought to be that of masculine importance.'[135] Until the eighteenth century, dinner parties had been hosted by men for men. During the nineteenth century, the responsibility for hosting the dinner party came to shift from the host to the hostess, but the event was still principally for the pleasure of the host and his male guests, and the room in which the meal was eaten was therefore a masculine stronghold.

English dining room furniture was ideally solid and serious, demonstrating stability and authority. Kerr argued: 'The style . . . is always somewhat massive and simple . . . on the principle, perhaps, of conformity with the substantial pretensions of both English character and English fare.'[136] Designer Lorenzo Booth felt that the dining room was a less interesting room to furnish than the drawing room because it was in the latter that luxury and taste were displayed, while the dining room was: 'suggestive of comfort and social convenience, for it is the apartment where the owner dispenses his hospitality'. He also advocated 'solid and substantial' furniture for the dining room.[137] *The Lady* published examples of dining room furniture, which avoided the frills associated with Victorian drawing rooms. Others used words like 'grave, rich and stately' to describe what they felt should be the attributes of the dining room furniture.[138] Wheeler advocated dark woods, such as old oak and old Spanish mahogany.[139] He also discussed the general appearance of the dining room, stating that the colours used should be stately and unobtrusive, and that if paintings were hung on the walls 'the selection should be limited to a few pleasant, rich and cheerful designs'.[140] Apart from when a meal was actually being eaten, the chairs would be placed along the walls. Kerr felt that this gave the room a 'substantial and hospitable aspect'.[141]

In France, historical styles of furniture were most desirable.[142] While architecture was modern and forward looking, the design of the dining room furniture looked to the past. Advising decorators, Simoneton gave illustration of possible dining room arrangements, advocating both the gothic and the Louis XIII styles as being particularly suitable, though his preference was for the gothic style, which he felt conveyed a 'lordly' hospitality.[143] Geroge Remon's dining rooms, obviously intended for the wealthier end of the market, owing to their large size, were decorated with beautifully painted wall panels and ceilings, and with mirrors. They were very ornate and elegant and, like English dining rooms, the chairs were lined against the walls.[144] The ideal dining rooms of both French and English architectural advice manuals were furnished with strong solid tables and chairs, and without the decorative elements associated with the feminised Victorian sitting room.

While the masculine identity of the dining room was represented in the furniture, the feminine mark was placed on the table setting. Hosting in the eighteenth century had been a masculine prerogative, but in the nineteenth century the burden gradually shifted on to women. By 1850, it was almost entirely a woman's responsibility to host a dinner party, and it behoved her to place evidence of the effort she had expended on her guests through a tastefully arranged table and flowers.[145] Advice writers generally agreed that there should be no outward signs of strain or effort on the part of the hostess and that to have appeared to have had too much to do with the cooking of the food itself was improper: the duty of the mistress of the house was to order the meal and oversee its preparation, but the actual cooking had to be done, or at least appear to have been done, by servants.[146] But decorating the table was a task which a woman could undertake with no risk to her reputation. In fact, it was generally advised that this was one of her principal duties, as servants would not have the aesthetic sense of their middle-class mistress when it came to tasks such as selecting and arranging flowers.[147] While furniture was expensive and tended not to be replaced very often, flowers were perishable, and it was therefore possible to change the fashion in flowers with every new season. Owing to the frequency of changes in fashion, advice about table decoration tended to appear in women's magazines more than in etiquette books.

Flowers and place settings were the principal elements of table decoration with which women were concerned. One author commented that: 'the best meal in the world is not appetising on a barren or soiled tablecloth'.[148] Mrs Loftie advised her readers to use restraint when setting the table. She warned against putting more glasses on the table than were likely to be needed: 'Many people, particularly old gentlemen, are fidgeted by finding five or six glasses at their elbow, all liable to be overturned or broken.'[149] She also discussed the important question of what silverware was appropriate for use at respectable dinner parties, referring to this as the 'knife and fork question': 'There is a serious question anxiously debated at many dinner parties as to the superiority of three prongs to four. The "three-prongians" hold their own against the "four-prongians," except in the matter of young peas.'[150] Mrs Loftie pointed out the practical dimension of floral decorations: 'Flowers and fruits are at all times desirable on the table . . . even to look at it is nice, and a bunch of sweet fresh flowers seems to give one appetite.'[151] An author in *La Salle à Manger* emphasised the more aesthetic principle, comparing a well-decorated table to a well-dressed woman: 'The arrangement of a table is like the toilette of a women, its success often rests on few things.'[152] Just as the organisation of house and furniture revealed the inner morality of household members, so the choice of cutlery and the arrangement of the table had moral as well as aesthetic implications.

The many articles on floral decoration which appeared in the French women's magazine *Le Pot-au-feu* reveal the extent to which aesthetic knowledge was considered an intangible possession, what we might now refer to as cultural capital, rather than something which could be acquired simply by following instructions. While giving hints on new floral fashions, these articles reiterated the point that decorating was a matter of personal taste. One article from 1895 stated: 'It is very difficult to say what is currently the fashion in terms of flowers for table decorations. Every hostess ingeniously surprises her guests with a new note, and there are no rules other than good taste and imagination.'[153] Another, from 1896, affirmed that it is up to the mistress of the house to determine exactly how to place all the elements of table decoration at her disposal, ending: 'We can state no rule on this subject other than the rule of taste.'[154] Yet another article, from 1904, confirmed the same belief, ending, however, on a more positive note, that the taste required could be learned by all, given the proper training.[155]

All commentators on women's good taste in decorating their tables did not share *Le Pot-au-feu*'s optimism. Many articles were highly critical of women who failed to use the rules of good taste when arranging flowers on the dinner table. One wrote: 'out of vain ostentation, tables are overloaded with centrepieces, with floral decorations with pieces so high that the guests on the right can no longer glimpse those on the left, and conversation, between people who cannot see each other, becomes impossible. The French table is one where one speaks, it attempts to mask no one.'[156] Another commented that if a woman had too many flowers on her table, she might be using them to distract her guests' attention away from the bad food she was serving them.[157] Floral decorations could reveal a woman's lack of aesthetic sense. A wrong choice in flowers could also suggest poor food and a deceitful hostess.

The men and women who wrote advice books for the middle-class market came from the same class and social environment as their intended audience. The advice they produced, in etiquette as much as in medicine and architecture, reflected the values, norms and moral standards they themselves aspired to. This accounts for the striking similarities in the advice contained in books which at first glance might appear to offer expertise in very different areas, such as dinner party conversations and the properties of a healthy diet. In the same vein, the expertise proffered in advice books published in London and Paris might differ in, for example, describing a house or an apartment as the ideal dwelling place, but were easily recognisable as proffering advice that stemmed from a transnational bourgeois culture of respectability and restraint. In both France and England, it was women who were expected to maintain health and morality within the home. Women's domestic knowledge formed a body of rules, which overlapped with the rules of advice writer, the study of which forms the subject of Chapter 2, and allows us some insight into the complex ways in which the ideals gleaned from prescriptive literature reflected but also competed with the daily mealtime preparation and rituals of individual families.

Notes

1 A. E. Douglas, *The Etiquette of Fashionable Life* (London: Easingwold, 1849) p. v.
2 D. Attar, *A Bibliography of Household Books Published in Britain, 1800–1914* (London: Prospect, 1987) p. 13.
3 The stability of advice as a genre, and the tendency for authors to copy one another, has been noted elsewhere. See for example J. Davies, *Dining in the Past, 1450–1700* (Bristol: Stuart Press, 2006) p. 2.
4 A. Bryson, *From Courtesy to Civility: Changing Codes of Conduct in Early Modern England* (Oxford: Clarendon Press, 1998) p. 6.

5 See for example: M. Eleb-Vidal, *Architecture de la vie privée [1]: maisons et mentalités XVIIè–XIXè siècle* (Bruxelles: Aux Archives d'Architecture Moderne, 1989); A. Adams, *Architecture in the Family Way: Doctors, Houses and Women, 1870–1900* (Montreal: McGill-Queen's University Press, 1996); G. Lees-Maffei, 'From Service to self-service: advice literature as design discourse, 1920–1970', *Journal of Design History* 14:3 (2001) 187–206; H. Long, *The Edwardian House: The Middle-Class Home in Britain, 1880–1914* (Manchester: Manchester University Press, 1993).

6 C. Kelly, *Refining Russia: Advice Literature, Polite Culture and Gender from Catherine to Yeltsin* (Oxford: Oxford University Press, 2001).

7 C. Dallett Hemphill, *Bowing to Necessity: A History of Manners in America, 1620–1860* (Oxford: Oxford University Press, 1999) p. 4.

8 L. Young, *Middle-Class Culture in the Nineteenth Century: America, Australia and Britain* (Basingstoke: Palgrave-Macmillan, 2003). Also: J. Kocka and A. Mitchell (eds), *Bourgeois Society in Nineteenth Century Europe* (Oxford: Berg, 1993); P. Pilbeam, *The Middle Classes in Europe 1789–1914: France, Germany, Italy, Russia* (Basingstoke: Macmillan Education, 1990).

9 G. Routledge, *Routledge's Etiquette for Ladies* (London: Routledge), 1864) p. 55. The same advice was given to gentlemen in *Routledge's Etiquette for Gentlemen* (London: Routledge, 1864) p. 59.

10 N. Elias, *The Civilising Process: The History of Manners* (Oxford: Blackwell, 1994).

11 A. St George, *The Descent of Manners: Etiquette, Rules and the Victorians* (London: Chatto & Windus, 1993) p. xi.

12 J. Trussler, *The Honour of the Table, or Rules for Behaviour During Meals; with the whole art of carving* (London, 1791) p. 7.

13 L. Davidoff, *The Best Circles: Society, Etiquette and the Season* (London: Croom Helm, 1973).

14 Agogos, *Hints on Etiquette and the Usages of Polite Society: With a Glance at Bad Habits* (London: Longman & Co., 1849) p. 11.

15 Davidoff, *The Best Circles*, p. 15; A. St George, *The Descent of Manners*, p. xiv.

16 P. Carter, *Man and the Emergence of Polite Society, Britain 1660–1800* (Harlow: Pearson, 2001).

17 Adams, *Architecture in the Family Way*.

18 Elias, *The Civilising Process*.

19 *The Caterer* (15 April 1882).

20 Bryson, *From Courtesy to Civility*, p. 6.

21 Dallett Hemphill, *Bowing to Necessity*, p. 4.

22 Bryson, *From Courtesy to Civility*, p. 2.

23 M. Visser, *The Rituals of Dinner: The Origins, Evolution, Eccentricities and the Meaning of Table Manners* (London: Penguin, 1992).

24 See for example: Eleb-Vidal, *Architecture de la vie privée*; Adams, *Architecture in the Family Way*, Lees-Maffei, 'From Service to self-service: advice literature as design discourse, 1920–1970', *Journal of Design History*, 14:3 (2001) 187–206; Long, *The Edwardian House: The Middle-Class Home in Britain, 1880–1914*.

25 C. J. Lawrence, 'William Buchan: medicine laid open', *Medical History* 19:1 (1975) 20–35; C. E. Rosenberg, 'Medical Text and Social Context: Explaining William Buchan's *Domestic Medicine*', *Bulletin of the History of Medicine* 57:1 (1983) 22–42; R. Porter, *Doctor and Society: Thomas Beddoes and the Sick Trade in Late-Enlightenment England* (London: Routledge, 1992); G. J. Barker-Benfield, *The Culture of Sensibility: Sex and Society in Eighteenth-Century Britain* (London: Chicago University Press, 1992); G. Smith, 'Prescribing the rules of health: self-help and advice in the late eighteenth century', in R. Porter (ed.), *Patients and Practitioners: Lay Perceptions of Medicine in Pre-Industrial Society* (Cambridge: Cambridge University Press, 1985).

26 H. Kamminga and A. Cunningham, *The Science and Culture of Nutrition, 1840–1940* (Amsterdam: Rodopi, 1995).

27 J.-P. Aron, *The Art of Eating in France: Manners and Menus in the Nineteenth Century*, trans. N. Rootes (London: Owen, 1975) p. 11.

28 M. Montanari, *The Culture of Food*, trans. C. Ipsen (Oxford: Blackwell, 1994) pp. 21–4.

29 C. E. Harrison, *The Bourgeois Citizen in Nineteenth-Century France: Gender, Sociability and the Uses of Emulation.* (Oxford: Oxford University Press, 1999).

30 M. J. Wiener, *English Culture and the Decline of the Industrial Spirit* (Cambridge: Cambridge University Press, 1981).

31 M. J. Daunton, ' "Gentlemanly capitalism" and British industry 1820–1914', *Past and Present* 122:1 (1989) 119–58; W. D. Rubenstein, *Elites and the Wealthy in Modern British History: Essays in Social and Economic History* (New York: St Martin's Press, 1987) pp. 172–214.

32 See for example A. Bennett, *The Letters of Arnold Bennett*, vol. II 1889–1915, ed. James Hepburn (London: Oxford University Press, 1968) p. 13 (letter to George Sturt, 28 Oct. 1894), p. 77 (Letter to George Stuart, 8 Feb. 1897), p. 95 (Letter to John Rickard, 8 Dec. 1897), p. 303 (Letter to Jane Wells, 17 Feb. 1912).

33 U. Bloom, *Sixty Years of Home* (London: Hurst & Blackett, 1960) p. 118.

34 See for example J. H. Curtis, *Advice on the Care of the Health* (London: Whittaker and Co., 1845) p. 12: *Cassell's People's Physician: A Book of Medicine and of Health for Everybody*, 5 vols. (London: Cassell, 1900–15).

35 Anon. *The Family Physician: A Manual of Domestic Medicine*, 2nd edn (London: Cassell and Co., 1882) p. 354. Also, Sir H. Thompson, *Diet in Relation to Age and Activity, with Hints Concerning Habits Conductive to Longevity* (London: Frederick Warne, 1902) Part I, p. 30.

36 E. Monin, *L'Hygiène de l'estomac: guide pratique de l'alimentation* (Paris, O. Doin, *c.* 1890) p. 385. Also W. Lovett, *Elementary Anatomy and Physiology, for schools and private instruction: with lessons on diet, intoxicating drinks, tobacco and disease* (London: Darton, 1851) p. 136.

37 Sir J. Crichton-Brown, *Delusions in Diet or Parsimony in Nutrition* (London: Funk and Wagnalls, 1910) p. 105. Also Monin, *L'Hygiène de l'estomac*, p. 25.

38 A. Haig, *Diet and Food in Relation to Strength and Power of Endurance, Training and Athletics* (London: Churchill, 1902) p. vii. Also, H. Dobell, *On Diet and Regimen in Sickness and Health* (London: H. K. Lewis, 1872) p. 4.

39 *La Salle à Manger* (June 1890).

40 *L'Art Culinaire* (15 Oct. 1889).

41 Crichton-Brown, *Delusions in Diet*, p. 2.

42 'La clef des champs', *L'Illustration* (5 May 1860).

43 Anon. *The Family Physician: A Manual of Domestic Medicine. By physicians and surgeons of the principal London hospitals*, 2nd edn (London: Cassell & Co., 1879), p. 382.

44 See for example Anon. *How to Dine; or, etiquette of the Dinner Table* (London: Ward, Locke and Tyler, 1879) p. 63; P. Donmer Stanhope, *Encyclopædia of Manners and Etiquette* (London: H. G. Bohn, 1850).

45 Stanhope, *Encyclopædia of Manners and Etiquette*, p. 79.

46 St George, *The Descent of Manners*, p. xi.

47 Routledge, *Etiquette for Ladies*, p. 60; Routledge, *Etiquette for Gentlemen*, p. 60; Anon, *The Lady's Manual of Modern Etiquette* (London, 1864) p. 6; E. Cheadle, *Manners in Modern Society: Being a Book of Etiquette* (London: Cassell, Petter and Galpin, 1972) p. 139.

48 A. de Bassanville, *Code du cérémonial: Guide des gens du monde dans toutes les circonstances de la vie* (Paris: Lebigre-Duquesne frères, 1867) p. 240.

49 Anon., *Table Etiquette, Domestic Cookery and Confectionary* (London, 1854) p. 11; Bassanville, *Code du cérémonial*, p. 230; P. Boitard, *Guide manuel de la bonne compagnie* (Paris: Passard, 1861) p. 276.

50 Routledge, *Etiquette for Ladies* and *Etiquette for Gentlemen*, p. 65; Bassanville, *Code du cérémonial*, p. 230 and 239; Boitard, *Guide manuel de la bonne compagnie*, pp. 42–3.

51 Bassanville, *Code du cérémonial*, p. 230.

52 Bassanville, *Code du cérémonial*, p. 240.

53 This and all the following rules appear in almost all etiquette books. References are only to some examples of each: Routledge, *Etiquette for Ladies*, p. 71, Anon. *The Lady's Manual of Modern Etiquette*, p. 10; Cheadle, *Manners of Modern Society: Being a Book of Etiquette*, p. 141; Bassanville, *Code du cérémonial*, p. 240.

54 Anon., *How to Dine*, p. 10.

55 Anon., *How to Dine*, p. 10; Routledge, *Etiquette for Ladies*, and *Etiquette for Gentlemen*, p. 66.

56 Anon., *How to Dine*, p. 11.

57 I. Beeton, *Mrs Beeton's Book of Household Management* (London: S. O. Beeton Publishing, 1861) p. 13.

58 S. Mennell, *All Manners of Food: Eating and Taste in England and France from the Middle Ages to the Present* (Oxford: Blackwell, 1985) p. 36; R. Spang, *The Invention of the Restaurant: Paris and Modern Gastronomic Culture* (London: Harvard University Press, 2000) pp. 38–41.

59 Arthur Crisp, an expert on the psychiatry of eating disorders, argued that Byron himself was probably anorexic and bulimic, based on what is known of Byron's attitude towards food and towards obesity. A. Crisp, 'Ambivalence towards fatness and its origins,' *British Medical Journal* 315 (1997) 1703.

60 Mennell, *All Manners of Food*, p. 39.

61 G. Cheyne, *The English Malady* (London: G. Strahan, 1733). Also Barker-Benfield, *The Culture of Sensibility*.

62 *Salle à Manger* (May 1893).

63 *The Travellers Journal and Hotel Gazette* (15 March 1880).

64 E. Chapus, *Manuel de l'homme et de la femme comme il faut* (Paris: A. Bourdilliat, 1861) p. 51.

65 E. Chapus, *Manuel de l'homme et de la femme comme il faut*, p. 51.

66 Crichton-Brown, *Delusions in Diet*, pp. 4–5.

67 W. Banting, *Letter on Corpulence, Addressed to the Public*, 3rd edn (London: Harrison, 1864).

68 Chapus, *Manuel de l'homme et de la femme comme il faut*, p. 56.

69 Chapus, *Manuel de l'homme et de la femme comme il faut*, p. 56.

70 Chapus, *Manuel de l'homme et de la femme comme il faut*, p. 56.

71 E. Boursin, *Le Livre de la femme au XIXème siècle* (Paris, 1865), p. 327.

72 Boursin, *Le Livre de la femme au XIXème siècle*, pp. 338–9.

73 Boursin, *Le Livre de la femme au XIXème siècle*, p. 353.

74 Boursin, *Le Livre de la femme au xixeme siecle*, p. 353. Similar ideas about the importance of a woman's appearance also appear in B. A. Macfadden, *The Power and Beauty of Superb Womanhood; How they are lost and how they may be Regained* (London: Macfadden Physical Development, 1901) pp. 11–12.

75 Boursin, *Le Livre de la femme au xixeme siecle*, p. 353.
76 Boursin, *Le Livre de la femme au xixeme siecle*, p. 354.
77 Boursin, *Le Livre de la femme au xixeme siecle*, p. 354.
78 See for example H. King, *The Disease of Virgins: Greensickness, Chlorosis and the Problems of Puberty* (London: Routledge, 2004); L. W. Smith, 'Imagining women's fertility before technology', *Journal of Medical Humanities* 31:1 (2010), 69–79.
79 J. Vernon, *Hunger: A Modern History* (London: Harvard University Press, 2007).
80 Brumberg, *Fasting Girls*, pp. 128, 134–7.
81 L.-V. Marcé, 'Notes on a form of hypochondriacal delusion, consecutive to the dyspepsias, and principally characterised by the refusal of food', trans A. Blewett and A. Bottéro, *History of Psychiatry*, V (1994) 273–83.
82 Monin, *L'Hygiène de l'estomac*, pp. 383–4.
83 Bloom, *Sixty Years of Home*, p. 116.
84 Bloom, *Sixty Years of Home*, p. 116.
85 E. B. Foote, *Dr. Foote's Home Cyclopedia of Popular Medicine, Social and Sexual Science* (London: L. N. Fowler, 1906), p. 77.
86 See for example Monin, *L'Hygiène de l'estomac*, p. 397.
87 J. A. Murray, *The Economy of Food: A Popular Treatise on Nutrition, Food and Diet* (London: Constable, 1911) p. 47.
88 Murray, *The Economy of Food*, p. 47.
89 Murray, *The Economy of Food*, p. 47.
90 Macfadden, *The Power and Beauty of Superb Womanhood*, p. 123.
91 R. Diprose, *The Bodies of Women: Ethics, Embodiment and Sexual Difference* (London: Routledge, 1994), p. viii.
92 E. Ross, *Love and Toil: Motherhood In Outcast London, 1870–1918* (New York: Oxford University Press, 1993). See also A. Davin, *Growing Up Poor: Home, School and Street in London, 1870–1914* (London: Rivers Oram Press, 1996).
93 Thompson, *Diet in Relation to Age and Activity*.
94 Mennell, *All Manners of Food*, p. 73.
95 *L'Illustration*, 'Hygiène et médecine de l'alimentation pendant la première enfance,' (11 Feb. 1865); Herbert Mayo, *The Philosophy of Living* 3rd edn (London: John W. Parker, 1851) p. 80; O. Bornand (ed.), *Diary of W. M. Rossetti, 1870–1873* (Oxford: Clarendon Press, 1877) p. 148; A. de P. D12Z/3 contains an advertisement *c.*1900 for a non alcoholised beer which was advertised as suitable for wet nurses.
96 See, for example: T. Marriott, *Female Conduct, Being an Essay on the Art of Pleasing* (London, 1759) pp. 258–60.
97 J. S. Forsyth, *The Natural and Medical Dieteticon* (London: Sherwood, Gilbert, and Piper, 1824) p. 16; T. Parry, *On Diet, with its Influence*

on Man (London: S. & J. Bentley, Wilson, and Fley, 1844) p. 1; J. H. Curtis, *Advice on the Care of the Health* (London: Whittaker, 1845) p. 6; W. Davidson, *A Treatise on Diet, Comprising the Natural History, Properties, Composition, Adulterisations and uses of Vegetables, Animals, Fishes & c. used as Food* (Glasgow: Blackie, 1846) p. 17.

98 *Le Pot-au-Feu* (1 Dec. 1901).

99 A. de P. D12Z/3.

100 Murray, *The Economy of Food*.

101 The important role of Roast Beef in articulations of British national identity is explored in B. Rogers, *Beef and Liberty: Roast Beef, John Bull and the English Patriots* (London, Chatto & Windus, 2003).

102 See for example: Monin, *L'Hygiène de l'estomac*, p. 391; Thompson, *Diet in Relation to Age and Activity*, p. 67; Anon., *Physicians and Surgeons*, p. 356.

103 Murray, *The Economy of Food*, pp. 2–3; Monin, *L'Hygiène de l'estomac*, p. 389. For a discussion of a similar phenomenon in the eighteenth century see: F. A. Jonsson, 'The Physiology of Hypochondria in Eighteenth-Century Britain' and A. C. Vila, 'The *Philosophe's* Stomach: Hedonism, Hypochondira, and the Intellectual in Enlightenment France', both in C. Forth and A. Carden-Coyne (eds), *Cultures of the Abdomen: Diet, Digestion and Fat in the Modern World* (New York: Palgrave Macmillan, 2004).

104 *The Hotel Review* (Oct. 1886).

105 See for example A. Gaultier, *L'Alimentation et le régime chez l'homme sain et chez les malades* (Paris: Masson, 1904), p. 353.

106 Mayo, *The Philosophy of Living*, pp. 90–1.

107 J.-B. Fonssagrives, *Hygiène alimentaire des malades, des convalescent et des valétudinaire* (Paris: J.-B. Baillière et fils, 1881) pp. 332–3.

108 *Dr Foote's Home Cyclopedia*, pp. 76, 82. The author uses words such as 'balance' and 'blockages', traditionally the lexicon of the humoral system.

109 B. S. Turner, 'The Government of the Body: Medical Regimen and the Rationalisation of Diet', *The British Journal of Sociology*. 33:2 (1982) 258, and Smith, 'Imagining Women's Fertility before Technology', *Journal of Medical Humanities*.

110 *Dr Foote's Home Cyclopedia*, p. 76.

111 *L'Illustration* (1 Jan. 1870).

112 L. Bourdeau, *Histoire de l'alimentation* (Paris: Alcan, 1894) p. 1.

113 Frykman and Löfgren, *Culture Builders*, p. 6.

114 L. Davidoff and C. Hall, *Family Fortunes: Men and Women of the English Middle Class 1780–1850* (London: Hutchinson, 1988) p. 359.

115 R. Dixon and S. Muthesius, *Victorian Architecture* (London: Thames & Hudson, 1978), p. 30.

116 M. Ponsonby, 'Ideal, Reality and Meaning: Homemaking in England in the First Half of the Nineteenth Century', *Journal of Design History* 16:3 (2003) 201.

117 B. Denvir, *The Late Victorians: Art, Design and Society, 1852–1910* (Harlow: Longman, 1986) pp. 14–15.

118 J. J. Stevenson, *House Architecture*, Vol. II. *House-Planning* (London: Macmillan, 1880) pp. 47–8.

119 E. Goffman, *The Presentation of Self in Everyday Life* (Harmondsworth: Penguin, 1974).

120 Chatillon-Plessis, *La Vie a Table a la fin du xixème siècle*, Paris, 1894, cited in Aron, *The Art of Eating in France*, p. 214.

121 For a discussion of the contrasting styles of domestic architecture in nineteenth-century London and Paris, and the importance of privacy in each city, see Sharon Marcus, *Apartment Stories: City and Home in Nineteenth-Century Paris and London* (London, University of California Press, 1999).

122 *L'Illustrateur* (June 1895).

123 The concern with smells and with the need for well-ventilated kitchens was in part motivated by the domestic sanitation movement, which is discussed in detail in Adams, *Architecture in the Family Way*.

124 G. Wheeler, *The Choice of a Dwelling: A Practical Handbook of Useful Information* (London: John Murray, 1872) p. 214; other examples can be found in R. Kerr, *The Gentleman's House; or, How to Plan English Residences from the Parsonage to the Palace.*, third edn, revised (London: John Murray, 1871) p. 107; Stevenson, *House Architecture*, Vol. II, pp. 56–7.

125 Wheeler, *The Choice of a Dwelling*, p. 214.

126 Beeton, *Mrs Beeton's Book of Household Management*, p. 25.

127 L. D'Alq, *Le Maître et la maîtresse de maison*. 2nd ed. (Paris: Bureau des Causerie Familiaire, 1875), p. 22. For comments on the importance of protecting the public areas of the house from cooking odours, see also: Kerr, *The Gentleman's House* pp. 107–9; Stevenson, pp. 56–7.

128 Davidoff and Hall, *Family Fortunes*, p. 383.

129 Mrs Loftie, *The Dining Room* (London: Art at Home Series, 1876) pp. 71–2.

130 *The Lady* (19 Sept. 1895).

131 Kerr, *The Gentlemen's House*, p. 114.

132 See for example, *The Lady* (19 Sept. 1895). See also S. Nenadic, 'Middle-Rank Consumers and Domestic Culture in Edinburgh and Glasgow 1720–1840', *Past and Present* 145 (Nov. 1994), 122–56.

133 Ponsonby, 'Ideal, Reality and Meaning: Homemaking in England in the First Half of the Nineteenth Century', *Journal of Design History*, p. 201.

134 Wheeler, *The Choice of a Dwelling*, p. 221.

135 Kerr, *The Gentlemen's House*, p. 105.

136 Kerr, *The Gentlemen's House*, p. 104.

137 L. Booth, *A Series of Original Design for Decorative Furniture* (London: Houlston and Wright, 1864) pp. 37–8.

138 T. Morris, *A House for the Suburbs, Socially and Architecturally sketched* (London: Simpkin, Marshall, 1870) pp. 161–2.

139 Wheeler, *The Choice of a Dwelling*, p. 217.

140 Wheeler, *The Choice of a Dwelling*, pp. 216–17.

141 Kerr, *The Gentlemen's House*, p. 105.

142 There were also English examples of using historical styles of decorating. See for instance *The Lady* (11 July 1895).

143 A. Simoneton, *La Décoration intérieur* (Paris: Aulanier, 1893).

144 G. Remon, *Intérieurs modernes* (Paris: Librairie de l'art ancien et moderne, 1907).

145 *La Salle à Manger* (Dec. 1890).

146 Bonnie Smith argues that while the bourgeois women of the Nord region of France never themselves cooked the meals they served at dinner parties, it was their reputation, rather than that of the cook, which was at stake, *Ladies of the Leisure Class: The Bourgeoises of Northern France in the Nineteenth Century* (Princeton: Princeton University Press, 1981) pp. 66–7. Also, for example Beeton, *Mrs Beeton's Book of Household Management*, p. 12; Boursin, *Le Livre de la femme au XIXème siècle*, pp. 275–7.

147 Alq, *Le Maître et la maîtresse de maison*, p. 212, Boitard, *Guide Manuel de la bonne companie*, p. 277.

148 *The Lady* (26 Dec. 1895).

149 Loftie, *The Dining Room*, pp. 102–3.

150 Loftie, *The Dining Room*, p. 91.

151 Loftie, *The Dining Room*, p. 34.

152 *La Salle à Manger* (March 1891).

153 *Le Pot-au-Feu* (15 April 1895).

154 *Le Pot-au-Feu* (15 Feb. 1896).

155 *Le Pot-au-Feu* (19 March 1904).

156 H. Le Roux in *Le Temps*, cited in *L'Art Culinaire* (1888).

157 *La Salle à Manger* (July 1898).

2

Family dinners: timekeeping, privacy and women's knowledge

In 1861, Isabella Beeton published her *Book of Household Management*, which would become one of the best known cookery books in the English language. While it included over a thousand recipes, cookery was not the only significant thing that Mrs Beeton offered her readers. As the title suggested, the hefty volume contained everything its 23-year-old author considered necessary for running an efficient and respectable middle-class home.[1] The *Book of Household Management* was uniquely successful, but the information it provided was not original.[2] Like the etiquette books examined in Chapter 1, Mrs Beeton's book brought together accepted ideas from a variety of sources, and presented them in a way that made them accessible to middle and lower-middle-class readers. Nevertheless, recipes provide the bulk of a book on household management, suggesting the extent to which food was the key component of successful family life. The dining room, and its adjunct the kitchen, held a key position in maintaining the bonds of family life. Successful family life was believed to require that members be shielded from the outside world, and that the house was a fortress and a sanctuary. Yet, at the same time, it provided a stage upon which the household could perform the rituals of domestic harmony, often to an audience who gathered around the dining table. So while private life was organised around mealtimes, the preparation and presentation of meals was also central in allowing a family to forge links with the wider community. This relationship of the private with the public followed two paths. First, timekeeping was essential for ensuring that meals which were often eaten in private could also frequently be shared with outsiders who adhered to the same timetable; and second, women possessed knowledge and expertise about cookery and nutrition which ensured their families' well-being and created a mode of communication between women from separate households. This chapter looks at the place – both literal and symbolic – occupied by food in the private sphere.

The concept of the family meal remained remarkably stable between 1850 and 1914. In a rapidly changing world, the family dining room was for many a place of safety and continuity. Changes in eating patterns occur more slowly than changes in public life, because of the emotional importance of food, which makes people cling to patterns they are already comfortable with.[3] Cultural and psychological factors must be understood alongside a parallel slowness in changes to the available food supply, and the unchanging nature of the body's physiological needs.[4] Private domestic meals shaped individual experiences of home and family. Memories of childhood often centred on the family dining table, while husbands and wives shared experiences of choosing and eating food.

There is no one model for who comprised the bourgeois household. Personal accounts, as well as inventories and census data all offer insights about who lived within the walls of the family home. But there was great variety between households and the composition of the household changed over time, depending on the family life cycle, as well as on the presence of long-term guests and the number of servants living in at any time. Typically, the bourgeois home was organised around the nuclear family. Parisian *inventaires après décès* can sometimes miss this, because many of the homes inventoried are of older people whose children were no longer in residence. First-hand accounts, be they French or English, often refer to the household as a general 'we', with no further details about who is included. Thus the 'we' who meet for lunch might be a smaller circle than the 'we' who assembled for dinner later on, but there is no way to be certain of this.

The bourgeois family, so central to historians' and contemporaries' understanding of nineteenth-century social organisation, has been the subject of extensive study and commentary. But how people came together in the private sphere to cook and eat remains largely obscure for the historian.[5] The daily routine of eating rarely held a prominent place in the writings of diarists. But, in memoirs, the family meal could take on symbolic significance, as a happy moment of unity and exchange.

Writing about his childhood in Paris in the 1850s, François Coppée remembered a harmonious scene: his father sat at the head of the table, surrounded by four loving children, while his mother carried in the soup. The father joyfully exclaimed: 'We're dying of hunger . . . sit down quickly, Mummy, and serve us our soup.'[6] While the mother served the meal, the father was the head, and in requesting that his wife hurry with the food, made his authority overt. John Tosh has argued that fathers, largely absent during the week, enjoyed key, ritualised moments, in which their authority over wife and children was made palpable, while John Gillis has argued that 'family time' was a Victorian invention.[7] In his painting of his daughter's birthday party, W. P. Frith represented his own position as head of the family by his location at the table (figure 3). The painting represents a joyful occasion on which a large family group are gathered to share a meal which they are clearly enjoying and which provides a focal point for the gathering. A warm glow seems to emanate on the faces of the eaters, reflecting the warmth provided by the food and drink. At the same time, family harmony is maintained by everyone knowing their place, with men and women grouped respectively at either end of the table, and the children ranging in between as they imbibe the lessons in how to become respectable men and women.

Recalling growing up in London in the 1880s, author and memoirist M. V. Hughes considered mealtimes part of her brothers' and her education. It was also a time when family bonds were solidified through exchanges of information: 'The main work of the day was over and the family pooled what gossip they had got from school or books or friends, discussing future plans and telling the latest jokes. Mother, pouring out at the head of the table, liked us to chatter freely.'[8] Childhood meals were, of course, idealised by adults in later years. What is significant about recollections of pleasurable childhood dinners is that writers endowed mealtimes with symbolic meaning, as a time when family solidarity was reinforced under the nurturing attention of the mother and the benevolent authority of the father. Dinner was family time, as well as an opportunity for children to learn about gender roles and social hierarchy.[9]

Middle-class memoir writers emphasised the harmony of the family gathered around the table. Published diaries similarly did not reveal any unhappiness, arguments or violence around the table, possibly because diaries that did mention such things were later destroyed, or, most likely, were never recorded at all. The principal discourse on bourgeois identity centred on the perfection of family life, casting the husband as provider and the mother as nurturer. To concede that one's own family did not conform to this ideal may have seemed to many to acknowledge that they were not truly part of the community to which they aspired to belong. First-hand accounts of disastrous meals or families who never sat down to dinner together are difficult to find. Extreme disharmony of the type that might lead to violence or divorce would form the whole subject of another book.

However, the high incidence of prescriptions against letting bad food in the home destroy family life can suggest the extent to which domestic meals were perceived as a potential site for tension and discord. Advice literature of various kinds and, in particular, domestic advice manuals written for a middle-class, female audience, abounded with cautionary tales and warnings to housewives about what would happen if they failed to provide good meals for their families. Though the domestic dining room was a private space, literature abounded on how life within it should unfold. The part to be played by the mistress of the house, in particular, was highly detailed. Housewives came under a great deal of scrutiny: theirs was the central role in maintaining balance and harmony in the home.

Images produced in the nineteenth century of families sitting down together can give us some additional information about how contemporaries perceived the importance of the family meal. Frith's 'Many Happy Returns of the Day' from 1856 (figure 3) depicting his daughter's birthday party, portrays an intergenerational party of well and respectably dressed people waited on by a servant, enjoying what is clearly a festive occasion, with flowers encircling the child who is being celebrated. Beyond showing us something of how children's birthdays were marked, it is revealing of the emotional bond which a shared meal can strengthen. It also gives us some insight into the ways in which the age and gender of the participants shaped mealtimes: the older generation are singled out as deserving respect, in particular the older man who sits apart and reads the newspaper, signalling his right to be somewhat removed from the women and children. Though boys and girls are mingled together, the women and men are grouped separately, with the older daughters sitting near their mother and grandmother, possibly because, as Carol Dyhouse argues, it was at mealtimes that girls learned from their mothers the role that they would go on to play in adulthood.[10]

Figure 3 'Many Happy Returns of the Day', 1856,
by William Powell Frith.

A French photograph taken in 1898 shows the Roger family
at dinner at a long table (figure 4). That there are no floral decorations may be due to this being a family meal, rather than a more
formal meal with guests. The family group is a large one, and
includes some children, with everyone sitting closely and comfortably together.

The extent of the advice offered on the importance of good food
for a happy family life suggests the extent to which this was not the
norm. Clubs, restaurants and cafés were held up to scare women:
if they could not satisfy their men, then the men would find refuge
in other places.[11]

> Not the least useful piece of advice – homely though it be – that we
> can offer to newly-married ladies, is to remind them that husbands
> are men and that men must eat. We can tell them, moreover, that
> men attach no small importance to this very essential operation, and
> that a very effectual way to keep them in good-humour, as well as
> good condition, is for wives to study their husband's peculiar likes
> and dislikes in this matter.[12]

Figure 4 Diner de famille Roger. Octobre 1898.

Mrs Warren advised young women wishing to marry, to: 'Diligently and zealously learn and practise every domestic duty and every feminine accomplishment'[13] which would encourage men to marry, 'and no longer will they say, "We cannot marry, our incomes will not suffice."'

To wives wishing to improve the quality of their marriage, Mrs Warren wrote:

> If you would retain your husbands' love with a deeper affection than when in its youthful freshness, cultivate every winning charm of mind and manner – every grace of proper attire, but let your household management be such as shall ensure comfort, pleasure, and recreation, and your own knowledge of simple cookery that which shall not only tempt the appetite, but as much as possible ensure health, by banishing indigestion and all the evils which arise from it.[14]

La Salle à Manger gave much the same advice to its French readers:

> I am convinced that if the father of the family comes home, feeling harassed by his affairs, to find his lunch or dinner served in an appetising and attractive manner, he will immediately get a sense of well-being and relaxation, and his strength and spirits will be lifted. If, however, you thrust onto a waxed cloth a stew brutally poured onto the plates, some bread with crumbs falling around it, badly folded and wrinkled napkins . . . his outlook will be black, his struggles will seem insurmountable . . . and he will look for a row with his wife.[15]

If prescriptive sources emphasised the importance of combining elegance with affordability, the reality was nonetheless rather different. In his diary in May 1872, William Michael Rossetti recorded a visit from his brother, Gabriel, who was worried about his household expenses 'On looking into household bills lately – merely those of butcher, baker, and other such purveyors – it was found that the annual expenditure on these accounts exceeds £1,000.' Gabriel was 'startled at this enormous amount'. In an attempt to economise he decided to 'now [hand] over to Emma £5 per week: she is expected to defray everything out of this sum, and keeps accounts accordingly with Dunn – sometimes a little within the £5, and sometimes a little beyond'.[16]

While men made the money, women were responsible for spending it, and they had to spend it wisely or they would jeopardise their marriage and the stability of their home. As well as being essential to a family's survival, economy was, itself, a highly prized value, for demonstrating restraint, stability and a sense of proportion. Many prescriptive sources emphasised the importance of good household economy as part of women's domestic expertise. Books such as *Mrs Beeton's Book of Household Management* (1861) and Mrs Warren's *How I Managed my Household on Two Hundred Pounds a Year* (1864) emphasised that a good meal was one which, as well as tasting good, was achieved within the means of the family's budget. In France, Mme D'Alq's *Le Maître et la maîtresse de maison* (1875), like her English counterparts, advised that a good housewife was hospitable within her means. Yet the importance of good food could collide with the value placed on domestic economy, as was apparent in an item appearing in *Le Figaro* in 1854, which claimed that only the French dined, while in other countries – and England in particular – people simply ate. The author went on to point out the importance for French women not to cut corners when serving food to guests, even when the guests in question were very close friends.[17]

It was in English domestic advice manuals, written for the housewife on a modest income, that money, economy and budgeting were brought to the fore. Early nineteenth-century French publications created the impression that for the French, economising was of no concern. But Anne Martin-Fugier points out that these French manuals were a continuation of the eighteenth-century genre of *ménagerie*, in which economic rationality and household management went together. For Martin-Fugier, this genre of writing is part of the trend towards investing in the possibility of happiness in the private life of the family. She argues that it was the woman's responsibility to manage the household effectively in order to allow this happiness to flourish.[18] As the editors of *La Salle à Manger* put it in 1895, 'Domestic science is, for women, the true science of private, happy, family life.'[19] And by mid-century, domestic advice manuals in France and England were very similar, and revolved around the same themes of order, economy and rational management.[20] As the guardian of the domestic sphere, the mistress of the house was entrusted with the burden of producing good food in a congenial environment within budgetary constraints. Family meals were recognised by contemporaries as a potential site for conflict, and the responsibility for avoiding this lay with the women.

The house and the dining room

Chapter 1 outlined several dimensions of the architecture and décor of the ideal dining rooms of London and Parisian homes.

These were designed to bring comfort to family and guests. They were intended to create harmony for the household, but also to impress strangers with the success and good taste of their owners. The ideal dining room contained reflections of the master and the mistress of the home. At the same time, the place of the dining room within the home was determined according to various precepts of middle-class respectability, notably the importance of keeping clean and dirty spaces separate, and the need to create semi-public spaces within the privacy of the home.

Evidence of actual interiors is scarce compared to the amount of evidence about the ideal provided by prescriptive sources. Margaret Ponsonby argues for the importance of considering how advice about interiors was mediated by readers, a point worth considering when reading any form of advice literature.[21] Once a family inhabited a home they could use it in ways different from those intended by the architect. Plans of homes designated a specific space for food consumption. First-hand accounts suggest that in this, at least, the reality measured up to the architects' intentions. References to people eating outside of prescribed areas are scarce, and generally only occurred in cases of illness.[22] This marks a change from how homes were used in the eighteenth century, when it had been usual to eat in all parts of the house.

Various writers have left clues about where food was prepared and consumed in their homes. Edmund Yates, a London journalist who also worked as a clerk for the General Post Office from 1847 to 1872, lived in his second house with his wife for six years though: 'The accommodation consisted of a narrow dining-room painted salmon-colour, and a little back room looking out upon a square black enclosure in which grew fearful fungi; two big drawing-rooms . . . two good bedrooms, and three attics.'[23] The dining room was narrow and its walls the wrong shade, but the kitchen was even worse, 'pronounced by the servants to be "stuffy," and the whole place "ill-convenient," there being no larder, pantry, nor the usual domestic arrangements.' Yet Yates's recollection was of being happy in that house, and of frequently entertaining guests. Ursula Bloom, in contrast, recalled that, 'All good dining-rooms had to be exactly alike.'[24] She remembered the carpets as 'varied . . . which matched nothing' and the furniture: 'easy chairs, lady's and gent's, set on either side of the hearth'. But mostly she recalled the colour scheme: 'red wallpaper and curtains and bevelled glass on the sideboard, Chenille cloths in red were on the table, and never could there be a redder room. If it faced south that did not matter, for all dining-rooms were RED.' Her somewhat scornful recollection of the homes of her childhood reflects her adult choice to become a writer and distance herself from the stuffy Victorian middle class in which she had been raised.

In Paris, in cases where a will was contested, a notary was called in to conduct an *inventaire après décès*. This was a very detailed inventory of all the objects within the home of the deceased person. These inventories give first-hand accounts of the layout of the home, as they were presented room by room. There is no equivalent for London homes, but the Parisian inventories offer similar insights to those from memoirs like Bloom's and Yates's. What is interesting is how individuals chose, at various moments in their lives, to conform more or less to the norms described by advice writers. The two greatest factors in determining how much emphasis was placed on the dining function of a house seem to have been age and wealth. Older people, it seems, may have opted out – or perhaps been excluded from – the rounds of dinner parties which had punctuated their younger lives. All dining rooms contained the basic furniture needed at mealtimes, which were table and chairs, and some sort of sideboard for storing dishes, flatware and glasses. But while M Goutant, who lived on the rue Descartes and was an employee of the École Polytechnique, owned several luxury items, such as a wooden sideboard laden with various carafes, glasses of various descriptions, teapots, sugar and milk dishes, a round table and over seventy plates, there were only two chairs in his dining room.[25] Leaving aside the possibility that some chairs had been removed from the room prior to the inventory being taken, the dishes suggest that there had once been dinner parties, while the lack of chairs suggest that they had not been taking place for some time.

Homes of modest dimension often had one reception room that served two purposes. While French manuals referred to this as a *salle à manger*, for the English, it was a sitting room. In each case, the function considered most central to family life was foregrounded, while the other was treated as secondary. Yet inventory takers made their own choices about what labels to use, based on their own observations. When Mme Brabant died in 1851, the home on the rue Jacob, shared with her husband, a financial clerk, contained two rooms. They were described as being, respectively, sleeping and sitting rooms. The sitting room contained a round walnut table, three straw-filled chairs, and two armchairs (*fauteuils*).[26] This furnishing is consistent with the suggestions of advice writers on how to use one room to fulfil two purposes, though for the inventory taker, the sitting function appeared more important than the dining function. In contrast to Mme Brabant's apartment, M Theodore Dumont Fontaine's inventory upon the death of his wife in 1870 revealed that their home on the rue du Temple had been arranged so as to have a dining room but no *salon* (sitting room). The dining room contained a round table with eight straw-stuffed chairs, a sideboard and small desk as well as a mirror and a clock.[27] Yet this room must have fulfilled the role of both public and family space.

What advice writers and architects could not account for was what people would do with the backstage or hidden areas of the home. In Mme Brabant's case, a kitchen table and several items used for cooking were kept in the bedroom. A choice had been made to have a private area in which to both sleep and cook, in order to maintain a public area where these backstage activities could remain hidden from visitors. And there were precedents making eating in bedrooms acceptable, such as the custom of having breakfast in bed. An inventory of a house in London whose contents were being sold by auction listed the following in the gentleman's room: 'A Spanish mahogany inlaid breakfast table, on pillar and claws, and a cloth table cover.'[28] In the case of M Dumont Fontaine's house, one of the two upstairs rooms contained, as well as a bed, four chairs. While the dining room may have doubled up as a sitting room, one of the bedrooms was also used as a private *salon*.

Mme de Chenevière, who died in 1876, had been married to a pharmacist described as *de première classe* (first class). Their home on Avenue de Wagram had several rooms, but no dining room. The rooms were described in the inventory as cellar, kitchen, toilet, bedroom, office and room. There were 100 litres of wine and 50 empty bottles in the cellar. The kitchen contained, among other things, two tables (one of which was described as a chrome kitchen table, and the other simply as table), two sideboards, and nine chairs. There was also a cupboard with 100 items of faience, porcelain and glass, and a sideboard with 12 place settings and 30 glass and crystal items.[29] Everything suggests that the inhabitants of this home, contrary to custom, had their meals in the kitchen. The large quantity of items suggestive of dinner parties may have been left over from a time when the de Chenevières were younger and more in the habit of entertaining. The decision to have an office but no dining room in the house seems to suggest that the people living in this home prioritised work above social engagements, and also that, unlike the majority of middle-class people, they did not choose to have any public spaces within their home.

In larger homes, there was often no need to group various activities into a single room. Landlord Jean Louis Félix de Conny, who died in 1851, had lived on the Champs-Elysées in a home with a dining room containing a table, a sideboard and a writing desk, though oddly not a single chair.[30] In M de Conny's home, the dining room could only be reached by walking through the salon (sitting room).[31] This would have been confirmation for English architecture J. J. Stevenson, that the French were inferior to the English in having homes in which each part was not isolated from the others.[32] Yet the inventory taker took a note of this particular layout, suggesting that this was unusual for a Parisian home. Like London houses, apartments in Paris generally allowed their inhabitants to separate space according to function and, most importantly, to keep front and backstage activities separate from one another.

Many inventoried homes reveal ways in which practice diverged from prescription. Others, though, did have room layouts that corresponded to the format of the respectable home, as prescribed by advice writers. Mme Eleonore Marguerite Celeste Collas requested an inventory of her home in 1866, on the death of her husband Cyrille Marie Louis Saderin, an officer of the *légion d'honneur* and Prefect of the *département de la Meurthe*. As his position suggests, this was the home of a rather well-to-do upper-middle-class couple, who lived on the rue Saint-Lazare. It contained a dining room used only for dining (the house also contained a well-furnished salon), which held a table with three boards to enlarge it, eight chairs, a large wooden sideboard, as well as several decorative items including heavy curtains, a barometer and a mirror.[33]

A household without a dining room could find itself excluded from socialising with other bourgeois families. Though restaurants were gradually gaining ground as a sociable space, the domestic dinner remained central to both private and public life. While most middle-class homes contained a space labelled as the dining room, the Parisian inventories suggest that diversity prevailed in terms of the spatial organisation of the home. Rather than strictly conforming to the intentions of architects and designers, individuals and families felt at ease with using spaces within their home in ways which were most suited to their specific needs.

The meals of the day

Meals and their hours, and the divisions of the day which they control, are of permanent and close personal interest to all of us.[34]

The day-to-day life of the bourgeoisie of London and Paris was punctuated and shaped by food and eating. Mealtimes were prescribed, but individual practices varied, and there was no single accepted norm for meals or their hours. However, in spite of the range of habits apparent in the sources, a certain regularity of eating schedules was adhered to by all. In order to be a part of a wider community of respectable and likeminded people, each individual and each household had to tailor their schedule to keep them in harmony with their wider community. Thus mealtimes demonstrate the extent to which even the most private of activities was affected by the importance of the social sphere in the creation and performance of bourgeois identity.

A modern family, living in an urban metropolis, had a daily routine detached from the exigencies of the agricultural cycle and the rising and setting of the sun. This may go some way towards explaining how clocks became increasingly central within the homes, and watches to personal attire. For knowing what to do when was increasingly a matter of social convention. By the 1850s, most middle-class men lived away from their work, and needed to organise their day into separate segments for domestic life and working life. Women – quite apart from the growing number of unmarried women with their own jobs – also divided their days, around the needs of the home, their role as consumers, and the important task of cementing the family's social position through paying and receiving visits. As various historians have argued, advances in technologies for lighting the home and public spaces extended the hours of the day in which social interaction could easily take place.[35] Thus mealtimes became more spread out throughout the day, compared to the previous century. The early modern practice was of dinner being served in the late morning and acting as the only hearty meal of the day, sometimes supplemented by a light evening supper. In the 1850s, there were several daily meals – breakfast, lunch, tea (for the English as well as some fashionable French Anglophiles), supper – and dinner was eaten in the early evening, lit by candles, gas and eventually electric bulbs.

Punctuality and accurate timekeeping were required of participants in the culture of respectability. Victorian town halls were crowned by enormous clocks to demonstrate the authority of the urban elites over all the hours of the day. Regularity of mealtimes was as central to good living as were the healthful properties of the food served.[36] This was true both for the private circle of the family, and as a way of demonstrating and enhancing its ties to the outside world. Meals taken throughout the day varied according to age and gender, social position and fashion. In many homes, a large clock encouraged good timekeeping in family members and their guests. In M. V. Hughes's childhood home the family 'went' by the dining room clock. While this clock encouraged routine and timeliness, it served the further purpose of maintaining the family's boundaries. Hughes's mother kept the clock ten minutes fast: ' "to be on the safe side", as mother said. She also confided to me once that it caused visitors to go a little earlier than they otherwise might . . . for she had observed that they never trusted their own watches.'[37]

There were important and obvious reasons why an individual or family could not eat at wildly different times from the rest of society. Time was dictated not only by family clocks, but also by work schedules, shop opening times, and the need to socialise with other families. Visits and 'at home' days were central to women's social lives, especially in the upper echelons of bourgeois society. Polite visits had to be made between prescribed times, and visitors were supposed to be conscious of not arriving at a time that would interrupt the meal of the family they were calling on.[38] One English etiquette book explained:

> visits are usually paid between the hours of two and four p.m. in winter, and two and five p.m. in summer. The object in view of observing this rule is to avoid intruding before the luncheon is removed, and leave sufficient time to allow the lady of the house leisure for her dinner toilette.[39]

Family meals were not the only meals in which people participated during an ordinary week. As Chapter 3 argues, meals with outsiders were a frequent part of bourgeois domestic life. Likewise, Chapters 4 and 5 explore the extent to which socialising over meals consumed in public spaces was integral to the social and cultural existence of respectable society. So while family meals were private, it was essential that they coincide with wider practices, so that families of friends or acquaintances could share meals with one another.

Mrs Beeton was clear on the importance of good timekeeping for the respectable mistress of any English home. She advised her readers of the various duties they needed to perform, and the times of day at which they needed to perform each one.[40] Readers who followed Mrs Beeton's advice could visually display their adherence to correct timetables through their choice of clothing:

> The dress of the mistress should always be adapted to her circumstances, and be varied with different occasions. Thus, at breakfast she could be attired in a very neat and simple manner, wearing no ornaments. If this dress should decidedly pertain only to the breakfast-hour, and be specially suited for such domestic occupations as usually follows that meal, then it would be well to exchange it before the time for receiving visitors . . . It is still to be remembered, however, that, in changing the dress, jewellery and ornaments are not to be worn until the full dress for dinner is assumed.[41]

Parisian women who followed the Contesse de Bassanville's advice column in *La Mode de Paris* through the 1870s received similar advice about the importance of a well-maintained timetable of daily chores and activities.[42]

Respectable women's letters and diaries leave no trace of daily wardrobe changes, but do suggest regular timekeeping, and that mealtimes provided the dividing line between morning, afternoon and evening. But women did keep regular timetables, and meals were a crucial element in punctuating the day. The Hugheses, as we have already seen, used their dining-room clock to time meals and other daily routines. Young Parisian Lucille le Verrier, writing in 1867, described her typical day:

> I generally wake up at 7:30 and I work until 10:30. Then I arrange my hair and we have lunch. I have free time from 11:30 to 2:00. Then I work until 6:30, at which time we have dinner. In the evening, I do catechism, and I go to bed around 11:00.[43]

Though this was an ordinary day, Thursdays and Sundays – being Mass days – were different, as were days on which visits were paid or received.[44] At midday and again after six in the evening Le Verrier would sit down for a meal with the rest of the household.

Francis Wey, a French visitor to London in the 1850s, noted that in London the 'smart' people did not dine before eight o'clock.[45] While this may have been true, most middle-class people were probably not particularly 'smart' and the majority of them probably dined much earlier than eight. In Paris, dinner was also at the end of the day, and was the most important meal. Fashionable people dined at around seven or eight o'clock. In order to fit in at least three meals each day, with a decent interval between them so that each could be faced with a reasonable appetite, it was necessary to respect some sort of schedule. Also, if family members, and sometimes guests, were to meet to share a meal, some sort of common timetable was essential.

Edmund Yates recalled visits with his maternal grandfather in the mid-nineteenth-century: 'We dined early – two o'clock – in Kentish Town, and had the most delightful hot suppers at nine.'[46] It was these suppers, rather than the more substantial dinners, which remained in Yates's mind as special events, being substantially different from his normal routine: 'sprats, or kidneys, or tripe and onions, with foaming porter and hot grog afterwards'. Yates's experience reveals the persistence of overlapping traditions for mealtimes, with his grandparents adhering to the fashion of their youth in eating a substantial meal part way through the day, while his parents kept to newer trends in eating dinner in the evening.[47]

Like the elderly, English children ate their main meal, dinner, in the middle of the day. At school, M. V. Hughes was made to sit through a sermon every Wednesday from 1 to 1:30, which was the last period of the school day:

> Most of us had breakfasted before eight, and it was considerably past two before we could reach home for dinner. Bessie Jones has told me she used to get back in such an exhausted state that she often had to lie down and rest before she could face dinner . . . one day during this sermon ordeal the girl next to me fainted.[48]

Regular mealtimes became a habit on which the body depended. Girls, who probably ate less than boys, could suffer if they did not get their meals on time.

According to medical advice, meals had to be eaten at specified intervals.[49] As in all medical advice, science and culture overlapped in the advice doctors gave about how often healthy people should eat. Doctors advocated meal intervals based on the needs and capacities of the human digestive system, while generally affirming that current fashions were in agreement with the needs of a healthy body.[50] French doctor Armand Gautier believed that the older custom of having the biggest meal in the middle of the day was the healthiest option, but that modern life could not accommodate itself to this, and that the current customs were satisfactory for combining the demand of modern life with the needs of the digestive system:

> The necessities of modern activity have caused the large midday meal to be replaced by a lighter meal which allows, without a rest, for intellectual and physical work to be resumed almost immediately, but which makes it necessary to have a second substantial meal in the evening, six or seven hours after the midday meal and three hours before bed time.[51]

In addition to the two main meals outlined above, Gautier stated that the French, the English and the Germans all ate a light breakfast, a snack (*goûter*) around five o'clock, and a light supper before bedtime.[52] According to Gautier, this combination of meals, spread throughout the day, was both practical and healthy. In 1897, L. Ducheron contributed an article on health and hygiene to *La Salle à Manger*, urging that older customs were preferable to modern ones from a medical perspective. While conceding that evening dinner was a harmless custom for many people, for the gourmets who were the principal audience of *La Salle à Manger*, late dinner could be harmful for digestion, as eating heartily from a number of dishes at a late hour could lead to 'insomnia, nightmares and even indigestion'.[53] French and English doctors agreed that health was a major factor in determining how frequently to eat but in London and Paris custom, fashion and practicality combined to shape the rhythm of the day and its meals.

The day began with breakfast. In London, this was a more substantial meal than in Paris, but in both cities something was taken first thing in the morning. After breakfast, snacks of various descriptions might be eaten, but the next proper meal was lunch, which was a modern, British, invention. In London, by 1850, lunch was an established part of the day, which elicited no comment. A hundred years earlier, lunch, or luncheon, had been controversial for it marked the move away from dinner as the mid-point of the day. It also added to the overall amount of food an individual ate, since it was lighter than dinner but still more than a snack. As the exigencies of the modern workday, and the separation of home and work, became entrenched, the need for lunch ceased to be called into question. In Paris, lunch was noted as a new arrival by one journalist in 1855. Another attributed this to the influx of English visitors at the time of Queen Victoria's visit to the French capital. He stated that though the English were leaving Paris in droves, the custom of having lunch would stay behind, as the French, he claimed, had adapted to it very readily.[54] Yet in spite of these journalists' perception, a midday meal had already been gradually incorporated into French practice, and was not such a novelty in the 1850s. In France, breakfast came to be known as the *petit déjeuner*, or small breakfast, while lunch was sometimes referred to as *déjeuner à la fourchette*, breakfast with fork, denoting a more substantial sort of food.

It was at lunchtime that men and women most often found themselves eating apart. Men, who spent the daytime hours away from home, ate at work or in a nearby restaurant. English advice books suggested that women with children should combine their lunch with their children's dinner, which continued to be a midday meal.[55] Many women, both French and English, chose lunchtime for socialising with other women. In Paris throughout the century, and in London from the 1860s, respectable women could also eat lunch out in a variety of restaurants or cafes, which were increasingly accessible to them, if they were in town for shopping or other leisure activities. While dinner was always considered a formal meal, lunch offered the possibility of greater freedom and flexibility.[56] According to Mrs Loftie, lunch should consist of 'a side table always laid with a few necessaries, so that a light meal can be had in five minutes at any hour of the day'.[57] This way, a family 'whose avocations are various, and whose business must be attended to at irregular times', could eat well without causing undue work either for the mistress of the house or for her servants.[58] Mrs Loftie recommended a system of self-service for lunch:

> If during the middle of the day there is always to be found on the side table a pat of butter, some bread, a jug of milk, a stilton cheese, a bottle of beer, and a small dish of cold meat, it will always be

possible for anyone to get a sufficient luncheon without feeling he is troublesome to either master or servant. It is quite shameful sometimes to see even in large wealthy establishments how difficult it is to get quickly a light meal for a person who is in a hurry, and how often members of the family would rather do without luncheon than ask for it at a different hour from the time appointed.[59]

To Mrs Loftie, it was clear that a family might be expected to always be together and punctual at the end of the day, but could well have a range of obligations which made communal lunch unlikely.

For the English, tea passed quickly from luxury commodity in the eighteenth century to everyday necessity in the nineteenth. While the word continued to denote the drink imported to England from its overseas empire it also came to refer to certain meals. While a working-class tea continued to be the evening meal (dinner being eaten at midday), for the British middle classes tea was a mid-afternoon meal most often eaten among women. The food was delicate, and often sweet, which was considered appropriate to feminine tastes and needs. Tea was generally served from a tray in the sitting room, where the hostess received her guests. The food could be served by a servant or the lady of the house, and was passed around to each lady where she sat, rather than everyone being seated around one table, as at every other meal. Tea was an English custom, though Parisians had a snack at around the same time, and in some circles it was fashionable to emulate the English tea.[60] English women from all levels of society drank copious amounts of tea, and for some the caffeine may have provided energy where food was lacking, whether out of choice or because of poverty.

The problem with tea, as evidenced by this article from *The Caterer*, in 1882, was that it was generally exclusive to women, which could be inconvenient to their men:

A correspondent launches a vigorous but amusing anathema against that beloved institution of the weaker sex. He complains that paterfamilias 'comes home to dine with his family, and he finds the adult female members have a most delicate appetite, pick at the fish, decline the entrée, look at the joint, and venture on the entremet sucré. Why? They have devoured two hours previously an unknown quantity of teacakes, crumpets, and tartines. Ten years ago they were quite happy without their afternoon tea, but tyrant fashion will do more than any man can – even make a woman do something against her will.'[61]

Women came under attack from this correspondent for both the sins of under- and of overeating. That women were frivolous victims of fashion was a common trope, coupled here with an expression of anxiety that women were enjoying the sensual pleasure afforded by good food, away from the supervision of the male head of the household.

Dinner, the most important meal of the day, came after tea and brought with it all the rules of etiquette and formal manners. Dinner was a meal usually eaten in mixed company. It was often a social event, with dinner parties being generally seen as essential to maintaining the bonds of society. Fashion and practicality each played a part in determining the dinner hour. In England, the fashion with regard to dinner times was often determined by people attempting to follow the times at which the Queen and the royal family ate their meals. However, it was similar to the dinner time in Paris, with the English royal family following where French fashion led. Dinner times ranged from six to eight o'clock for respectable people. To some commentators, it seemed as if the dinner hour got continually later, though in fact it never went past 8 p.m.[62] One reason for it not to get progressively later was that there were further social obligations to be fulfilled after dinner, often in the form of receiving evening visits. In 1891, *La Salle à Manger* announced that the Prince of Wales was advocating moving the dinner hour back from 8 p.m. to 7 p.m. because late dinner, from which people only rose at around ten o'clock, was preventing many from going out in the evening.[63]

Supper, for those who ate it, was the last meal of the day. In the early modern period, it consisted of a light evening meal, necessary to those whose dinner hour may have been as early as mid-morning. By 1850, supper had disappeared from the daily routine of many household, and was instead reserved for special occasions such as evening parties or balls. For the elderly, or those living in rural areas, who ate their dinner at midday, supper continued to be a necessary meal, but in London and Paris it was a matter of elegance and luxury, rather than a satisfying of appetites.[64]

Food preparation and women's knowledge

Making meals was about more than just cooking. Great emphasis was placed on decisions about what to eat and how food should be presented, as well as the division of labour between women, their servants and, sometimes, middle-class men. Where money was sufficient, the bulk of the cooking was done by servants, yet even in such homes, mistresses and even masters still had a direct and important role to play in choosing menus, as well as in training servants to cook specific dishes, and in overseeing the running of the kitchen and dining room. Cooking was a backstage activity and Londoners and Parisians all agreed on the need to keep the kitchen far away and shut off from the dining area. It was only in the 1950s that British families began to accept the idea of an open-plan kitchen, allowing for back- and frontstage areas to be joined.[65] But though the kitchen might be far away, even below ground, its importance loomed large. Family happiness depended on healthy and tasty meals and such meals, it was generally believed, could be best produced in modern, rationally organised kitchens.

The extent to which a bourgeois housewife engaged in physical work depended in part on what she could afford. According to Boursin, in France the gentry and bourgeoisie could define their women as 'maîtresses de maison', that is mistresses of their homes, while the petite bourgeoisie and working-class women were only 'ménagères' or housewives, because they had to perform more than a managerial role within their homes.[66] For most writers, the role of a middle-class wife was essentially managerial. In 1861, Mrs Beeton's famously began her book: 'As with the commander of an army, or the leader of any enterprise, so is it with the mistress of a house'[67] while, in 1895, La Salle à Manger published a series of lessons on domesticity that promised to 'demonstrate that domestic science is for women the true science of happy, familial, private life'.[68] Many women chose to do some of their own cooking, but limited this to special and delicate foods, such as sweets, or recipes to nurture sick family members. If she did have to get her hands dirty, a woman might attempt to hide this from public view.[69] But as she was also believed to be naturally endowed with the desire and ability to nourish her family, the unlucky housewife found herself pulled in opposing directions.[70] She was expected to have a comprehensive knowledge of cooking and of the nutritional needs of all her family, but at the same time to show herself to be entirely distant from anything resembling work in the kitchen. The tension between these two opposing tendencies characterises many of the attitudes towards women and cooking in this period, while first-hand accounts suggest that the reality of most women's lives obliged them to have a hands-on knowledge of cooking, as well as a supervisory one.

Criticising a woman's understanding of food and cooking was tantamount to attacking the core of her identity. Middle-class men, and especially women, had for many decades been determined to show working-class wives and mothers how to run their homes. By suggesting that working-class women were not capable of feeding their families, middle-class observers were implying that in some sense these were not true women. The ability to feed was associated with women's most basic biology, since from the beginning of pregnancy and through a child's infancy the mother actually nourished the child from her own body. Underlying the criticism of working-class cooking may have been the belief that industrialisation and urbanisation had distanced people from their natural and innate abilities. The ongoing critique of middle-class women's domestic competence was part of the same tradition, which implied that the trappings of modern, civilised life – wealth, education, fashion – corrupted women and led them to neglect their duties.

While the mistress of a house was seen by some as a manager, there were many who believed that she should possess an innate ability to cook. The Parisian press abounded with articles denouncing the paucity of upper- and middle-class women's culinary knowledge. Critics of the modern world could blame progress for removing women from their natural sphere. One author, the self-styled *vieux monsieur difficile* (fussy old man) complained that modern education was responsible for the bad meals he was served in the homes where he was a guest. He blamed female education for girls' ignorance of cooking, but also found fault with boys' education. This, he claimed, taught them many things, but left them ignorant about 'the structure of their stomach and the quality of foods that suit it'.[71] Tensions around knowledge about food highlighted the fact that cooking could be considered as part of a range of different types of knowledge, from natural, to tradition, to modern and scientific. While women were the experts on domesticity, men's knowledge, being more scientific, might be considered to be of a superior kind, allowing them to criticise and oversee women's domestic arrangements.

As in Paris, in London the press also made frequent references, both humorous and earnest, to the poor state of middle-class women's knowledge of cookery. Young housewives were frequent targets:

> Young Mistress: 'All behind with the dinner again, Sarah? Why you haven't even done the salad! Here, give it to me – I'll wash it, where's the soap?'[72]

Yet in both London and Paris, middle-class women were involved with food preparation on a range of levels.[73] Many of the diaries of girls growing up in the period revealed an awareness of, and involvement with, domestic food preparation. In the 1840s, Amélie Weiler, the daughter of a Strasbourg doctor, cooked with her mother, and after the latter's death in 1842 the young Amélie took responsibility for preparing various foods herself. Most of the food Amélie and her mother made was sweet, for example desserts for special occasions.[74] In addition, they undertook big yearly projects such as preparing jams and preserves. The everyday cooking of savoury and other foods was left to the servant, while Amélie, as a very young woman, was expected to take over her mother's managerial role. In the 1870s, M. V. Hughes, whose father was a stockbroker, but not a wealthy one, observed her mother's domestic work, which involved: 'putting out sheets, counting the wash, ordering the dinner, arranging which tradesmen would be blamed for something'.[75] In the week before Christmas, Hughes's mother would be busy in the kitchen, 'presiding over mincemeat and puddings', while Hughes herself 'was set to clean currants, squeeze lemons, and cut up candied peel.'[76]

In Paris, when Emilie de Montbourg received the gift of a large bag of potatoes from Charles de Cerilley, in 1892, she was grateful, as there were at that time 32 mouths to feed in her house and the cook was having trouble satisfying everyone on the money she was given.[77] Emilie de Montbourg did not intend to do any day-to-day food preparation herself, but was closely aware of all food preparation within her home. When her daughter Marthe was ill, Emilie would go to the butcher's herself, to buy the meats required to cook the broth recommended by the doctor.[78] Even this late in the century, the overlap between recipes and remedies persisted, and women were assumed to possess some expertise on treating illness within their own family. Around the turn of the century, Ursula Bloom, whose family were solidly middle class, recalled that her mother could herself cook and also instruct her servants about cooking. However, Bloom framed this as a recollection of a 'golden age' for women in the kitchen, claiming that her mother 'was the product of an era when it was important that the mistress of the house could do everything better herself, for when in a quandary she could show a girl how it was done'.[79] Like the journalists who bemoaned women's loss of knowledge about food and cookery, Ursula Bloom placed women's ability to cook in a past era, in which women had more of the skills which were believed to be 'natural' to them in the nineteenth century.

M. V. Hughes contrasted the way that cooking was taught to her in school, where the lessons 'were entirely theoretical, as there was neither kitchen nor laundry at our disposal, and I darkly suspect that our teachers had never entered such places',[80] with what she learned at home from her mother. It was from her mother and not her teachers that Hughes learned how to feed her family. 'Nothing whatever remained to me of those recipes at school, nor of the elaborate menus for a family of seven, and I never had any idea whether my sons were consuming nitrogen or carbon or what.'[81] For Hughes, the teachers' scientific approach had nothing to do with the instinctive way in which a mother knew how to nourish her children.

In contrast with her schoolteachers, whom she suspected of being incapable of putting their lessons into practice in a real kitchen, Hughes saw her mother as a true cook, with no need for theoretical knowledge. According to Hughes, visitors who enjoyed her mother's food sometimes asked for her recipes:

'How do you manage to get such good rice pudding, Mrs Thomas? My cook is so uncertain – one day we can swim in it, and the next day we can dance on it. Do tell me exactly how you get it just right like this.'
'You take a pie dish.'
'What size?'
'Oh, the ordinary size. Put some well-washed rice in it.'
'How much?'
'Enough to cover the bottom. Then add a bit of butter.'
'How big a bit?'
'As big as a walnut. Then add salt and sugar.'
'How much?'
'Oh, as much as you think will do. Then bake in a *very slow* oven.'
'For how long?'
'Until it seems done.'

The curious part about this recipe was the complete satisfaction shown by the visitor, who nodded her head at each item of information, for mother took care to emphasise the really important points.[82]

Hughes distinguished between the theory and the practice of food preparation. While her teachers could explain the rules of cooking, her mother could cook by instinct. This in effect made her mother more of a woman than the female teachers. At the same time, it brought her mother admiration from other women who were further removed from their instincts to feed and nurture. Whatever role a woman chose to play in her life, she could expect to be judged by her peers according to how close she came or how far she strayed from the ideal of feminine domesticity. At the same time, a woman's knowledge of cookery could provide her with a currency with which to exchange and interact with the wider community to which she belonged.

Though servants might be expected to carry out the physical work of cooking, it was generally agreed that all but the very best were ignorant and needed to be educated by their mistresses. A series of articles in *Cornhill Magazine* in 1901 offered advice on how to live comfortably on budgets of £800, £1,800 and £10,000 per year.[83] In the first two cases, emphasis was placed on the need for the mistress to train her servants in culinary matters. Only the wealthiest families were assumed to be able to hire perfectly trained servants:

A constant acquiring of knowledge is the one thing that redeems housekeeping from being intolerably uninteresting; without this its daily monotony is very trying to many characters. I heard the other day of a lady who said she was getting rid of her cook for no fault, but merely because she was so tired of seeing the same face every day. I do not believe that sort of feeling would come over anyone who tried daily to teach her to cook something.[84]

Ursula Bloom recalled a 'pile of recipe books' in the kitchen of her childhood, of which 'Mrs Beeton took pride of place', even though 'it was already thought that she was a trifle extravagant, for the modern trend of 1900–14 was more careful'.[85] As well as owning cookery books and domestic advice manuals, many bourgeois women kept personal books of recipes and remedies. Bloom recalled 'an old laundry book into which my mother had herself copied our recipes'.[86] These handwritten notebooks of favourite recipes could be passed through several generations. The contents of manuscript cookbooks could vary; each was the unique creation of the woman who owned it. Women's handwritten records of recipes, sometimes with notes indicating that a particular dish had been tried, indicate that at least some women were actively involved in thinking about food preparation in the home. Women collected recipes from a range of sources, including publications as well as friends and relatives. Manuscript cookery books also contained remedies for various ailments, which were useful for women who took charge of nursing sick family members. Feeding and healing were equally essential in a woman's job of maintaining a happy and healthy household.

Like Mrs Beeton, women who kept manuscript cookbooks used them not just for recipes, but as repositories of a range of useful knowledge about housekeeping. A book might include several recipes for food and drinks, interspersed with remedies for a variety of illnesses such as: 'For a cough when very troublesome' and 'To cure deafness,' as well as instructions for household chores such as: 'To scour boot tops' or 'varnish for boxes'.[87] Manuscript cookbooks show that women were actively involved in food preparation, through knowledge of and curiosity about recipes. Women exchanged recipes that then became part of their collections. Sarah Alice Ede's book included 'Aunt Mary's pudding'[88] and Elizabeth Pease included several recipes and remedies attributed to people she knew, such as 'Mr. Stokwell's Beer or rather small ale'.[89] Women also included others that they had cut out or copied from published sources. For example, Ede clipped a series of columns on Sunday Dinners: 'How to select it, how to buy it, and how to cook it.'[90] Clipping and copying recipes and menu plans was an indication of women's involvement with domestic food preparation, as was putting annotations next to particular recipes. Next to a recipe for sheep's head pie, someone had added the comment: 'A few hard boiled eggs introduced into the pie is a great improvement.'[91] Manuscript cookbooks demonstrate bourgeois women's willingness to involve themselves with household chores, in terms of the creation of a body of knowledge, if not in the actual labour.[92]

Servants were, ideally, expected to be responsible for the majority of household chores, including cooking. According to income and preference, families could have different numbers of servants responsible for a variety of different chores. It was once assumed that having servants was one of the defining characteristics of the middle classes, though this belief has now been refined, as it appears that some families who can be considered middle class by other measurements did not have live-in servants, while some working-class families actually did have servants within the household.[93] Because of the smaller size of homes in Paris, Parisian families tended to have fewer servants than Londoners, unless they were very wealthy.

Mrs Beeton was one of many advice writers to provide timetables for daily, weekly and monthly chores, and suggest which servants should carry them out.[94] She gave advice on kitchen servants in a section separate from that outlining the general duties of domestic servants, confirming the importance of food and eating within the general scheme of the household. According to Mrs Beeton, the cook was the head of the kitchen, and where there were also a kitchen maid and a scullery maid, the cook was to act as a good example for them to follow. Like the mistress of the house, the cook had to rise early and keep her domain in order.[95]

Dinner, the evening meal, was the most demanding time of day for both mistress and cook:

> It is in her preparation of the dinner that the cook begins to feel the weight and responsibility of her situation, as she must take upon herself all the dressing and serving of the principal dishes which her skill and ingenuity have mostly prepared . . . When the dinner-hour has arrived, it is the duty of the cook to dish-up such dishes as may, without injury, stand . . . but such as are of a more important or *recherché* kind, must be delayed . . . Then comes haste; but there must be no hurry – all must work with order.[96]

Only families wealthy enough to hire several servants would have a cook who did nothing else. A female cook was less expensive than a male one, because she was considered less skilled. Cooks sometimes advertised for positions in periodicals such as the *Pot-au-Feu*, and included details such as age, marital status, and the skills they possessed, as well as their willingness or otherwise to undertake tasks such as cleaning.[97] Hiring a male cook was considered by many a mark of distinction, available only to the very rich. In his diary, Arnold Bennett referred to a male servant, skilled in the art of cookery. In May 1897 he wrote: 'After wonderful experiences, we have obtained the very prince of manservants, who cooks like an angel & is the terror to thieving London tradesmen.'[98] Men were thought to be the only ones capable of producing haute cuisine, while women could produce good, wholesome bourgeois fare. The elitist journal *L'Art Culinaire* suggested that a male chef would be instructed by the man of the house rather than a woman. As a highly qualified professional he needed no advice on how to cook particular dishes but 'The first duty of the master of the house who hires a cook (*cuisinier*) is to inform this artist of the kind of works necessitated by his particular tastes.'[99] The cook was hired to please the master of the house and his guests and a 'good conference with the chef can avoid many future disasters; for the talent of a cook is to please his master while maintaining the standards of his art'.[100] Once the master's preferences had been imparted, the cook would do the rest, without female interference.

In instructing women on how to use their servants during everyday meals, writers advised them to require the same standard of service as they would at a dinner party. The reason for this was twofold. In the first place, it was seen as important to make every meal a pleasant occasion. Contesse Loetitia advised the readers of her *Salle à Manger* column 'even for the family or its closest intimates, the table must be set with care . . . And let no one tell me that in families of meagre fortune details are impossible. There is time for everything and one always does what one <u>wants</u> to do.'[101] A husband had to be treated properly in his own home, and sloppiness at dinner could detract from his enjoyment. At the same time, many writers advised that daily dinners were the perfect opportunity to practise for a dinner party. Servants who were accustomed to doing things properly every day would have no trouble with more formal occasions. And it was widely acknowledged that a great deal of anxiety surrounding the dinner party concerned the difficulty of training servants to do things right.

Though tasty family meals and attention to husbands' needs were crucial to the women of London and Paris, it was in France that the importance of practising for dinner parties was often noted. Servants were to act as an extension of the mistress in the preparation of family meals. Ideally, the mistress was responsible for ideas, aesthetics and organisation, while her servants were left to do the actual work. In reality, there may have been a greater level of interaction between mistresses and servants than the available sources reveal. At the same time, individual households are likely to have differed in the extent to which servants, and cooks in particular, could influence the diet and mealtime rituals of their employers.

Men's involvement in culinary matters was discussed in quite different terms in London than in Paris. In London, as in Paris, male chefs were highly prized, and received higher wages than their female counterparts. But the men who employed them had little if any part to play in kitchen. Yet, given the extent to which English historians have argued that middle-class domesticity was exclusively a female concern in the second half of the century, it is perhaps surprising that even a few men were knowledgeable about cooking. In France it was another matter. The separation of male and female spheres was espoused in France as in England. For Chatillon-Plessis this represented 'truth and beauty' to which he added that 'as long as we seek a different solution for social or personal well being, we will find only misery'.[102] But in France cuisine was seen less as a mundane aspect of domestic life, and more a matter of national and masculine pride. Thus while French men might not get their hands dirty, the need to maintain a reputation for understanding gastronomy was keenly felt and an understanding of good food, and the ability to order a perfect dinner, were essential elements of the masculine body of knowledge.

A reviewer of the first edition of *Mrs Beeton's Book of Household Management* expressed the pleasures that a man could derive from reading cookery books:

> It may be a strange taste, perhaps, but ours, in a literary way, runs upon Cookery books . . . and I believe in this predilection that I am a fortunate man – that is to say if there be any truth in what has often been said, he who keeps his heart the longest the heart of a boy is the happiest man. For I have seen a certain youth, a son of mine, within the last few days turn over the pages of a cookery book which has been sent to me to review . . . and examine the recipes and count the illustrations, and criticize with such a determined and thorough manner that it proved to me two things, – Firstly, that Frederick was, indeed, the son of his father; secondly, that he evidently and distinctly feasted of the flavours indicated in his expectant and watering palate by the turkey and sausages.[103]

Father and son shared in the pleasure of anticipating the enjoyment of eating the dishes suggested in the cookery book. They suffered no anxiety in reflecting on the cost or difficulty of preparation of tempting meals. But they had sufficient knowledge of food preparation to be able to understand how the words on the page would translate to the dish on the table. While for a woman a cookery book was a didactic text, for a man it could be a source of imagination and enjoyment.

Sir William Hardman wrote of a foreigner visiting London, a friend of a friend, to whom he wished to demonstrate English hospitality and cuisine. After the roast beef, by which the foreigner was duly impressed, there followed another course: 'It was a "plat" devised by myself, viz. "Curried Maccaroni" . . . I can assure you it is most delicious, and by far the best method of employing curry.'[104] Hardman is unlikely to have cooked the dish himself. However, he had 'devised' it, presumably considering himself to be a man of taste, and who understood the arts of the table. There was clearly no shame in making public his knowledge of things culinary, and in fact Hardman appears to have expected to gain credit from his 'most delicious' dish. As shown in Chapter 5, English men revealed much more of their knowledge of all things culinary when they sat on the various committees which ran the gentlemen's clubs of London.

In the family home men, women and children shared privacy and emotional bonds. Responsibility for cooking and making choices about what to eat were shared by middle-class men and women and the servants they employed, but most observers felt that domestic food arrangements required feminine expertise. Women's knowledge about food and cooking allowed their family to enjoy mealtimes, and was also a source of social connections with other women, playing a part in the creation of social networks. While each family had choices to make about what meals to eat, and how to organise their time, participation in these social networks was facilitated by members of the bourgeoisie's shared ideas about mealtimes and the importance of orderly timekeeping throughout the day. Chapter 3 reveals that mealtime sociability, and dinner parties in particular, were a regular and important feature of the lives of most members of the middle classes.

Notes

1 I. Beeton, *Book of Household Management* (London: S.O. Beeton Publishing, 1861).

2 It has been published in numerous editions, most recently as *The Best of Mrs Beeton's Easy Everyday Cooking* (London: Weidenfeld & Nicolson, 2006).

3 D. Oddy and D. Miller (eds), *The Making of the Modern British Diet* (London: Croom Helm, 1976) p. 7; H. J. Teutberg (ed.), *European Food History* (Leicester: Leicester University Press, 1992) p. 6.

4 For a general discussion of the difficulties in periodising changes in diet in accordance with accepted historical periodisation see H. J. Teutberg, 'Periods and Turning Points in the History of European Diet: A Preliminary Outline of Problems and Methods', in A. Fenton and E. Kisbàn (eds), *Food in Change: Eating Habits from the Middle Ages to the Present Day* (Edinburgh: John Donald, 1986); M. Montanari, *The Culture of Food*, trans. C. Ipsen (Oxford: Blackwell, 1994) p. xi; C. Geisser and D. Oddy (eds), *Food, Diet and Economic Change Past and Present* (London: Leicester University Press, 1993) p. 8.

5 This paucity of source material is also discussed in S. Mennell, *All Manners of Food: Eating and Taste in England and France from the Middle Ages to the Present.* (Oxford: Blackwell, 1985) p. 211.

6 F. Coppée, *Souvenirs d'un parisien* (Paris: A. Lemerre, 1910) pp. 19–20.

7 J. Tosh, *A Man's Place: Masculinity and the Middle-Class Home in Victorian England.* (London: Yale University Press, 1999) p. 84; J. Gillis, *A World of their Own Making: Myth, Ritual and the Quest for Family Values* (New York: Basic Books, 1996) pp. 168–9.

8 M. V. Hughes, *A London Child of the 1870s* (Oxford: Oxford University Press, 1977) pp. 10, 56; M. V. Hughes, *A London Girl of the 1880s* (Oxford: Oxford University Press, 1978) p. 3.

9 N. Charles and M. Kerr, *Women, Food and Families* (Manchester: Manchester University Press, 1988) pp. 17, 113; also E. Ross, *Love and Toil: Motherhood in Outcast London, 1870–1918* (New York: Oxford University Press, 1993).

10 C. Dyhouse, 'Mothers and Daughters in the Middle-Class home c.1870–1914', in J. Lewis (ed.), *Labour and Love: Women's Experience of Home and Family, 1850–1940* (Oxford: Blackwell, 1986) p. 33.

11 J.-B. Fonssagrives, *Hygiène alimentaire des malades, des covalescents et des valétudinaires* (Paris: J.-B Baillière et fils, 1881) pp. 190–3.

12 Anon., *The Etiquette of Courtship and Matrimony: with a complete guide to the forms of a wedding.* (London, 1865) pp. 61–2; see also Mrs Warren, *How I Managed my Household on Two Hundred Pounds a Year* (London, 1864) p. iv; Mme D'Alq, *Le Maître et la maîtresse de maison*, 2nd edn (Paris: Bureau des Causerie Familiaire, 1875) p. 17.

13 Warren, *How I Managed my Household on Two Hundred Pounds a Year*, p. vi.

14 Warren, *How I Managed my Household on Two Hundred Pounds a Year*, p. vi; French women were offered similar advice in D'Alq, *Le Maître et la maîtresse de maison*, p. 221.

15 Comtesse Leotitia in *Salle à Manger* (Dec. 1890). See also D'Alq, *Le Maître et la maîtresse de maison*, p. 213. Similarly, Mrs Loftie advised that even the most homely of dinners should not be served without a menu, *The Dining Room*, Art at Home Series (London: Macmillan and Co., 1876) p. 105.

16 W. M. Rosetti, *The Diary of W. M. Rosetti, 1870–1873*, ed. O. Bornand (Oxford: Clarendon Press, 1977) pp. 195–6.

17 *Le Figaro* (30 July 1854).

18 A. Martin-Fugier, 'Bourgeois Ritual', in M. Perrot (ed.), *A History of Private Life. Vol. IV. From the Fires of Revolution to the Great War*, trans. A. Goldhammer, (London: Belknap Press, 1990) pp. 268–9.

19 *La Salle à Manger* (May 1895).

20 See for example: *La Salle à Manger* (Jan. 1899); E. Boursin, *Le Livre de la femme au XIXème siècle* (Paris, 1865) p. 300.

21 M. Ponsonby, 'Ideal, Reality and Meaning: Homemaking in England in the First Half of the Nineteenth Century', *Journal of Design History* 16:3 (2003) 203.

22 See, for example, Rossetti, *The Diary of W. M. Rossetti 1870–1873*, pp. 131, 137, 217.

23 E. Yates, *His Recollections and Experiences* (London: R. Bentley & Son, 1884) pp. 266–7.

24 U. Bloom, *Sixty Years of Home* (London: Hurst & Blackett, 1960) pp. 89–90.

25 AN MC ET/XCIII/855. This inventory was taken at the time of his wife's death in 1851.

26 AN MC ET/XCIII/638.

27 AN MC ET/IV/1447.

28 Green and Stansby, Auction Catalogue for no. 21 Old Bond Street (Lambeth: H. Kemshead, 1858) p. 8.

29 AN MC ET/IV/1506.

30 AN MC ET/XLVI/1013.

31 AN MC ET/XLVI/1013.

32 Stevenson's views are discussed in Chapter 1.

33 AN MC ET/IV/1403.

34 *The Hotel Review* (June 1886) p. 61.

35 See for example W. Schivelbusch, *Disenchanted Night: The Industrialisation of Light in the Nineteenth Century*, trans. A. Davies (London: University of California Press, 1995); L. Nead *Victorian Babylon: People, Streets and Images in Nineteenth-Century London* (London: Yale University Press, 2005).

36 E. B. Foote, *Dr. Foote's Home Cyclopedia of Popular Medicine, Social and Sexual Science* (London: L. N. Fowler, 1906) p. 92; Anon. *Cassell's People's Physician: A Book of Medicine and of Health for Everybody*, 5 vols (London: Cassell & Co., 1900–1915) p. 80; *The Caterer* (15 Sept. 1881); Boursin, *Le Livre de la femme au xixème siècle*, p. 342.

37 Hughes, *A London Child*, p. 61.

38 Anon. *How to Dine; or, etiquette of the Dinner Table* (London: Ward, Lock and Tyler, 1879) p. 23.

39 Anon. *How to Entertain; or etiquette for Visitor* (London: Ward, Lock and Tyler, 1876) pp. 56–7. Also *How to Dine*, p. 23.

40 Beeton, *Book of Household Management*, pp. 5–9.

41 Beeton, *Book of Household Management*, p. 5.

42 Comtesse de Bassanville, 'Du Domestique', *La Mode de Paris* (Nov. 1871).

43 L. Le Verrier, *Journal d'une jeune fille Second Empire: 1866–1878*, ed. L. Mirisch (Paris: Cadeilhan, 1994) p. 33.

44 Le Verrier, *Journal d'une jeune fille*, p. 33.

45 F. Wey, *A Frenchman sees the English in the Fifties*, trans. and ed. V. Pirie (London: Sidgwick & Jackson, 1935) p. 161. The fashionable dinner hour in restaurants was equally late.

46 Yates, *His Recollections and Experiences*, pp. 38–9.

47 See Chapter 4 also for midday dinners as a form of nostalgic and exclusive masculine sociability.

48 Hughes, *A London Girl*, p. 47.

49 See for example: E. Monin, *L'Hygiène de l'estomac* (Paris: O. Doin, 1888) p. 399; Anon. *The Family Physician*, 2nd edn (London: Cassell & Co., 1879) pp. 383–4.

50 Boursin, *Le Livre de la femme au xixeme siecle*, p. 342; *The Caterer* (15 Sept. 1881); *Salle à Manger* (Oct. 1897 and Dec. 1897).

51 Gautier, *L'Alimentation et le régime chez l'homme sain et chez les malades* (Paris: Masson, 1904) p. 351.

52 Gautier, *L'Alimentation et le régimes*, pp. 351–2.

53 L. Ducheron, 'Hygiène de la table', *La Salle à Manger* (Dec. 1897).

54 *L'Illustration* (1 Sept. 1855). See also J.-P. Aron, *The Art of Eating in France: Manners and Menus in the Nineteenth Century*, trans. N. Rootes (London: Owen, 1975) p. 146.

55 Because working women were not part of the ideal of the middle-class family, their lunchtime needs were not considered by advice writers.

56 Indeed, some sources suggested that one reason for keeping everyday dinners as formal as possible was that this would keep mistress and servants in good practice for dinner parties. *Le Pot-au-Feu* (1 Feb. 1901 and 2 Jan. 1904).

57 Loftie, *The Dining Room*, p. 36.
58 Loftie, *The Dining Room*, p. 36, also *L'Art Culinaire* (Feb. 1888).
59 Mrs Loftie, *The Dining Room*, p. 37.
60 Gautier, *L'Alimentation et le régimes*, p. 352.
61 *The Caterer* (15 Sept. 1882).
62 *The Hotel Review* (June 1886); *La Salle à Manger* (Oct. 1897 and Dec. 1897). Also, Mennell, *All Manners of Food*, p. 130.
63 *La Salle à Manger* (Feb. 1891).
64 Aron, *The Art of Eating*, pp. 147–8; *L'Illustrateur des Dames* (5 Oct. 1869).
65 G. Lees-Maffei, 'From Service to Self-Service: Advice Literature as Design Discourse, 1920–1970', *Journal of Design History* 14:3 (2001) 187–206.
66 Boursin, *Le Livre de la femme au XIXème siècle*, p. 277.
67 Beeton, *Mrs Beeton's Book of Household Management*, p. 1.
68 *La Salle à Manger* (May 1895).
69 B. Smith, *Ladies of the Leisure Class: The Bourgeoises of Northern France in the Nineteenth Century* (Princeton: Princeton University Press, 1981) pp. 66–7.
70 For example Mlle Marianne, *La Bonne Cuisine pour tout le monde de la ville et de la campagne* (Paris: C. Douniol, 1862) pp. 3–5; also *La Mode de Paris* (27 Oct. 1872).
71 *La Salle à Manger* (June 1890). Also *Pot-au-Feu* (14 Oct. 1877).
72 *The Caterer* (5 July 1879).
73 See for example: Le Verrier, *Journal d'une jeune fille Second Empire: 1866–1878*, p. 238 (1878).
74 A. Weiler, *Journal d'une jeune fille mal dans son siècle*, ed. N. Stroskopf (Strasbourg: La Nuée bleu, 1994) pp. 25–6.
75 Hughes, *London Child*, p. 41.
76 Hughes, *London Child*, p. 27.
77 B. de Fréminville, *Marthe: Recueil de lettres extraites d'une correspondance familiale, 1892–1902* (Paris: Seuil, 1981) p. 24.
78 de Fréminville, *Marthe*, p. 24.
79 Bloom, *Sixty Years of Home*, p. 65.
80 Hughes, *London Girl*, pp. 42–3.
81 Hughes, *London Girl*, pp. 42–3.
82 Hughes, *London Girl*, pp. 42–3.
83 *Cornhill Magazine*, 'Family Budgets, Eight Hundred a Year' (1901); *Cornhill Magazine*, Mrs Earle, 'Family Budgets, Eighteen Hundred a Year' (1901); *Cornhill Magazine*, Lady Agnew, 'Family Budgets, Ten Thousand a Year' (1901).
84 *Cornhill Magazine*, Mrs Earle, 'Family Budgets, Eighteen Hundred a Year' (1901).

85 Bloom, *Sixty Years of Home*, p. 68.

86 Bloom, *Sixty Years of Home*, p. 68.

87 Wellcome MS 3824.

88 Wellcome MS 2280.

89 Wellcome MS 3824. See also MS 5853.

90 Wellcome MS 2280.

91 Wellcome MS 3318.

92 Early modern scholars have done some work on the importance of manuscript cookbooks with regards to transmission and social relationships. See: S. Pennell, 'The Material Culture of Food in Early Modern England, *c.*1650–1750', Oxford DPhil thesis, 1997; L. Smith, 'Women's Health Care in England and France, 1650–1775', University of Essex, PhD thesis, 2001; J. Stine, 'Opening Closets: The Discovery of Household Medicine in Early Modern England', Stanford University, PhD dissertation, 1996.

93 E. Higgs, *Domestic Servants and Households in Rochdale 1851–1871* (London: Garland, 1986) pp. 98, 103. G. Crossick and H.-G. Haupt argue that servants were common in petit bourgeois homes. They suggest that servants were present both through a desire to emulate the bourgeoisie but also, and more importantly, because their work formed an important contribution to the family enterprise. *The Petite Bourgeoisie in Europe 1780–1914: Enterprise, Family and Independence*, London, 1995, pp. 104–5.

94 Beeton, *Mrs Beeton's Book of Household Management*, pp. 961–1024. Also Comtesse de Basanville in *La Mode de Paris* (Nov. 1871).

95 Beeton, *Mrs Beeton's Book of Household Management*, pp. 40–4.

96 Beeton, *Mrs Beeton's Book of Household Management*, pp. 42–3.

97 See for example, *Pot-au-Feu* (15 Feb. 1896).

98 A. Bennett, *The Letters of Arnold Bennett*, Vol. II, ed. J. Hepburn (Oxford: Oxford University Press, 1968) p. 85.

99 *L'Art Culinaire* (1886).

100 *L'Art Culinaire* (1886).

101 *Salle à Manger* (Dec. 1890).

102 *Salle à Manger* (May 1898).

103 *The Queen* (28 Dec. 1861).

104 W. Hardman, *A Mid-Victorian Pepys*, 2 vols. ed. S. M. Ellis, (London: Cecil Palmer, 1923–25) p. 164. See also Yates, *His Recollections and Experiences*, p. 251.

3

Dinner parties:
ideal versus experience

The dining room, central to the private living space of a bourgeois family, was also for receiving visitors. The same room that could keep a family united could also be used to expand its social horizons. It could be cosy, impressive or even intimidating, as the case required. In both London and Paris, dinner parties were a frequent and integral part of sociability. Yet 'dinner party' is perhaps too narrow a term to encompass the wide range of situations, from the highly formal and elegant, to the casual and even sometimes unplanned, in which members of the middle classes entered one another's homes to share a meal. While some historians have highlighted the important role of the highly formalised and ritualised dinner party in bourgeois life, contemporary accounts reveal a far more nuanced and varied situation.[1] By looking at the wide range of occasions on which bourgeois people ate in with each other, it is possible to begin to understand the complex ways in which meals shaped bourgeois sociability. Cultural capital was created and displayed through food and drink, ornament and architecture. This chapter illustrates how the dinner party existed on two levels: the imagined and the experienced.

The imagined dinner party was present in etiquette books, which laid out rules and rituals. The experienced dinner party gave participants the opportunity to conform to social norms or to challenge them. In looking at French and English sources, the extent to which the middle classes shared a similar culture is apparent. Etiquette books published in the two countries presented a set of idealised behaviours which would have allowed individuals who were aware of the rules to easily move between the two countries, and to recognise the respectability of their cross-Channel neighbours. In first-hand accounts of dinner parties, what emerges, in contrast, are more individualised sets of behaviour suggesting that social networks or groupings held common practices which resembled but did not slavishly follow the highly idealised practices set out in the prescriptive literature.

By following a recognisable formula, the bourgeois dinner party acquired a meaning shared by all participants. The codification of behaviour that began in the Middle Ages, referred to by Norbert Elias as the progress of civilisation, reached its apex in the second half of the nineteenth century.[2] In the idealised image created in the pages of advice literature, dinner parties were regulated from the moment a potential host or hostess sat down to decide whom to invite until the moment when the last guest finally left the house. And even beyond, the regulation continued, since accepting an invitation to dinner in effect meant accepting the obligation of a return visit and a reciprocal invitation. For French etiquette writer Pierre Boitard there were two sorts of dinners: with or without ceremony.[3] Only those in possession of a large home and a full staff of servants were advised to attempt the first type. Yet in spite of the gallons of ink and reams of paper devoted to the topic of dinner party etiquette, there was tacit acknowledgement that no one could be expected to follow all the rules all the time. While first-hard accounts reveal a world of informal socialising interspersed with occasional formal dinners, etiquette writers went so far as to adjust the rules depending on the sex of the diners – single-sex parties could dispense with many formalities – the type of occasion, economic sphere, and whether or not only close friends and relatives would be present. Much of the meaning of a social meal was created through choices about which rules to abide by and which to ignore. Meals described in first-hand accounts resembled the dinner party of the rule books enough to be recognisable as the same phenomenon, even though rules were often only loosely applied.

Though dinner parties were frequent, references to them in diaries are relatively rare. Sir William Hardman, a lawyer and a writer, provides a notable exception. In 1862 he wrote:

> To-morrow we give a wild sort of supper-party . . . Champagne cup at supper and punch afterwards, with cigars in the dining room. All ladies have been warned that they will be expected to stand tobacco smoke, and must dress accordingly. It is a nervous business, but we hope it will go off well.[4]

After the supper had taken place, Hardman wrote again:

> We sat down to supper about half-eleven, and very well it went off. The boned turkey was admirable. My concoction of champagne and punch was universally admired, and I think we have acquired fresh laurels. We had cigars after supper, and it was actually a quarter past two before any of the party left.[5]

The English convention of the men staying behind in the dining room to smoke while the ladies went ahead to the drawing room was flouted. The convention of wearing formal attire – usual at large supper parties – was also dispensed with on this occasion.

In his description of the supper party, his feelings about and his perceptions of his guests' reactions Hardman seems to confirm many etiquette writers' assumptions. The hosts suffered anxiety as to how the meal would go and how they would be perceived by their guests. Women and men were understood to have different roles to play, even in a case like this in which part of the meaning was being created through breaking down the barriers between the sexes. At the same time, there was the question of display: Hardman and his wife, in hosting a dinner party that challenged several of the rules of polite society, had decided on the kind of reputation they wished to make for themselves among their circle of acquaintances. At the same time, Hardman showed concern about the quality of the food and drink, commenting on specific items, and that everyone seemed to have enjoyed the food and drink served. Food was, after all, the central feature of a meal, even if the purpose of the meal was to show off some aspect of the hosts' characters. In this instance, Hardman's conclusion was that having challenged the rules of the dinner party, he had succeeded in enhancing his social standing: 'I think we have acquired fresh laurels.'[6] Hardman's 'wild sort of supper-party' is a useful though rare illustration of the way in which people consciously shaped the meanings of social domestic meals. The rules of etiquette could be useful for those who needed to learn how to behave properly. However, to those who possessed a knowledge of the rules, they were also useful as a way to shape identity and create reputation, by breaking with traditions and reinterpreting protocols.

Both Londoners and Parisians entertained friends and acquaintances over meals and the social purposes of these meals varied little between the two cities. Where differences did exist they were small matters of protocol and procedure. Needless to say that in spite of mutual influences on each other's diets, the food served was different on either side of the channel.[7] But the principal contrast is one of terminology: the term dinner party exists in the English-speaking world. It implies both a shared meal and a festive atmosphere. The assumption is that the party element will be of at least equal importance to the meal. In French, there is no phrase equivalent to this. Dinner parties were often referred to in French as simply '*un dîner*' with the article signalling the difference between this and a domestic dinner (presumably referred to as '*le dîner*'). They were sometimes referred to as '*dîner en ville*', implying an outing, to distinguish it from dinner at home, or in its more formal incarnations, as '*dîner avec cérémonie*' or '*dîner prier*', implying a meal in which rules would have to be adhered to and certain types of food and service could be expected.

While these various terms were effective in demarcating the boundary between everyday meals and social occasions, there is less emphasis on a festive mood. There is no obvious explanation for this linguistic disparity beyond the simple fact that the French language does not have a direct translation of the English 'party'. While this fact may in itself have a cultural explanation, to seek it is beyond the scope of this book. It is possible that French diners placed a greater emphasis on food, while in England a dinner was more of an excuse for a social event. English architects sometimes commented on the fact that French dining rooms were more austerely decorated than English ones, and attributed this to the greater importance placed on food in that country.[8] The difference in terminology may, in part, reflect the difference in emphasis in French and English meals, in spite of the overall similarities in respectable mealtime manners.

Few scholars have chosen dinner parties as an object of study. Some works on sociability and etiquette touch on the subject of mealtime manners, though none have investigated the way that dinner parties function beyond the rules of good behaviour.[9] Work on ritual, though relevant to the way dinner parties are examined in this chapter, has tended to be undertaken by anthropologists, who have focused on non-Western cultures and on religion.[10] More recently, historians of early modern Europe have also become interested in ritual, noting how many activities of the daily and annual life cycle were standardised and given meaning.

Edward Muir argues that dining, in particular, was a ritual and was particularly 'formative of social identity'.[11] Sociologists have also become interested in the meal as ritual. Margaret Visser and John Gillis, in particular, have each examined the ways in which all meals have to follow certain rules in order to provide shape and meaning to participants.[12]

As part of the bourgeoisification of the domestic interior, dining rooms were gradually incorporated into domestic architecture from the eighteenth century.[13] The dining room was used to make a good impression, whatever that might mean to a particular individual or group. For Hardman, to be 'wild' was a good thing, but for others something more restrained might be in order. Table decorations were one way of creating an appropriate environment.[14] Mrs Loftie commented, with a degree of irony which, however, was not intended to detract from the seriousness of the issue, that well-folded napkins not only looked good but also 'may sometimes afford a subject for dinner conversation when the weather has been exhausted'.[15] Aside from physical objects, an appropriate aesthetic environment was also created through lighting. Wolfgang Schivelbusch has looked at the impact of lighting on private life and on the imagination, with a particular emphasis on technology, but also some keen insights into how the availability of light at night expanded bourgeois sociability both within and outside the home.[16] As gas lighting gradually replaced candles, and eventually electric light overtook gas, advice writers discussed the benefits of each for facilitating social interaction, as well as for allowing female guests to appear in the most flattering light.[17]

For some families in London, but not in Paris, special objects were reserved for the sole purpose of making an impression. According to Ursula Bloom:

> The very best articles were preserved under lock and key for parties and for company. The Crown-Derby tea-set, the Spode dessert service, Grand-mamma's rat-tailed spoons and forks, Great-grandmamma's ivory handled knives.[18]

Though the custom of locking things away for 'best' may have been widespread, advice writers frowned on it. They reasoned that a family should use the best objects they could afford every day, as this would make the home a more beautiful place and therefore enhance the quality of family life. At the same time, they advised that what was good enough for the family should also be good enough for the guests.[19]

Whether it was the house and its objects, or the food consumed, which was most important in creating a good impression is very debatable. Food, though, could communicate many things about those who offered it: from financial wealth to the possession of cultural capital, much could be conveyed about a family's status via their dinner party menus. In the first instance, food provided nurture and nourishment. French sources in particular emphasised the vital role of the hostess in feeding her guests. She was intended to provide not only a tasty feast, but one that took into account the nutritional and health needs of her guests.[20] The dangers of '*dîner en ville*' to the digestive system was widely bemoaned, as many hostesses were accused of not being adequate to the task of providing good food as well as an elegant surrounding.[21] Pierre Boitard was especially scathing of the supposedly polite practice of passing along to the next person the plate given to one by the hostess. For one thing, only the hostess was aware that among her guests could be 'a Hussard captain who eats for four, a young lady suffering from chronic gastritis, a priest in danger of dying of . . . apoplexy' and so on, and that as well as taking their various needs into account, it was also within the hostesses' rights to choose which choice morsels to serve to each of her guests.[22]

Food also constituted a display of wealth. This was so much the case that families who were not in a position to provide better meals for their guests than they themselves usually ate often felt unable to invite outsiders to a meal. This was a view set forth by prescriptive literature. However, Marion Sandborn, whose husband was an illustrator for *Punch*, recorded in her diary that she and her husband accepted invitations to dine with wealthy friends, and were then comfortable reciprocating on a much more modest scale.[23] Food was also a medium for demonstrating taste, both in the choice of dishes and the composition of menus. 'It is the sheen of colours, the brilliance of the sauces, the transparency of the jellies, the limpidity of the wines and above all the aroma of it all which demonstrate the good taste of the host and the culinary talent of the artist.'[24] The execution of the dishes was generally the accomplishment of a servant, rather than the hosts, but the possession of a good servant could also reflect favourably on the masters. Lastly, food was representative of the possession of what we might refer to as cultural capital, since knowledge about food and drink were considered to be acquired through good taste, success and good living.[25] It is therefore understandable that it was widely agreed that people could gain a public reputation from the quality of food they served at their dinner parties.

In the history of European dinners there are two types of service: *à la française* and *à la russe.* The older French 'style as observed in early modern royal banquets makes opulence highly apparent as each course is made up of a huge number of dishes, placed around the table in accordance with a map drawn up by the chef. This type of service was gradually replaced by the more modern Russian style, in which a succession of courses were put on plates by servants. In the French style, all male diners could help themselves to dishes, though women, because of the restraint expected of them, were to be helped by their male dinner companions. While it allowed for great displays of conspicuous wealth, the older service had some disadvantages, namely in the difficulty of getting a taste of any dish placed out of reach, and the fact that dishes could become cold sitting on display on the table.

À la russe service was also more democratic, as it allowed for elegance to be attained in the more modest homes of the middle classes, where the number of dishes needed even for one course of an *à la française* meal would have been prohibitive. But we cannot be too definite in arguing for the succession of one service style by another, since even once it was no longer spoken of, the French style left its mark, especially on informal or family style meals where dishes placed on the table were served by the hostess, perhaps with the host contributing by carving the roasts.[26] At a more formal dinner, dishes were placed on the table for all to see, then promptly removed by servants who carved any joints of meat, and put the food onto plates or platters behind the scenes, then brought it back ready to eat.[27] At dinner parties where formal rules applied, the menu was a series of individual courses, which were described, or at least named, to diners on menu cards, which in France were often taken home and kept as souvenirs.[28]

The number of guests at a dinner party could vary as much as the nature of the party itself. However, advice writers generally focused on parties of even numbers, generally between six and twelve, when providing sample menus. Mrs Beeton provided her readers with menu suggestions for dinner parties of twelve:

FIRST COURSE
Soupe à la Reine   *Julienne Soup*
Turbot and Lobster Sauce   *Slices of Salmon à la Genevese*

ENTREES
Croquettes of Leveret   *Fricandeau de Veau*
Vol-au-Vent   *Stewed Mushrooms*

SECOND COURSE
Forequarter of Lamb   *Guinea Fowls*   *Charlotte à la Parisienne*
Orange Jelly   *Meringues*   *Ratafia Ice Pudding*
Lobster Salad   *Sea Kale*
Dessert and Ices[29]

Mrs Beeton provides a clear example of the overlap between the older and the more modern style of service, with the course comprising several dishes and the menu laid out as a diagram rather than as a list. Yet this was a very modest menu if compared to the standards of even a few decades earlier. The diagram did more than bring to mind the elegance of French style service. It had the added advantage of informing readers who were perhaps not well-versed in fashionable dining, which elements of the meal to group together. While some of the dishes had French names, this was a rather traditional English menu with few genuinely foreign elements.

Readers of *Le Pot-au-Feu* were offered similar schemes, with the added convenience that prices were included for consideration. A menu proposed in 1896 was for twelve people who were 'relatives or intimate friends, not dressed up and without truffles, but a "good dinner"'.[30] This description was given in order to distinguish this meal from more ceremonial and elegant ones. The cost was estimated at 70 francs.

Potage Crécy
Canapés de kilkis
Turbot sauce mousseline
Chartreuse de perdrix
Gigot dans son jus
Dinde rôtis
Salade
Haricots verts
Praliné à la crème
Dessert[31]

This menu was presented without headings for each course, unlike that found in Mrs Beeton. Appearing some three decades later, it reflects the total abandonment of the service *à la française*, while Mrs Beeton's earlier menu still embodied the principles of that form of serving. The simple ordering of the dishes also reflects the fact that this was a menu for a simple, unceremonial meal. Unlike Mrs Beeton's menu, the dishes are not grouped together, so the hostess planning the meal needed more prior knowledge to decode the list.

A menu which appeared in *Le Pot-au-Feu* in January 1901 was for a 'simple but chic' dinner, which had to be good but also as economical as possible. The goal of any self-respecting bourgeois hostess was to create the impression of an expensive dish without the expenditure, and housewives who overspent on dinner parties were widely criticised.[32] This particular dinner was priced at around 100 francs.

> Potage crème de santé
> Barbue sauce génevoise
> Poulardes demi-deuil
> Selle de chevreuil sauce muscovite
> Mauviette en caisse en chaudfroid
> Salade en saison
> Petits pois à la française
> Pudding de marrons
> Dessert[33]

The order of the simple but chic dinner of 1901 is not very different from the informal meal of 1896. The order of the service was similar, though by 1901 one item fewer appeared. Menus were gradually becoming shorter and simpler through the course of the century, a progression which continued into the twentieth century, ending eventually with the three-course dinner with which diners today are familiar.

The ideal dinner: rules of etiquette

The ideal dinner party could only exist in the perfect world imagined by etiquette writers and their readers. At such dinner parties everyone knew her role and played it perfectly. But awareness of the potential dangers and pitfalls awaiting both hosts and guests was ever present. The dinner party, as it appeared in the vast numbers of advice books and articles published in this period, was in many ways a piece of theatre. The interest of the performance came from the tension of trying to attain perfection and avoid disgrace. In the dinner party performance the roles were divided between hosts and guests and between men and women.

The role of the host could be played by almost any member of the respectable bourgeoisie.[34] It was seen by some as a possible source of pleasure,[35] but others perceived it as causing untold anxiety. English advice writers considered it a social duty for every household to host a dinner party at least once a month. Single men were excused from the duties of formal entertainments, but could still expect to receive frequent invitations themselves. However, couples who could not afford to offer proper dinners were warned against accepting invitations they could not reciprocate.[36] The existence of independent unmarried women was not acknowledged by the writers of prescriptive literature. Widows, however, could host dinner parties as they had done during married life.

The perfect dinner party was presided over by both host and hostess. Each had complementary but distinct parts to play. Comtesse de Gencé suggested that when hosts ignored their duties, it led to the unhappiness of all: 'Hosts, solely preoccupied with the brilliant appearance of the meal, forget about comfort, intimacy, well being, and real enjoyment.' She went on to urge greater care: 'I would very much like it if the master of the house would look after his menu, his wine cellar, the *male* things, while madam, with a feminine delicacy, would think of the multitude of details that she alone is capable of administering.'[37] As de Gencé suggested, both host and hostess had a role to play in the entertainment of guests, and each part was essential to the success of the evening.

Yet the hostess bore a heavier burden than the host, which represented a rather recent transition.[38] According to English etiquette manuals, hosting a dinner was a male privilege and obligation in the final decades of the eighteenth century. By the early 1800s, there began to be signs that women were taking more responsibility in this area, and by mid-century, the transition was complete, with women receiving all the blame or credit for the meals they hosted.[39] The dining room, as discussed in Chapter 1, remained a masculine space, with women receiving guests on their husbands' behalf. And men did not lose interest in hosting meals, but instead made use of new, commercial spaces such as clubs and restaurants, to invite one another to eat, and display their taste and wealth.

The first duty of the hostess was to make a guest list. As well as the number of guests, the character of each had to be considered in order to ensure that the party gathered around the table would be well balanced, congenial and interesting.[40] For the duty of the hosts was not simply to feed their guests, but also to entertain them, which was achieved by seating everyone next to someone whose conversation they would enjoy. Once the guest list had been decided upon, invitations needed to be made. Advice on how to do this varied. Some situations called for a written or even printed card, while for others oral invitations sufficed.[41] In France, Mme Raymond stipulated that 'Dinner invitations are made with printed cards for a formal dinner . . . they are made in writing for somewhat less formal dinners, orally if it is a case of bringing together a few guests who are intimate friends.'[42] Comtesse de Bassanville, however, insisted that written invitations were adequate for inviting people of the same social rank as the inviter, but that their social superiors should be invited in person.[43] Similar advice was presented to English readers. Invitations needed to be made anywhere between two days and two weeks in advance, though longer notice than that was never recommended, and the same rule applied for wedding invitations.[44] This is a shorter interval than twenty-first-century readers might anticipate, and indicates that social engagements of all kinds must generally have been organised within these time limits, allowing people to be free to accept dinner invitations at short notice.

On the day of the dinner party, the hostess, and her servants if she had them, were required to be extremely organised.[45] Though many bourgeois women managed their home without help from a full domestic staff, etiquette books often operated on the assumption that the majority of their readers did have such a staff. It was, presumably, up to the readers themselves to discover how to compensate for the lack of helping hands in the kitchen on dinner-party days. As readers of *La Salle à Manger* were instructed: 'The woman who takes most care of the interior of her home, must arrange to appear not to put her hand to anything.'[46] After a very full and busy day of preparation, when the guests finally arrived 'out of consideration for her guests, all things have to have been foreseen and prepared so that . . . the hostess need not disturb herself for anything'.[47]

The host might also have some duties to perform on the day of the dinner party. In 1891, readers of *La Salle à Manger* were informed:

> Truly great lords take loving care of their table themselves.
>
> The Duke of Mauchy never receives guests without having personally been to inspect the table setting and the food preparation.[48]

Other writers insisted that it was the host who had to take responsibility for choosing the wines to serve with dinner:

> Almost every gentleman has wine at his table, whenever he has invited guests. Indeed, wine is considered an indispensable part of a good dinner, to which a gentleman has been formally invited.[49]

However, unlike his wife, the host could choose how much or how little he involved himself in such preparations. Shirley Nicholson found evidence in Linley Sandbourne's diary that he looked after the wine that was served at the dinners he and his wife hosted and also drew up the seating plan and made notes on all the guests.[50]

On the arrival of the guests, everyone was supposed to gather in the drawing room until a servant announced that dinner was served.[51] However, owing to the great importance placed on punctuality, the interval in the drawing room was not expected to be long.[52] In that short time, an important task had to be carried out by either host or hostess: to quietly inform each guest about how to proceed to the dining room. Generally, each male guest was assigned to accompany a female guest into the dining room, and to sit beside her. The host and hostess entered with the most honoured female and male guests, respectively. All this had to be done strictly according to the rules of precedence, which could be found in numerous advice books to avoid confusion.[53]

When all the guests were seated it was finally time for the food to take centre stage. The food, as we have seen, was important in many ways. Even if everything else was perfect, bad or badly served food could affect the reputation of both host and hostess. Meals could consist of several courses, and the ideal meals of the etiquette world tended to be lavish. *How to Dine* contained an extended description of 'A Fashionable Dinner-Party':

There were two soups (white and brown) standing on a side-table. Each servant handed the dishes in his white kid gloves, and with a damask napkin under his thumb . . . After the soup, Hock and Moselle were offered to each guest, that they might choose either. A dish of fish was then placed at each end of the table . . . then the appropriate sauce for the fish, also cucumbers to eat with the salmon . . . Directly after the fish came the *entremets*, or French dishes . . . Afterwards a saddle or haunch of Welsh mutton was placed at the master's end of the table, and at the lady's end a boiled turkey . . . The poultry was not dissected – nothing being helped but the breast. Ham and tongue were then supplied to those who took poultry; and currant jelly to the eaters of the mutton. Next came the vegetables . . . Next, two dishes of game . . . Then placed along the table were the sweet things – Charlottes, jellies, frozen fruit . . . A lobster salad dressed and cut up large was put on with the sweets. On a side-table were stilton and cream cheese . . . After this, port wine . . . Next, the sweets were handed round.[54]

Boitard advised a different order for meals in France: 'After the roasts, the fish is served (because salad no longer dares to show itself at a *dîner de cérémonie*), and these are carved by the *écuyer tranchant* with a silver slice. Then come the sweet *entremets* which are served by the hosts.'[55] Mme D'Alq was most explicit about the order in which the dessert ought to be served: 'the cheeses, starting with the salty ones, preserves, raw fruit, compotes, light pastries, bonbons and ices'.[56]

Dinner came to an end once all the guests had finished eating. Host and hostess were reminded not to send away their plates until all the guests had finished theirs.[57] When the plates had been cleared away (one by one, never stacked),[58] the hostess stood up.[59] In France, the hostess was instructed to take 'the arm of one of her neighbours, either the one who accompanied her in, or the other one who is placed on her left, if she wants him to have an equal part in the *honours* she is bestowing'.[60] There was an art to bestowing this honour, 'she will abstain from approaching too directly the guest to whom she wishes to give her arm; she will turn towards him and incline her head slightly. If, however, this should not suffice, she can add a few words to this mute invitation, and invite him to accompany her to the living room.'[61] The rest of the guests would then rise and follow their hostess to the *salon* where coffee was served, while the men withdrew to the *fumoir*, or smoking room.[62] In London, when the hostess rose from the table, only her female guests followed her to the drawing room. The men stayed at the table, drinking and smoking, before eventually joining the women for coffee.

Just as everyone could potentially host a dinner party, so everyone could also be a guest at one. The duties of the guest were less onerous than those of the hosts, and the potential for enjoyment proportionally greater. Nonetheless, at the idealised dinner parties described by etiquette writers, guests were participants in an elaborate ritual and, like their hosts, had to play by the rules. A guest's obligation began when an invitation was received. Politeness required a prompt response, especially if the invitation was to be declined.[63] But dinner invitations, crucial as they were to creating and maintaining the bonds of respectable society, were not to be turned down lightly; refusal was only acceptable on genuine and important grounds.

Nothing was expect of a guest, between accepting an invitation and appearing at dinner. It was not customary in either London or Paris for guests to bring gifts or offerings of any kind to the meal, though some people did bring gifts. One French author suggested that at informal dinners it was nice to bring a bouquet of flowers to the hosts.[64] Food itself could also often be made as a gift between close friends and relatives.[65] In a letter to his wife, Parisian, M. Labaty wrote that whenever he dined with their friends the Geoffroy, 'I bring them grapes.'[66] His wife was staying in the country and the grapes were in lieu of a return invitation. But reciprocity was created through the exchange of invitations, and gifts were not needed.[67] Since a dinner party was the hosts' opportunity to demonstrate their abilities and possessions, contributions would in any case have been unwelcome. Guests' principal tasks were to arrive on time and to be gracious to whomever they were seated next to, which could be a chore if a diner felt slighted or disappointed by the choice their hostess had made in seating them.[68]

Bad or insufficient conversation at a dinner party was generally blamed on the hosts. French advice writers were keen to advise would-be hostesses on the important skill of directing conversation.[69] Politics was seen as a dangerous area, to be avoided at all costs.[70] A French cartoon appearing in *Le Figaro* in 1899 (figure 5) depicted a pleasant family dinner that turned into a brawl once the Dreyfus affair – *the* hot political topic of the day – was discussed. This satirical image in which a numerous, respectable family were

Figure 5 Affaire Dreyfus. 'Un dîner en famille' (1899).

served dinner by a male servant showed men and women coming to blows over politics. It was intended to illustrate the ridiculous extent to which the Dreyfus affair had divided French opinion, but in placing the argument at the dinner table it also played on fears about social impropriety and the importance of sticking to appropriate topics of conversation at mealtimes.

This French concern with avoiding political disagreements at the dinner table may have been a consequence of the French Revolution and ensuing decades of political instability. In England, where politics were less divisive, less concern was expressed over the rudeness of bringing politics to the dinner table. But French etiquette writers did not make reference to history; rather, their concern was the belief that certain types of intellectual and emotional strain were harmful to the digestion process. Also, as both host and hostess wanted their guests to go away with a happy memory of the dinner party, it was in their interest to steer clear of topics that might leave guests upset or uncomfortable. Guests had a part to play in keeping talk both lively and polite.[71] While both men and women conversed, it was men who were entitled to take the lead,[72] and it was principally towards their enjoyment that both food and conversation were directed.[73] While only men had the ability truly to appreciate food and drink, women were more ornamental.[74] Their charm and beauty could be a great accompaniment to a dinner, but they also had to be careful not to speak at the wrong moments, thereby distracting men from their gustatory pleasures.

While enjoying the food, wine and conversation, men had also the responsibility of looking after the needs of their female companions.[75] As dinner was generally served *à la russe*, this principally meant being polite and pouring wine.

> During the whole course of the meal, the men placed near the women must do all the little favours for their neighbours which they may require in order to avoid for them any effort or inconvenience; they will pour wine and water for them, they will do all these favours quickly, since a well brought up woman can in no case ask for them.[76]

Through conversation, men hoped to entertain but also to impress. To this end, they were advised to cultivate certain areas of knowledge. To avoid embarrassment, 'it is quite necessary that every gentleman should be able to converse, intelligently, upon the character and quality of the various wines in use.'[77] The lull in conversation that a lack of response could cause was bad enough, but there were further worries, as 'ignorance of the history and quality of wines may impress gentlemen with the idea that you have not been much in good company'.

After a meal, dinner guests were expected to stay for the evening, and were sometimes joined by new arrivals.[78] These would be guests who had been formally invited, but not for the meal itself. They might be close friends and family, who on other occasions were meal guests but on this particular occasion in question were simply coming to spend the evening. Likewise, they might be acquaintances whom the hosts wished to entertain, but with whom they were not on sufficiently close terms to warrant an invitation to dinner. It was customary to invite people to spend an evening in one's home, where they would be given refreshments and entertainment.

Male and female guests were, as we have seen, expected to fulfil somewhat different roles at the table. An extension of this was found in the fact that single-sex meals were subject to slightly different rules from mixed ones. If women entertained on their own, according to advice writers, it was generally either for lunch or tea.[79] In either case these were meals with few formalities, and it was sufficient for all the women present to behave with decorum, and not to overstay their welcome. Neither tea nor lunch, both associated with feminine and single-sex sociability, were meals at which complicated or elegant food needed to be served, which fitted with the idea that food in itself was a primarily masculine pleasure. What was essential at meals, and which united groups of women, were pleasant surroundings and a sociable atmosphere.

Men on their own might well invite one another to dinner parties. These would be less formal than mixed dinner parties. According to advice writers, men could afford to do away with many of the formalities of good behaviour when no women were present.[80] Women only were believed to have delicate sensibilities. Among men, intelligent conversation was considered more important than the rules of good behaviour. When men met for dinner the food was essentially the same as that served at mixed dinner parties with one exception: men could do without any sweet courses at dinner. While men and women were each considered to be part of the same system of rules governing behaviour at the table, single-sex groups were felt to be able to relax their application of the rules. However, both men and women, in a variety of situations, revealed themselves to be at once aware of the rules of polite behaviour but also willing and able to bend, break or ignore the rules, depending on the circumstances.

Real dinners: some first-hand accounts

The parts to be played by all the participants at a dinner party were clearly defined in the prescriptive literature. In reality, however, these did not necessarily coincide with the way people behaved. The rules of dinner-party etiquette were numerous and difficult to follow. It is hard to imagine any instance where all the rules would have been followed and, if such occasions did occur, it is clear that they would have been stiff and unpleasant. First-hand accounts of dinner parties paint a different picture, with a slightly different set of meanings. Food and display were still at the heart of the ritual, but so were amusement and enjoyment. Contrary to expectation, many a dinner party was a comfortable and familiar event, extending the sphere of mealtime intimacy beyond the family circle.

Parisian journalist Georges Montorgueil – the pseudonym of Lyon-born Octave Lebesque – received frequent invitations to dine with friends and colleagues. These provide a unique insight into the way in which at least one section of the bourgeoisie socialised over food in the domestic sphere. The fact that invitations were received from numerous sources indicates that the literary and journalistic acquaintances of the Montorgueil family participated in a shared culture of dining. The several large boxes of Montorgueil's correspondence preserved in the *Archives National* reveal a man who was socially active and very sought out. Both as a friend and as a journalist, he was often in demand:

> My dear friend,
> I know that you are very busy. If however, one time exceptionally you could come and dine with us it would make me very happy it would be next Thursday 7:30 and if needs be we could wait till a little later it would be altogether without ceremony as there will be no other ladies than my wife and daughter but only a few interesting friends Say yes I pray you.[81]

This letter from circa 1910, was from a friend or acquaintance named Eugene Revillout. The invitation, one of several Montorgueil received from Revillout, implies familiarity by its informal style, though also allows for a certain distance, in using the formal *vous* rather than informal *tu* in addressing Montorgueil. At the same time – especially when seen alongside other invitations from Revillout to Montorgueil – the slightly imploring tone suggests that Revillout wished to impress Montorgueil and win his friendship. Although dinner was planned for 7:30, Revillout offered to delay it to suit Montorgueil, suggesting that Montorgeuil's needs were more important than those of the host and his other guests, and also seemingly refusing to take no for an answer.

Other invitations from Revillout are similar in tone, including phrases such as: '[since] you will only be free a few days later we will see each other then if you prefer 7:30 then we can have dinner at 7:30 . . .'[82] Or: 'As we have discovered that Saturday would suit you better, we will await you Saturday evening 2nd July . . .'[83] Changes to invitations already extended suggest that the Montorgueils were very much in demand as guests in the Revillout household. It is impossible to determine to what extent this was reciprocated, though it cannot have been entirely one-sided, as one letter survived in which Revillout accepted an invitation from Montorgueil:

> My dear friend,
>   My wife and daughter and I will be faithful next Sunday to the gracious appointment which you and Mme Montorgueil have given us.[84]

Revillout, like many of the people who wrote to Montorgueil, was happy to fit his mealtime around his guest's preferences. The rules of dining as set out in advice publications always stressed punctuality and inflexibility as to time, but the invitations Montorgueil received from Revillout reveal that dinner times could be shifted to accommodate different timetables.

Revillout's invitations to Montorgueil accord with the rules of etiquette concerning the different needs of men and women in relation to good manners. In the first invitation cited above, Revillout wrote that dinner 'would be altogether without ceremony as there will be no other ladies than my wife and daughter but only a few interesting friends'.[85] The rules, as we have seen, insisted on the greater need for formality where women were present. Stressing that no women from outside his household would be present at the meal was his way of reassuring Montorgueil that there would be no need for rigid formality if the invitation were accepted. It may also have been a way of indicating to Montorgueil that his wife was not included in the invitation, but that no offence was intended by this omission, since it would have been awkward for her to be the only female guest at an all-male dinner party. Women from within the household did not, by Revillout's calculations, hold the same status as female guests, and could be ignored in setting the informal tone of the evening.

Montorguil's invitations provide an example of a social set happy to break from the convention of women issuing dinner invitations and women being the first named recipient of invitations. Of twenty invitations in the Montorgueil archive, twelve are addressed to Montorgeuil alone[86] and eight to himself and his wife.[87] The invitations came from men as well as women. While much of the correspondence in the archive is from professional colleagues, only one of the twelve invitations addressed to Montorgueil alone, from his editor Henri Beraldi, is specifically to a working lunch.[88] Some invitations, though, did conform to the formal rules of etiquette, like the one to tea at the Hammonds, in which the women were listed before their husbands, and the time was firmly specified:

> Mme and M A. Hammond pray Mme and M Montorgueil to come take tea on Sunday 7th July from 4 till 6.[89]

From their name, it was likely that the Hammonds were English, though it was not unheard of for fashionable French women to host English style teas. The invitation included directions to their house in Neuilly, a respectable upper-middle-class suburb of Paris.

While some writers included a request for greetings to be extended to Mme Montorgueil, invitations that did not include her were unapologetic and offered no explanation. In a society in which same-sex meals were commonplace there was no reason to make excuses. Many of the invitations from which Mme Montorgueil was excluded were ones which Montorgueil received from colleagues and professional acquaintances, regardless of whether the colleague was male or female. Where one of the purposes of the meal was to discuss a work-related matter, Mme Montorgueil was generally not included in the invitation. Invitations received from couples, and ones whose motivation was exclusively social, tended to invite the Montorgueils as a couple.

Two women, both known feminists as well as fellow journalists, extended invitations to Montrogueil. These women, Jeanne Schmahl and Marguerite Durand, were neither of them typical bourgeois *maitresse de maison*, yet each was still operating within the boundaries of respectable society. Schmahl always wrote, herself, even though her letters indicate that her husband was present at the meals. She generally invited Montorgueil to lunch rather than dinner, and these were very informal meals, suggesting the possibility that Schmahl and Montorgueil were on terms of close friendship. Four letters from Schmahl were invitations. The first was written in May 1893:

My dear sir,
Would you do us the pleasure of coming to lunch with us (and a few friends) Sunday May 28th at noon?[90]

This invitation is neither formal nor overly familiar. Rather it is a simple statement, where time and date, though nothing else, are clearly specified. The second letter is dated 15 July 1894:

Dear friend,
Would you like to do us the pleasure of coming to lunch with us next Sunday the 22nd at noon. We could then chat a bit about all our shared interests.
My husband joins me in sending you his affectionate compliments.[91]

This second letter is friendlier than the first, saluting 'friend', rather than 'Sir'. Again time and date are specified, and it seems that in spite of the friendship and informality, Montorgueil was expected to be punctual. Possibly other guests were invited, though clearly the main purpose of lunch was for Schmahl to have a chance to chat with Montorgueil. This was even more evident in the following letter, from circa 1896. It was a longer letter, and the invitation to lunch was only a small part of it:

Could you not come to lunch with us, alone, the day when you are going to work with our friend Boulet?
We are always at home for lunch and you will always find an omelette done my way to complete the meal if the main course is a bit meagre.[92]

There are several interesting aspects to this invitation. This was a respectable invitation to have lunch with her and her husband, in their normal routine, on a normal workday. In such a case, the fluidity of the boundaries of the home are clear. There are instances of outsiders being invited to share in the daily routine of the household. Schmahl was prepared to cook an omelette, if the main course on the day when Montorgueil came over was insufficient, revealing that in spite of the rules of etiquette, not all women were at pains to hide either the humble nature of their daily fare, nor their role in preparing food for guests. Another interesting point is Jeanne Schmahl's emphasis on Montorgueil coming to lunch alone – she seemed to crave intimacy and informality, as opposed to a more polite social setting.

The final invitation was the only one from Schmahl that included Mme Montorgueil. It was for lunch with other guests. The time was a quarter of an hour later than the usual time of Mrs Schmahl's lunch invitations, probably reflecting the fact that it was a more formal occasion:

> My dear friends,
> Would you like to do us the pleasure of lunching with us Sunday, 3rd of April, at a quarter after noon.
> We will have a few friends, among whom my dear Mme d'Alzès. She will, she tells me, have great pleasure in spending some moments with you both.[93]

The tone of the invitation suggests a social occasion, rather than an intimate one. Mutual acquaintances would be present, and someone had already heard that the Montorgueils would be invited, and had expressed pleasure at the prospect of seeing them. Avoiding the formality of addressing the invitation to the lady first and then the man, the invitation is informally addressed to 'My dear friends'.

Marguerite Durand's initiations were different in tone to the ones received from Schmahl. But like the Schmahl invitations, they are remarkable for being written from a woman to a man without any sign of the unusualness of the friendship or collegiate relationship crossing the gender divide. There are two invitations from Durand, both made in the summer of 1898. It is impossible to know if these were the only invitations there were, but they are the only ones to have survived.

The first invitation was written in June:

> Dear Sir,
> You would give me great pleasure if you would kindly come, with Mrs. Montorgueil, to dine with me this week, on the day of your choice.
> In intimacy, without dressing, as I am in the country . . .
> I am living at the Chateau de Madrid, where I have rented an apartment to put my baby within reach of the Bois de Boulogne; it's the country in Paris, as you see.[94]

Durand had separated from her husband in 1891, and so was unusual in being both a woman who wrote to male colleagues as an equal, as well as a single mother. While etiquette writers never acknowledged the existence of women outside the roles of daughter, wife or widow, the Montorgueils' social etiquette allowed women into the social sphere without such strict limitations.

As with Revillout's invitation, time was treated flexibly. Even the day was open to discussion. Although the timing of the event was left up to Montorgueil, Durand's invitation differs significantly from Revillout's. It is more polite and less imploring. Although she is a woman writing to a man, she seems to put herself on a more equal footing with him than did Revillout. Like Revillout, Durand specified that formal dress was not required at dinner. Revillout's reason was that since no female guests would be present, formal attire could be dispensed with. Durand's was that, although she and Mme Montorgueil would both be there, there was no need to dress for the occasion, since they would be in the 'country'.[95] Durand used the country in this context to denote informality. By referring to her home as being in a rural setting, Durand implied that the dinner would be outside the rules governing Parisian behaviour. In fact, she was exaggerating the rural nature of home, since it was, at most, a suburb of Paris.

Her second invitation came in July:

> I would be very pleased, dear Sir, if you would do me the pleasure of coming, with Mme Montorgueil, to dine at Madrid next Thursday.
>
> The weather is good and the pleasure of crossing the woods after a day of heat and of work may compensate for the chore of coming to dinner so far away.
>
> I am counting on this and on your extreme friendliness to make you accept my invitation.
>
> Remember me fondly, I beg you, to Mme Montorgueil . . .[96]

Again the tone was polite, without being particularly formal. The time was more specific than in the previous invitation. The day was specified, and in a postscript, Durand added: 'We will dine between 8 and 8:30.' There could be a variety of reasons for Durand being more specific about time in this second invitation, though the most likely one seems to be that other people must have been coming to the second dinner, while the first one was just going to be herself and the Montorgueils, as well, of course, as other members of her household who would normally present at dinner, though we do not know who, if any, these were.

Not all the dinner and lunch invitations received by Montorgueil, and to a lesser extent by his wife, were for them to attend meals at other people's houses. At least one friend felt close enough to the couple to regularly invite himself to meals at their house. This was Samuel Rousseau, a writing colleague of Montorgueil's. He wrote several letters, all very informal, often scribbled hurriedly on random bits of paper. His letters were all fairly similar, and a few examples should suffice to illustrate their tone and content. None of the letters is dated, but all are thought to have been sent between 1895 and 1915:

> Dear friend,
>   I'm intending to have lunch with you on Sunday – I'll be at your house around noon –
>   If that day happens to be devoted to Mme Montorgueil (which would be very natural) leave me a note in Paris, at my house . . .
>   Therefore do not change one iota of your plans, I would be saddened to make Mme Montorgueil cross.[97]

Rousseau simply announced his intention of coming to lunch, a meal not usually intended for entertaining guests. Though not stated in any prescriptive sources, it seems likely from Schmahl and Rousseau's letters that Sunday was the day of the week, if any, for having friends over for lunch. Yet Rousseau's letter also suggests that Sunday may have been a day devoted to family, when he stated that it would be entirely natural for him to be an unwanted guest on that day if the Montorgueils were devoting time to each other.

Rousseau was clearly on very close and informal terms with the Montorgueils.

> I will dine with you next Sunday between 9:30 and 10 o'clock – when you come home from *L'Eclair* – If you do not go home don't worry about me – I will dine somewhere in the neighbourhood.[98]

This letter is very similar to the first, though it is for dinner rather than lunch. Interestingly, it suggested a dinner time of between 9:30 and 10 p.m., considerably later than what was considered the usual bourgeois dinner time of 7 or 8 p.m. Although this may simply have been the custom of the Montorgueil family, or perhaps more widely of the journalistic circles to which they belonged, Rousseau implied that the reason was actually that Montorgueil would be working until then (*L'Eclair* was the newspaper of which he was editor).

The next self-invitation from Rousseau was addressed not to his colleague, but to Mme Montorgueil:

Dear Mme. Montorgueil,

Has M. Montorgueil told you that I have the intention of asking you for lunch tomorrow morning, Thursday?

If not, I am announcing myself. I beg your forgiveness for imposing myself like this without warning but it has been so long since I've been able to come up without Victor Masse and to chat during a whole lunch![99]

Given our assumption that respectable families in this period guarded the privacy of their homes very closely, it is surprising to find Rousseau inviting himself to dinner with the Montorgueils, and on more than one occasion. Rousseau's letters raise more questions than they provide answers for. Why was it acceptable for Rousseau to invite himself for dinner? Was he a bachelor, and if so, did this allow him to take liberties which women and married men would not have done? Perhaps Rousseau's behaviour was acceptable within the context of journalistic and literary circles, but would not have been accepted in other bourgeois environments. However, we must also consider the possibility that people did invite themselves into the homes of close friends, rather than always waiting to be asked.

According to etiquette writers, putting invitations in writing was only one of several options. Equally valid was making invitations in person. It is therefore likely that the preserved invitations in the Montorgueil archive represent only a small fraction of the total number of invitations received by Montorgueil and his wife. As a prominent journalist, Montorgueil's papers were thought to be of interest to the public, and were therefore preserved. Similarly, the letters and diaries of other men of letters have been preserved and even published. These cannot be taken as representative of the middle classes as a whole, since these people were part of circles which were in some cases unusually sociable and sometimes avant-garde. Nonetheless, since the segment of society subsumed under the umbrella of the middle classes is so large and varied that no single practice can be seen as representative of the whole, and these examples are as good as any for exemplifying how practices differed from ideals. At the same time, we can see many ways in which the real and the ideal intersect, giving shape and meaning to the ritual of the dinner party.

Three decades before the Montorgueil correspondence was taking place, William Rossetti, the less well-known brother of Dante

Gabriel and Christina, kept a diary in which he referred to many meals that he and others in his circle attended. The highlight of each of these occasions, and the reason why each seems to merit mention in the diary, was the people present and the topics discussed: 'Took tea with Boyce, Wallis, Scott, and Miss Boyd there also . . . Wallis tells me that Peacock regards Hogg's *Life of Shelley* as little better than a caricature'[100] in March 1871; or: 'Dined with some others at Brown's – principally for the purpose of meeting Andrieu of the Paris commune'[101] in May 1872. As we have seen, conversation was the principal element of entertainment at sociable meals, and was therefore a consideration of central importance in selecting guests. The conversations Rossetti commented on were mostly about art and literature, the main occupations of the people in his social circles, though he was also preoccupied with discussions of people's health.[102] Sometimes unusual occurrences warranted a mention, such as in the case of a dinner at his brother Dante Gabriel's in July 1870:

> On the present occasion some very surprising things were certainly done, in the way of making the somnambule do and think whatever Bergheim chose. Three men (Leyland, I, and Whistler) also submitted to Bergheim's manipulations, but not one of us was in the slightest degree affected.[103]

Bergheim, described by Rossetti as a 'German Jew or German Arab by parentage', added an exotic flavour to the evening, which was heightened by the seance after the meal. As with Hardman's 'wild' supper party, choosing to hold a seance at dinner was a way for those involved to stake out their unique identity and establish themselves as challengers of the boundaries of social convention.[104]

Sophia Beale, who published her memoirs under the title *Memoirs of a Spinster Aunt*, though she was in fact also a successful painter, often wrote about dinner parties, but never mentioned the food she ate there. Of interest to her were the people she encountered, and the conversation topics. These were not serious or enlightening conversations. On one occasion, at a dinner in March 1882, she merely wrote 'conversation about ghosts'.[105] At other times dinner table talk was nothing more than gossip, as in December of 1883 when 'The conversation . . . turned upon conceit' and Beale regaled her companions with an anecdote about a writer, Mr Buckle, who was the most conceited person she had ever met.[106] Dinner parties were amusing in themselves, and offered amusing anecdotes to write about afterwards.

Rossetti wrote about a great many meals, but in only one case – at a dinner he attended in January 1883, and at which the food was foreign and exotic – did he refer to the food he was served:

> Miller gave us American oyster soup and American salmon: the former with a strange gamey taste – no doubt highly agreeable to many palates and not obnoxious to mine; the latter uncommonly fine and delicate.[107]

Alongside Rossetti was another guest, referred to as Knight. The three men ate soup and fish and perhaps other courses. As no women were present, they are unlikely to have had a sweet course. Whatever else they ate, it was these first two courses which were noteworthy for being new and somehow exotic.

Rossetti, a single man, never referred to any domestic meals he himself hosted. Montorgueil's letters are far more revealing of his frequent invitations, than of how often he did the inviting. But William Hardman, host of the 'wild' supper party and a married man, frequently received dinner guests. In his diary, he makes passing reference to 'our weekly dinners', suggesting that these were indeed both regular and frequent, and no cause for anxiety.[108] As with Rossetti, Hardman enjoyed talking about 'literary matters' over dinner.[109] Dinners with close friends were probably very informal, as in February 1863 Hardman wrote:

> Meredith's birthday . . . A letter arrives from him announcing his acceptance of our invitation to dine and stay all night, and suggesting an appropriate Bill of Fare.[110]

A guest suggesting a menu to his host is perhaps even more surprising than a friend who invites himself for dinner. Hardman's diary entry, like Montorgueil's letters from Revillout, raises questions which are difficult to answer. We assume that it was not the norm for guests to suggest bills of fare, and that this was an exceptional case of a close friendship in which such a breach of manners was overlooked. That the Hardman's consciously fashioned themselves as breakers of social rules makes it plausible that they would have enjoyed this kind of inversion of protocol. However, this diary entry is also interesting in suggesting that men corresponded about menu plans in a way that one might more readily expect of women, whom we have seen were more directly involved in the domestic food preparation process.

From the evidence of his memoirs, Edmund Yates, another Londoner who travelled in literary and artistic circles, spent a great deal of his time and social life over food. As well as writing extensively on the eating places of London, he made several references to meals eaten in with others.[111] When he was only 16, he was invited to a dinner where he made the acquaintance of, among others, 'the famous editor of the *Times*'.[112] As a young married man, Yates often ate with friends. In particular, he referred to Sundays, which he and his wife 'almost invariably spent in the company of the Keeley's, either dining in their house at Brompton Square, or joining them in some excursion to Richmond, Hampton, Thames Ditton &c'.[113] Yates was also in the habit of receiving friends at home, even when, as noted in Chater 2, his dining room and kitchen were very modest:

> We were very happy in that little house, and neither we nor our friends took much heed of its smallness or lack of conveniences. Our ménage was humble enough, and our 'good plain cook' was not always to be trusted. I recollect one day, when a boiled leg of mutton had made its appearance in a very 'gory' state, Albert went into the kitchen, and with his own hands prepared an excellent broil. I could not afford good wine, and would not give bad; but there was an ever-flowing barrel of Romford ale, and some Irish whiskey . . . which was highly esteemed.[114]

Similarly, other men of letters, in France as well as in England, left traces of having been participants in a social life that was played out over many meals in many private homes. All of these meals were a mixture of business and pleasure, in that the people mentioned as being present, either as hosts or fellow guests, were generally not only friends but also colleagues and professional contacts.[115]

Much of the evidence presented here has been preserved because it was produced by prominent men whose papers have been deemed worthy of preservation or publication. But young women, who frequently kept diaries during their youth, referred to similar practices. In some ways, young women were the members of bourgeois society who were most involved in dinner parties as a form of sociability and entertainment. Men of all ages had access to several forms of commercial entertainment and venues for socialising.[116] Married women could socialise accompanied by their husbands, and thereby gain access to venues such as restaurants and theatres. In addition, their responsibilities as shoppers took them out of the house, and could lead to lunches and teas taken in commercial venues. While young women had access to all the same places as their mothers, their lack of independence meant that they tended only to participate in meals in commercial venues by invitation rather than through their own initiative.[117] Lucille Le Verrier, for example, commented that her brother was less affected by their mother's illness, since he could come and go from the house and find entertainment at the theatre and elsewhere while she was obliged to remain at home. At the same time, some historians have argued that dinner parties were one of the key places where the marriage market operated.[118]

Caroline Brame was a young woman from an upper-middle-class Parisian family living in the Faubourg St-Germain. Frequent diary entries written in the years before her marriage reveal a daily routine in which social dinners featured as frequently as, or more frequently than, private family meals. These were not formal dinners as described by the etiquette books, but they were rituals, nonetheless, and followed patterns and rules known to the participants. The daily routine of meals brought Brame into the homes of close friends and relatives, and brought those same people into her home. These meals were ordinary, yet remarkable enough to be mentioned by Brame in her diary. For the most part the meals were described with pleasure: 'Paul and I dined at Mme de Bréda's, where we spent a delicious evening', from December 1864, was a typical entry.[119] Similarly, in May 1865: 'Thérèse wanted to have me over for dinner. She did not need to implore me very much, I like her so much.'[120] These dinners with people whom Brame saw on a regular basis were a source of pleasure and entertainment. However, they were also a form of obligation, and on occasion – as in May 1865, a week after the dinner mentioned above – she complained about it:

> My uncle, my aunt, Marie, M de Layre, Achille and his wife, Mme de la Morelie were all dining at our house; I had to make conversation, chat, and while I was very happy to receive all these people, I admit, I was very tired![121]

Whether or not she was enjoying herself, Brame never questions the routine of giving and receiving dinners on such a frequent basis. There is no indication that anyone in Brame's wide circle of dining acquaintances felt that the bourgeois family should be more private than this routine allowed. Far from the home being treated as a fortress, the French upper-middle-class home provided a border which was constantly being crossed from both directions. It has long been accepted that the aristocratic home was one where duty and choice led to its simultaneous use for public and private functions. It would appear that the same could be said about the upper-middle-class home.

Many of the meals evoked in first-hand accounts were planned, with formal or informal invitations being made in advance. However, there were also frequent occasions when guests arrived unexpectedly at mealtimes.[122] On one occasion in 1869, Lucille Le Verrier received word from her friends the Denis family that, though she had declined their invitation, a place would be kept for her at the table until the very last minute, in case of a sudden change of heart.[123] Rossetti referred to two instances in the early 1870s where unexpected dinner guests were easily accommodated. In 1871 he wrote: 'Dined with Brown. Somewhat to the surprise of everyone at table, Swinburne came in. He looks not well – but still not very particularly ill.'[124] Though there was surprise at Swinburne's arrival, it seemed to relate more to his presumed poor health than to any difficulty about accommodating an extra person at dinner. In 1873, Rossetti described an instance in which a quick visit to his friends the Howells turned into an unexpected dinner invitation: 'I was so much pressed to stay to dinner that at last I consented – not without some ensuing repentance, as the thing was kept dragging on till 9:15 before any dinner appeared.'[125] Women were warned to be prepared to extend a meal to accommodate a last-minute arrival. Advertisements for canned foods emphasised that by keeping some nice items in the cupboard, an elegant meal could easily be thrown together at the last minute if guests arrived unexpectedly.[126] The arrival of an unexpected guest could be remarked on as a surprise.[127] Still, domestic meals were often easily extendable, as some hosts were described as encouraging uninvited guests to stay.[128] However, politeness could also force a hostess to extend a family meal when she could ill afford to do so, as happened to M. V. Hughes's mother on one occasion:

> At another time of poverty my mother had bought a pair of kippers
> for supper, to regale my father after the children had gone to bed

. . . Just as all was ready, who should arrive but Aunt Polly, 'only for a minute, dear,' But the savoury smell was too much for her, and she consented to stay to supper.[129]

Out of politeness, the hostess was obliged to claim that kippers did not agree with her, and do without supper altogether.

Whatever a family's financial constraints, it seems clear that belonging to polite society required a certain amount of mealtime sociability. Men and women's experiences of dinner parties varied, and included both the formal and the routine. Dinner parties could be dull or lively, and the unexpected, either in the form of an encounter with a new person, idea or even dish, or through the arrival of an uninvited guest, suggest that the rules of etiquette did not govern all mealtime sociability. Yet the rules of etiquette found a wider readership, as people enjoyed the fantasy of a highly fashionable and elegant life punctuated by receiving guests and being received at highly formal dinner parties. Throughout the second half of the nineteenth century, dinner parties continued to be central to most people's social lives. But new commercial venues, mostly in the form of restaurants, but also in club dining room, gradually emerged, which could compete with the respectability and good taste of the domestic dinner party.

Notes

1 On the highly formal aspects of the Victorian dinner party, see for example: S. Freeman, *Mutton and Oysters: The Victorians and their Food* (London: Victor Gollanez, 1989); J. Burnett, *Plenty and Want: A Social History of Diet in England from 1815 to the Present Day* (London: Nelson, 1966) pp. 176–7, Davidoff, *Best Circles* (London: Croom Helm, 1973).

2 N. Elias, *The Civilising Process – The History of Manners*, trans. E. Jephcott (Oxford: Blackwell, 1994).

3 P. Boitard, *Guide Manuel de la bonne compagnie* (Paris: Passard, 1851) pp. 297–8.

4 Hardman, *A Mid Victorian Pepys*, 2 vols, ed. S. M. Ellis (London: Cecil Palmer, 1923–25) p. 229.

5 Hardman, *A Mid Victorian Pepys*, p. 229.

6 Hardman, *A Mid Victorian Pepys*, p. 229.

7 Norbert Elias's seminal study on European etiquette treats all of Western Europe as one subject. While there are small differences between French and English ways of doing things, they are generally

treated in this chapter, as one set of rules. Thus it is the differences rather than the similarities that are highlighted.

8 The major differences in architectural advice between England and France are discussed in R. Rich, 'Designing the Dinner Party: Advice on Dining and Décor in London and Paris, 1860–1914', *Journal of Design History* 16:1 (2003) 49–61.

9 See in particular Davidoff, *The Best Circles*.

10 See for example: E. Morales, *The Guinea Pig: Healing, Food, and Ritual in the Andes* (Tucson: University of Arizon Press, 1995); S. Wilson, *The Magical Universe: Everyday Ritual and Magic in Premodern Europe* (London: Hambledon and London, 2000); V. W. Turner, *The Ritual Process: Structure and Anti-Structure* (London: Routledge & Kegan Paul, 1969); M. Douglas, *Purity and Danger: An Analysis of the Concepts of Pollution and Taboo* (London: Routledge & Kegan Paul, 1966).

11 E. Muir, *Ritual in Early Modern Europe* (Cambridge: Cambridge University Press, 1997) p. 126. See also, for example: D. Cressy, *Birth, Marriage, and Death: Ritual, Religion, and the Life-cycle in Tudor and Stuart England* (Oxford: Oxford University Press, 1997); J. Adamson (ed.), *The Princely Courts of Europe: Ritual, Politics and Culture Under the Ancien Regime, 1500–1750* (London: Weidenfeld & Nicolson, 1999); R. Hutton, *The Rise and Fall of Merry England: The Ritual Year, 1400–1700* (Oxford: Oxford University Press, 1994).

12 M. Visser, *The Rituals of Dinner: The Origins, Evolution, Eccentricities, and Meaning of Table Manners* (London: Penguin, 1992); J. Gillis, *A World of their Own Making: Myth, Ritual and the Quest for Family Values* (New York: Basic Books, 1996). See also, for example: M. Douglas, 'Deciphering a Meal', *Daedalus* 10 (1972) 61–81; R. C. Wood, *The Sociology of the Meal* (Edinburgh: Edinburgh University Press, 1995).

13 In early modern homes, especially those belonging to the aristocracy, the public uses of the home could often take precedence over more private uses. See for example: R. Neuman, 'French Domestic Architecture in the Early 18th Century: The Town Houses of Robert de Cotte', *The Journal of the Society of Architectural Historians* 39, 2 (May 1980) 128–44; K. B. Neuschel, 'Noble Households in the Sixteenth Century: Material Settings and Human Communities', *French Historical Studies* 15, 4 (Autumn, 1988) 595–622.

14 See for example 'L'Art de faire son menu,' *L'Art Culinaire* (Oct. 1889).

15 Mrs Loftie, *The Dining Room*, Art at Home Series (London: Macmillan and Co., 1876) p. 91.

16 W. Schivelbusch, *Discenchanted Night: The Industrialisation of Light in the Nineteenth Century* trans. A. Davies (London: University of California Press, 1995).

17 See for example: Loftie, *The Dining Room*, p. 41, R. Edis, *Decoration and Furniture of Town Houses* (London: C. Kegan Paul and Co., 1881) p. 186; *Le Pot-au-Feu* (May 1893 and May 1902); Comtesse De Gencé, *Madame est servie* (Paris, 1910) p. 19, Comtesse Drohojowska, *De la Politesse et du bon ton, ou devoir d'une femme chrétienne dans le monde*, 7th ed. (Paris: V. Sarlit, 1878) p. 37.

18 U. Bloom, *Sixty Years of Home* (London: Hurst & Blackett, 1960) pp. 12–13.

19 Loftie, *The Dining Room*, pp. vii–viii.

20 *Le Pot-au-Feu* (6 Jan. 1906).

21 *L'Art Culinaire* (Nov. 1883) and (Oct. 1889); *La Salle à Manger* (Nov. 1890); *Le Pot-au-Feu* (6 May 1902, 6 April 1907 and 1 Feb. 1908).

22 Boitard, *Guide Manuel*, pp. 42–3.

23 S. Nicholson, *A Victorian Household* (London: Barrie and Jenkins, 1988) pp. 123–4.

24 *L'Art Culinaire* (Oct. 1889). See also *L'Art Culinaire* (Jan. 1883 and March 1883).

25 Serving good and elegant food, as well as keeping up with fashion trends, were positive attributes, though they could go too far. A story in *L'Illustration* described a dinner party given by an unnamed famous man, who served various 'Chinese' delicacies to his dinner guests including sharks fins and marinated dog. The author ended by saying that although the host of this dinner was clearly avoiding anything banal at his table, the author would prefer to dine at the house of a '*simple bourgeois*' (18 Feb. 1865).

26 See for example *L'Art Culinarire*, which published a series of articles on the art of carving in Feb. 1889.

27 Anon. *How to Dine; or, etiquette of the Dinner Table* (London: Ward, Lock and Tyler, 1879) p. 46.

28 C. Parr, *L'usage et le bon ton de nos jours* (Paris: Rueff, 1892) p. 23; A. de Linière, *Faites Ceci Dites Cela: guide pratique du savoir vivre et des usages mondains* (Paris, 1913) p. 75; J. de Bargny, *Code de la Femme du Monde, Journal d'une américaine* (Paris: Bureaux de la Mode pour tous, 1890) p. 120. The Montorgueil archive contains some menus kept as souvenirs, as do several of the *fonds privées* in the Archives de Paris. As well, the BHVP holds an uncatalogued collection of dinner party menus saved by dinner guests (The collection is called '*Service Actualité*'). These various sources suggest that it was indeed common practice for people to take menu cards home after dinner parties.

29 I. Beeton, *Mrs Beeton's Book of Household Management* (London: S. O. Beeton Publishing, 1861) p. 922. This is one of several sample menus, for parties of six to twelve. Mrs Beeton's menus are arranged

according to the months of the year, and the sample one reproduced here was intended to be served in April.

30 *Le Pot-au-Feu* (15 Dec. 1896).

31 *Le Pot-au-Feu* (15 Dec. 1896).

32 See for example: Boitard, *Guide Manuel*, p. 297. In spite of this criticism, it may well have been a widespread practice to scrimp on family dinners in order to spend more on impressing guests. This practice was sneeringly described in the periodical press: *L'Illustration* (8 Jan. 1870).

33 *Le Pot-au-Feu* (15 Jan. 1901).

34 Une Parisienne, *Les Usages du siècle: lettres, conseils pratiques, savoir vivre* (Paris, 1908) p. 88.

35 L'Homme qui lit, *L'Art Culinaire* (1888).

36 De Gencé, *Madame est servie*, p. 51.

37 *L'Art Culinaire* (Nov. 1890).

38 Parr, *L'usage et le bon ton de nos jours*, pp. 14–15; de Linière, *Faites Ceci Dites Cela*, p. 63; E. Dufaux, *Le savoir-vivre dans la vie ordinaire et dans les cérémonies civiles et religieuses* (Paris: Garnier frères, 1883) p. 224; de Bargny, *Code de la Femme du Monde*, p. 117; E. Cheadle, *Manners in Modern Society: Being a Book of Etiquette* (London, 1872) p. 139.

39 *How to Dine*, published in 1879 stipulated that invitations should be addressed by the hostess, and replies sent directly to her.

40 Anon., *Table Etiquette, Domestic Cookery and Confectionary* (London, 1854) pp. 34–5; A. Hayward, *The Art of Dining* (London: Murray, 1852) pp. 53–4; *La Salle à Manger* (Oct. 1890); Parr, *L'usage et le bon ton de nos jours*, p. 14; Une Parisienne, *Les Usages du siècle*, p. 87; de Gencé, *Madame est servie*, p. 56.

41 Parr, *L'usage et le bon ton de nos jours*, p. 3, Une Parisienne, *Les Usages du siècle*, pp. 82–3.

42 E. Raymond, *La Civilité non puérile, mais honnête* (Paris: Firmin-Didot frères, 1865) p. 52.

43 Comtesse de Bassanville, *Code du cérémonial guide des gens du monde dans toutes les circonstances de la vie,*. 4th edn (Paris: Lebigre-Duquesne frères, 1868) p. 227.

44 Bassanville, *Code du cérémonial*, p. 227; *How to Dine*, p. 7; Une Parisienne, *Les Usages du siècle*, p. 81; De Gencé, *Madame est servie*, p. 54; De Linière, *Faites Ceci Dites Cela*, p. 64; Dufaux, *Le savoir-vivre*, pp. 183–4; Drohowska, *De la Politesse et du bon ton*, p. 35; De Bargny, *Code de la Femme du Monde*, p. 113.

45 Une Parisienne, *Les Usages du siècle*, p. 95.

46 *La Salle à Manger* (Dec. 1890).

47 *La Salle à Manger* (Dec. 1890).

48 *La Salle à Manger* (Oct. 1891).

49 Anon., *How to Entertain; or etiquette for Visitor* (London: Ward, Lock and Tyler, 1876) p. 88. Similarly, in France De Bargny, *Code de la Femme du Monde*, p. 130.

50 Nicholson, *A Victorian Household*, p. 124. For the French case see, for example Une Parisienne, *Les Usages du siècle*, p. 101.

51 *How to Dine*, p. 44. Mme Raymond remarked that the servant should always inform the hostess, and not the host, that dinner was ready, a statement which reinforces the impression that women were held more responsible than their husbands for hosting domestic dinner parties, *La Civilité non puerile*, p. 56. See also, for example: Parr, *L'usage et le bon ton de nos jours*, p. 22; Drohojowska, *De la Politesse et du bon ton*, p. 37; De Bargny, *Code de la Femme du Monde*, p. 118.

52 Une Parisienne, *Les Usages du siècle*, p. 103.

53 De Gencé, *Madame est servie*, pp. 70–3; Drohojowska, *De la Politesse et du bon ton*, p. 38; De Bargny, *Code de la Femme du Monde*, pp. 119–20; M. de Saverny, *Le Femme chez elle* (Paris: Bureaux de la 'Revue de la Mode', 1876) p. 57.

54 *How to Dine*, pp. 46–9. Though the dishes were initially placed whole on the table, implying service *à la française*, these were in fact immediately carried to the side by servants, who then plated and served them. The only exception was the game, which was carved by host and hostess at opposite ends of the table, because the ability to carve at table was still considered a sign of good breeding.

55 Boitard, *Guide Manuel*, p. 289. The *écuyer tranchant* was a servant whose sole function at a dinner party was to carve the various meats and fishes. See also, for example: Une Parisienne, *Les Usages du siècle*, pp. 98–100.

56 Mme D'Alq, *Le Maître et la maîtresse de maison*, 2nd edn (Paris: Bureau des Causerie Familiaire, 1875) p. 217.

57 Boitard however also reminded guests that they should not eat too slowly, in order not to hold up the progress of the meal, p. 59.

58 Une Parisienne, *Les Usages du siècle*, p. 89; de Linière, *Faites Ceci Dites Cela*, p. 67; *Le Pot-au-Feu* (2 Jan. 1904).

59 Boitard, *Guide Manuel*, p. 62; Une Parisienne, *Les Usages du siècle*, p. 112; de Linière, *Faites Ceci Dites Cela*, p. 74; Drohojowska, *De la Politesse et du bon ton*, p. 119.

60 Raymond, *La Civilité non puérile*, pp. 63–4. Similar advice was given in Boitard, *Guide Manuel*, p. 62: Dufaux, *Le savoir-vivre*, p. 208.

61 Raymond, *La Civilité non puérile*, pp. 63–4.

62 *L'Illustration* (12 Jan. 1895 and 18 Feb. 1905); Parr, *L'usage et le bon ton de nos jours*, pp. 11–2; Une Parisienne, *Les Usages du siècle*, p. 117; de Gencé, *Madame est servie*, pp. 78–81; de Linière, *Faites Ceci Dites Cela*, p. 75; de Bargny, *Code de la Femme du Monde*, p. 132.

63 Parr, *L'usage et le bon ton de nos jours*, p. 15; de Gencé, *Madame est servie*, p. 57; Dufaux, *Le savoir-vivre*, p. 184; Drohojowska, *De la Politesse et du bon ton*, p. 113; de Bargny, *Code de la Femme du Monde*, p. 114; de Saverny, *Le Femme chez elle*, p. 229.

64 Une Parisienne, *Les Usages du siècle*, p. 93.

65 See for example: Wellcome MS 3318, M. V. Hughes, *A London Child of the 1870s* (Oxford: Oxford University Press 1977) pp. 137–8. See also M. Lane, *Jane Austen and Food* (London: Hambledon Press, 1995).

66 A de P Fonds Privée Famille Labaty (DE1/11/120).

67 Drohojowska, *De la Politesse et du bon ton*, p. 121.

68 On punctuality see: Bassanville, *Code du cérémonial*, p. 237; Mme Raymond, *La Civilité non puérile*, p. 52; *Le Pot-au-Feu* (21 Oct. 1877); Anon. *How to Dine*, p. 7; Boitard, *Guide Manuel*, p. 55; Parr, *L'usage et le bon ton de nos jours*, p. 5; Une Parisienne, *Les Usages du siècle*, p. 101; de Gencé, pp. 68–9. On seating arragements and the obligations entailed see: Boitard, *Guide Manuel*, p. 56; Anon., *How to Dine*, p. 7; Une Parisienne, *Les Usages du siècle*, p. 111; de Linière, *Faites Ceci Dites Cela*, p. 69; Anon, *L'Art de plaire et de briller en société* (Paris, 1879) p. 161.

69 Parr, *L'usage et le bon ton de nos jours*, p. 11.

70 *L'Illustration* (13 Nov. 1880); De Linière, *Faites Ceci Dites Cela*, p. 70; Une Parisienne, *Les Usages du siècle*, p. 112.

71 Parr, *L'usage et le bon ton de nos jours*, p. 24; de Gencé, *Madame est servie*, pp. 77–8; Dufaux, *Le savoir-vivre*, pp. 225–7.

72 However, Pierre Boitard did enjoin his male readers not to speak too loudly at dinner in a manner which might be obtrusive to others, *Guide Manuel*, p. 57.

73 Une Parisienne, *Les Usages du siècle*, pp. 87 and 93.

74 De Saverny, *Le Femme chez elle*, p. 113.

75 Boitard, *Guide Manuel*, p. 59.

76 Raymond, *La Civilité non puérile*, pp. 58–9; also: Une Parisienne, *Les Usages du siècle*, p. 109; de Gencé, *Madame est servie*, p. 47; Anon., *L'Art de plaire*, p. 162; Dufaux, *Le savoir-vivre*, p. 207; de Saverny, *Le Femme chez elle*, p. 58.

77 Anon., *How to Dine*, p. 30; Parr, *L'usage et le bon ton de nos jours*, p. 11.

78 Dufaux, *Le savoir-vivre*, p. 228; De Saverny, *Le Femme chez elle*, p. 65; De Bargny, *Code de la Femme du Monde*, p. 133.

79 Une Parisienne, *Les Usages du siècle*, pp. 122–4. There are some indications that this was true in practice as well as in prescription: Rossetti, W. M., *The Diary of W. M. Rossetti, 1870–1873*, ed. O. Bornand (Oxford: Clarendon Press, 1977) p. 143; A. Schlueter, *A Lady's Maid in Downing Street*, ed. Mabel Duncan (London: T. Fisher Unwin, 1922) p. 85.

80 Anon. *L'Art de plaire*, p. 166.
81 AN Fond Montorgueil 428/AP/3 *c.*1910. Punctuation as in the original.
82 AN Fond Montorgueil 428/AP/3 *c.*1900.
83 AN Fond Montorgueil 428/AP/3 June 30th, *c.*1900–10.
84 AN Fond Montorgueil 428/AP/3 *c.*1900–5.
85 AN Fond Montorgueil 428/AP/3.
86 To Montorgueil alone: AN Fond Montorgueil 428/AP/1 *c.*1890s and May 1895 from Henri Beraldi, AN Fond Montorgueil 428/AP/3 May 1893, July 1894 and *c.*1896 from Jeanne and Henri Schmahl, AN Fond Montorgueil 428/AP/2 March 1895 and April 1899 from Dr Gilles de la Tourette, AN Fond Montorgueil 428/AP/1 *c.*1884–1922 from Henri Boutet, AN Fond Montorgueil 428/AP/2 *c.*1886–96 from Pierre de la Pommeraye, as well as the invitations from Revillout cited above.
87 To Montorgueil and his wife: AN Fond Montorgueil 428/AP/3 *c.*1896 from Jeanne Schmahl, AN Fond Montorgueil 428/AP/1 June 1898 and July 1898 from Marguerite Durand, AN Fond Montorgueil 428/AP/2 July 1901 from Mme et M A. Hammond, AN Fond Montorgueil 428/AP/2 March 1908 from Marie Guillaume-Lami, as well as the ones from Revillout cited above.
88 AN Fond Montorgueil 428/AP/1 May 1895.
89 AN Fond Montorgueil 428/AP/2.
90 AN Fond Montorgueil 428/AP/3.
91 AN Fond Montorgueil 428/AP/3.
92 AN Fond Montorgueil 428/AP/3.
93 AN Fond Montorgueil 428/AP/3.
94 AN Fond Montorgueil 428/AP/1.
95 The fact that city people felt that the country required less formality than the city should not be taken to suggest that country people felt the same way. However, this book focuses on London and Paris, and rural dinner-giving customs are therefore outside of its scope.
96 AN Fond Montorgueil 428/AP/1.
97 AN Fond Montorgueil 428/AP/3 *c.*1895–1915.
98 AN Fond Montorgueil 428/AP/3 (*c.*1895–1918).
99 AN Fond Montorgueil 428/AP/3 (*c.*1895–1914). There were also two more letters in which Rousseau invited himself to eat with the Montorgueils, both from the same period as the others.
100 Rossetti, *The Diary of W. M. Rossetti*, p. 50.
101 Rossetti, *The Diary of W. M. Rossetti*, p. 200.
102 Rossetti, *The Diary of W. M. Rossetti*, pp. 40, 45–6, 157–8, 232, 233, 247–8, 275.
103 Rossetti, *The Diary of W. M. Rossetti*, p. 19.

104 Seances and mesmerism were quite popular in the nineteenth century. See for example: L. Henson, ' "Half Believing, Half Incredulous": Elizabeth Gaskell, Superstition and the Victorian Mind', *Nineteenth-Century Contexts* 24:3 (2002) 251–69; E. S. Ridgway, 'John Elliotson (1791–1868): A Bitter Enemy of Legitimate Medicine? Part 1: Earlier Years and the Introduction to Mesmerism', *Journal of Medical Biography* 1:4 (1993) 191–8.

105 S. S. Beale, *Recollections of a Spinster Aunt* (London: William Heinemann, 1908) p. 56.

106 Beale, *Recollections of a Spinster Aunt*, p. 78.

107 Rossetti, *The Diary of W. M. Rossetti*, p. 227.

108 Hardman, *A Mid Victorian Pepys*, p. 148. Arnold Bennett also hosted dinner parties. See for example: *The Letters of Arnold Bennett*, Vol. II. ed. J. Hepburn (Oxford: Oxford University Press, 1968) p. 112. L. Le Verrier mentions her family hosting monthly balls preceded by dinner parties, *Journal d'une jeune fille Second Empire: 1866–1878*. ed. Lionel Mirisch (Paris: Cadeilhan, 1994) p. 32.

109 Hardman, *A Mid Victorian Pepys*, pp. 148, 229.

110 Hardman, *A Mid Victorian Pepys*, p. 262.

111 E. Yates, *His Recollections and Experiences* (London: R. Bentley & Son, 1884), see for example: pp. 129–30, 224–5, 251–3, 225, 258–9.

112 Yates, *His Recollections and Experiences*, p. 225.

113 Yates, *His Recollections and Experiences*, pp. 251–2.

114 Yates, *His Recollections and Experiences*, p. 251.

115 See for example: *L'Illustration* (1 Apr. 1865); Bennett, *Letters*, Vol. I, p. 52: Bennett, *Letters*, Vol. II, p. 86; G. Claudin, *Mes souvenirs, les boulevards de 1840–1870* (Paris: C. Lévy, 1884) p. 163.

116 The specific cases of restaurants, clubs and banquets as forms of this will be discussed in detail in chapters 5 and 6.

117 Le Verrier, *Journal d'une jeune fille Second Empire*, p. 82.

118 See for example: A. Martin-Fugier, *La bourgeoise: femme au temps de Paul Bourget* (Paris: B. Grasset, 1983); Davidoff, *The Best Circles*; J. J. Brumberg, *Fasting Girls: the Emergence of Anorexia Nervosa as a Modern Disease* (London: Harvard University Press, 1988); Le Verrier in her diary frequently refers to the fact that there was a lot of flirtation between the young people at the dinner parties she attended, *Journal d'une jeune fille Second Empire*, pp. 34, 36, 38, 217.

119 C. Brame, *Le Journal intime de Caroline B.*, ed. Georges Ribeill and Michelle Perrot. (Paris: Montalba, 1985) p. 25.

120 Brame, *Le Journal intime de Caroline B.*, p. 59.

121 Brame, *Le Journal intime de Caroline B.*, p. 62.

122 See for example: Nicholson, *A Victorian Household*, p. 73.

123 Le Verrier, *Journal d'une jeune fille Second Empire*, p. 71.

124 Rossetti, *The Diary of W. M. Rossetti*, p. 54.
125 Rossetti, *The Diary of W. M. Rossetti*, p. 277.
126 See for example: A de P, D12Z/3 Which contains two advertisements from *c*.1890s canned foods which can be quickly prepared when unexpected guests appear.
127 Rossetti, *The Diary of W. M. Rossetti*, p. 54.
128 Rossetti, *The Diary of W. M. Rossetti*, p. 277; Le Verrier, *Journal d'une jeune fille Second Empire*, p. 71.
129 Hughes, *London Child*, pp. 18–19.

4

Respectable restaurants and the commercialisation of dinner

Auguste Escoffier and Cesar Ritz arrived in London in 1889, at the behest of Richard D'Oyly Carte, whose ambitious Savoy hotel project began to flounder soon after opening. D'Oyly Carte understood what was needed to create a modern, enticing place of leisure: his Savoy theatre, opened in 1881, was the first electrically lit public building in Britain. But it was Escoffier and Ritz, who had worked together at some of the finest hotels on the continent, who best understood the hotel and restaurant trade and could make the Savoy a huge success. Escoffier's talent for haute cuisine was unquestionable. He was the author of many now classic dishes, and saw his role – about which he was never modest – as giving French cuisine the international supremacy it clearly (according to him) deserved. At a time when professionalisation was occurring in many fields, and the role of the expert was exalted, Escoffier claimed the same position for those working in the catering trade as for any other highly trained professionals. In this he was part of a broader trend that saw chefs go from being domestic servants to specialised workers in the leisure sector.

The Savoy attracted the wealthiest and most distinguished guests, and was a favourite dining place of the Prince of Wales and his set. But Escoffier was intelligent, modern, a capitalist, and he did not stop at attracting those elegant diners already well versed in the language and mores of the French restaurant meal. Early in his stay at the Savoy, Escoffier saw that many English diners, intimidated by the French in general use on the menus of fine restaurants, eschewed making choices and let themselves be guided instead by the maitre d'hôtel. To enhance the eating out experience for these guests: '[We] agreed to change this by creating a *prix fixe* menu that contained most of the items offered on the á la carte menu. There had to be a minimum of four people at the table . . . and I took care of composing the menu myself.'[1] The host came early in the day – the normal way to order in a restaurant – and having requested the *prix fixe* could then rest assured of impressing his guests with the finest meal, since it would be composed by one of the greatest culinary minds in Europe. And Escoffier, who thought of everything, kept a note of each meal served in this way, so that no one who ordered it would ever face the embarrassment of being served the same meal twice.

Escoffier's rise to prominence within the world of haute cuisine is part of the story of the emergence and growth of the restaurant as a regular part of bourgeois eating habits. While dinner parties continued to be a central stage upon which to display taste, manners and a tasteful home and palate, from mid-century, and increasingly in the 1880s and 1890s, eating out became a socially accepted leisure activity. Like a dinner party, a restaurant meal afforded an opportunity to display cultural capital. Further, it also allowed diners to be seen in public, and some sources explicitly cast diners at neighbouring tables as forming an audience in front of whom to perform. Because the restaurant was a French invention, which was later imported into England, the form meals took, and the knowledge required to order and eat them successfully, were largely the same in London and Paris. Sources ranging from menus to travel guides and from architectural plans to reviews in the press reveal the growth of dining as a leisure activity well suited to the middle-class way of life. The principal difference between London and Paris, as Escoffier recognised, was that for English diners, restaurants could be unfamiliar and intimidating, while to the French there was a recognisable continuity in language and food with the meals people ate at home.

The first restaurant was invented in Paris in the eighteenth century, to cater to wealthy gentry caught up in the fashion of romantic sensibility.[2] This new type of establishment, where restorative (hence 'restaurant') broth was served to the fashionably unhealthy, gradually expanded the range of foods on offer.[3] In the nineteenth century, what had begun as a pastime of the elite was adopted by increasing numbers of middle-class people, for whom restaurants became one of many locations in which entertainment was available to those who could afford it.[4] Earlier historians credited the French Revolution with creating the social conditions in which restaurants suddenly appeared.[5] They reasoned that at the same time as luxurious food items were becoming available to a widening bourgeoisie,[6] Paris and London were suddenly flooded with out-of-work chefs who were formerly employed by the aristocracy. Yet Rebecca Spang has found restaurants gaining popularity in pre-Revolutionary Paris, while it took until the 1860s for them to become commercially or culturally a success in London. Rather than interpreting the invention of the restaurant as a response to a crisis in aristocratic life, we need to consider it as a cultural artefact of a society bent on commodifying all aspects of leisure and sociability.

Modern restaurants are not the same, and need to be distinguished from the wide range of other places where people ate out. Several innovations made the restaurant different from – and more typically bourgeois – than its competitors. In the first place, restaurants allowed diners to sit at separate tables. This meant that a restaurant meal was effectively a private party, which just happened to be located in a public space. A second key feature was the simple formula for ordering and paying, brought about by printed menus, which included prices for each item. This meant that, at least in theory, anyone with money could inhabit the space and eat the food provided by a restaurant. As we shall see, however, a certain amount of knowledge was required to navigate the printed menu. A third feature of restaurants was their conformity with middle-class domestic pattern of architecture and design, including the separation of space according to function, and the creation of back and front stage areas for the performance of eating dinner. Restaurants were neither public nor private, but were a new and ambiguous space. Eating was taken into the public sphere in restaurants and other catering establishments whose sole function was to provide meals. It was also inserted into other public spaces: refreshment rooms began to appear in railway carriages, museums and galleries, at the theatre, and even in stores.[7]

Writing about French gastronomy, Jean-Paul Aron mistakenly assumes that middle-class women's domestic role prevents them from the privilege of enjoying fine food, asserting that: 'Those who flaunt themselves in restaurants are nothing but whores.'[8] But women did eat out, and were mostly welcomed by restaurateurs, for whom profit was surely as important as any other consideration. But the discourse surrounding women who ate out was anxious, ambivalent and sometimes very negative, and it is important to both distinguish, and understand the connections, between this discourse and the experience of the many women who did eat in restaurants. By bringing eating out of the house and into the commercial arena, restaurant-goers were blurring the boundaries between public and private. Both sociability and food consumption patterns were affected by this shift, as the public gaze influenced the choices people made. In *Dining Out*, Joanne Finklestein, argues that by bringing eating into the public sphere, diners abdicate the responsibility of making choices for themselves by adhering to pre-scribed behaviours. On the contrary, nineteenth-century restaurant-goers were conscious of making decisions on many levels from where and when to eat, to what to order from menus which were often long and complicated.[9]

While London spread outward, Paris grew upward. Different trends in urban development led to different styles of dwelling places, and also different ways of organising restaurants. Often larger than in Paris, London restaurants often comprised several rooms each offering diners slightly different menu options. The majority of restaurants in Paris contained a single large space, in which all diners chose from the same set of menu options, with the addition, in some cases, of *cabinets particuliers*.[10] These *cabinets* were small rooms, accommodating from two to twenty people, which could be booked for private dinners. Though some were large enough to host dinner parties, their private nature caused *cabinets particuliers* to be associated with illicit encounters, especially sexual ones. Respectability could be found only in the main dining room, under the gaze of fellow diners. In Paris, if one can believe contemporary remarks, those whose object was good food ate in the main room, while those with other goals ate in the *cabinets*.[11]

London's restaurants, which were often connected to hotels, were divided into several functionally distinct rooms. Some of the rooms a restaurant might contain were the dining room, the ladies' dining room, the coffee room and the grill room, as well as the billiard room, smoking room, bar and a winter garden. In most cases, the name of the room suggested the type of meal that would be eaten or the activity carried out in a particular part of the restaurant. In its 1886 building plans, the Hotel Providence in Leicester Square had a dining room, a ladies' dining room and a smoking room. Ladies' dining rooms in London restaurants might partially seclude women from the public gaze, but were primarily a way of allowing those men who did not want to dine with ladies to avoid their presence. In Paris, there are no mentions of ladies' dining rooms in any written sources, though the blueprint of the Brasserie Universelle from 1921 had men's and ladies' dining rooms.[12] In 1889, the Café Monaco on Piccadilly Circus contained the Regent Room, a café and international hall, a banqueting hall and, in a later plan from 1905, a room simply called the restaurant. In 1897, The Hotel de Paris (later renamed Queen's Hotel) also on Leicester Square had a grill room, a restaurant, a buffet and a table d'hôte (although the name of the latter was relabelled 'restaurant' at a later date).[13] Figures 6 and 7 show the layout of the basemen and ground floor, which housed the various rooms listed as well as the storage and service areas. The plan shows a modern approach to spatial division, with areas of the building clearly separate according to purpose.

Private tables allowed diners to partake of a private meal, which could in many ways resemble the domestic dinner party, outside the home, combining various advantages of the new sphere of commercialised leisure with a more traditional sociability. One of the advantages of eating in a restaurant was that it could allow the host to offer a better standard of food, service and environment than he or she could provide in the domestic sphere. Paradoxically, though the restaurant was a particularly bourgeois construction, it was here that the middle classes came closest to emulating the aristocratic dinner party. Unlike in the home, the food in the restaurant was genuinely entirely prepared and served by the staff, with no need for the hosts to exert themselves beyond selecting the menu, choosing the guests, and keeping the conversation flowing. The private table also offered another advantage to patrons of restaurants: by keeping each party distinct, it increased the facility with which people could display themselves and observe others.

Performance was an important aspect of respectable life. Respectability was almost entirely based on appearance, and behaviour was assumed to be a clear indicator of moral worth. The role of performance in shaping identity, a matter that has long been of interest to sociologists, has recently come to engage historians.[14] Restaurants were perfectly designed for performing: separate tables, all within view of several others, allowed diners to be both performer and audience at the same time. Richard Sennett argues that, in nineteenth-century London and Paris, the frequency with which

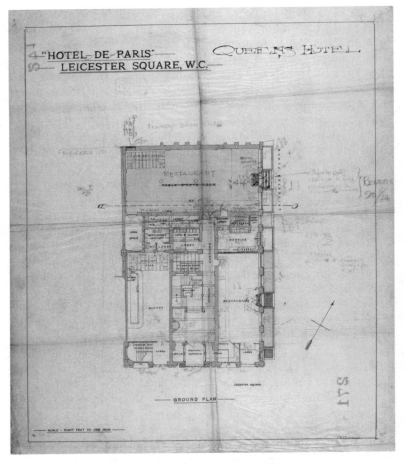

Figure 6 Queen's Hotel, Leicester Square, 1890.

an individual could expect to encounter strangers led to an increase in the importance of creditable appearances, in order to gain legitimacy for what a person said about him or herself.[15] Finklestein, who is particularly critical of people's choice to make eating a public activity, has argued that 'the interweaving of the personal with the practices of the social domain is characteristic of a bourgeois sensibility concerned with the presentation of self, the opinions of others, and the appearance of being in control of the material

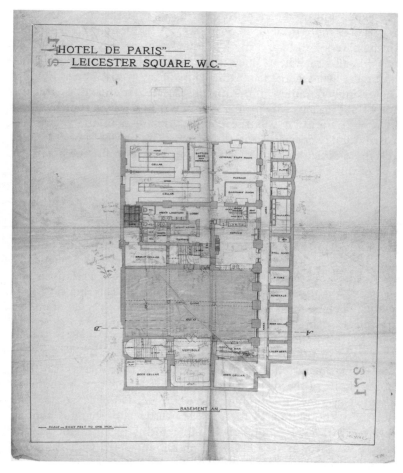

Figure 7 Queen's Hotel, Leicester Square, 1890.

world'.[16] Thus the display of oneself as a diner in an appropriate venue, and making knowledgeable choices about what to order, was an important element in building a reputation for respectability and success.

By the second half of the nineteenth century, eating out was becoming an increasingly complex activity. The proliferation of restaurants, and of other types of eating establishments, as well as the expansion of choice as to what foods to eat, made restaurant meals ever more difficult to negotiate.[17] Yet through the expansion of the catering industry, there gradually emerged types of restaurant whose aim was to make eating accessible to a wider public, and there also emerged an eating-out culture whose norms became increasingly common to the middle classes. As shown, one of the important reasons why people ate out was as a way of showing their taste and status. It was the complexities of both the social and gastronomic aspects of eating out which made this possible, and it is these difficulties and their solutions that form the subject of the rest of this chapter.

Why people ate out

There were many reasons to eat in a restaurant and many kinds of restaurants to visit. Not least among the reasons for eating out was that it was a pleasure, a break from domesticity, and a chance to imbibe new tastes and new sights. Restaurants were a relatively late arrival to the urban landscape. More traditional catering establishments, such as inns, taverns or pastrycooks' shops had catered to travellers or single men. These businesses continued to exist, but with the introduction of the bourgeois restaurant the concept of eating out just for fun gradually took hold. Robert Thorne argues that increasing numbers of people needing to have meals away from home is one of the surest indicators of modernity and restaurants' clientele also took in working people who needed to eat somewhere nearby in the middle of the day, as well as suburbanites coming into town to enjoy shopping or other forms of amusement.[18] By the 1870s there existed in both London and Paris wide ranges of catering establishments to provide for the needs of people of all income levels.

In London in the 1850s, there were those who felt that eating out was not quite as respectable as eating in, and evening dinners largely continued to be served at home,[19] but lunching out was becoming an increasingly normal part of everyday life. In the early part of the decade, Edmund Yates worked for the Post Office in London. When he started working there, lunch was delivered to the men in the office each day. Their boss found it inconvenient having delivery boys walking through the building carrying dishes of hot food and so instituted a policy of allowing the workers to leave work and get their lunch from nearby restaurants instead: 'a quarter of an hour – a marvelously elastic quarter of an hour – was allowed us in which to go and procure luncheon at a neighbouring restaurant.'[20] The 1850s was a transitional period in London catering, and Yates's early career at the Post Office coincided with this time of change.

In his journal several decades later, in July 1897, Arnold Bennett described the Rainbow Room as the sort of place where men went to eat their lunch in the middle of the working day: 'Here come lawyers and other *hommes d'affaires* of middle age to whom luncheon is a serious meal, not to be ordered without minute instructions to the obsequious waiter.'[21] Money as well as cultural capital might dictate that clerks would lunch in different places from business-men, but in the intervening years, the most significant change was the huge increase in the number of venues for ordering a meal. While Londoners lunched out regularly because many of them lived far from where they worked, Parisians, who were less likely to live in suburbs, used restaurants in different ways.

Compared to Londoners, Parisians appear to have dined out more frequently, if the references to restaurant dinners than lunches are to be believed. As with lunch in London, dinner eaten out in Paris could be a work-related meal. There was more than one invitation to a work dinner in Montorgueil's papers. These were from colleagues who were also friends and the meal was often offered as an opportunity to discuss both work and more personal topics:

> My dear friend . . . I am alone and I will dine on Friday 31st at the Brasserie Universelle at the corner of rue St. Roch and avenue de l'Opéra. It would be kind of you to join me for dinner at 7:30 when we will speak of many things . . . of the future and best of all, of us two good friends.[22]

While men were widely recognised to need a lunch break from work, there were those who characterised shopping as women's work, as in 'Where to eat when Shopping' from *The Lady* in 1888:

> The lady shopping, or going the round of some of the Art Galleries, knows that she has a long day to get through and arduous duties to perform. She requires substantial support mid-way, and knows by experience the fatuity of endeavouring to get through the task on a scrambled meal, probably taken standing at a pastrycook's.[23]

When diarist Sophia Beale moved from London to Paris to follow art classes, she discovered another reason why a young woman might find herself eating out. She wrote to her cousin Mary, describing the various local restaurants where she ate her daily meals. She had little choice but to eat out during her time in Paris, which meant that the cost of a meal was of no little importance. However, she also felt it was important to balance good price with good food, having found that some inexpensive options were not worth while.[24] Beale never felt, nor perceived those around her to feel, anything untoward in her eating alone in public.

Not only men and women, but whole families in Paris ate in restaurants as a leisure activity. In July 1865, Caroline Brame ate out on the Champs-Elysées on one of her younger brother's visits home from school.[25] On another occasion she went to Tortoni, a famous Champs-Elysées establishment, for ice cream with some girlfriends and the mother of one of the girls. Constant de Tours observed how, during summer weekends, Parisian families were out in number, some picnicking, while others filled the many restaurants and *guinguettes* on the outskirts of the city.[26] In London dining out was a pleasure generally reserved for adults rather than for family outings.

Whatever other reasons someone might have for going to a restaurant, the desire to demonstrate good taste, discernment or social standing could influence their choice. Donald Shaw, writing under the pseudonym 'One of the Old Brigade', recalled how in the 1860s, in London, there were strict rules governing behaviour in elite catering establishments: 'If you dined at Simpson's or Linner's you were served on silver, and no waiter ventured to ask you who won the 3:45 race.'[27] Yates recalled similar places from his youth: 'For the aristocratic and the well-to-do there was Dolly's Chop House, up a little court out of Newgate Street . . . with good joints, and steaks and chops and soup served in a heavy old-fashioned manner at a stiff old-fashioned price.'[28] Restaurants, like their patrons, could be divided into various categories. The bourgeoisie, who could afford to make choices about where to dine, came from a broad range of economic levels. Some were well-established members of the middle classes, while others might be on the margins, and aspiring to a greater level of distinction. Some could visit a restaurant secure in the knowledge that it was frequented by like-minded people, but for others the choice of restaurant was more a matter of aspiration. In the latter case, all aspects of the meal could be a test, as anxiety was provoked through the experience of dining in the public eye.

Many writers emphasised the importance of choosing to eat in venues where the other patrons would be of interest. Eavesdropping was a motivation for some,[29] while others went to socialise. Parisian diarist Gustave Claudin loved the Café Riche in the 1860s and 1870s because of the people he encountered there: 'journalists, novelists, playwrights, musicians, painters, lawyers . . . we would discuss . . . politics, literature, the arts . . . everything.'[30] Restaurants allowed those who aspired to higher, or simply different, levels of distinction to place themselves side by side with those whom they sought to join. In offering this opportunity for display, restaurants played a part in the creation of bourgeois identities that could be adapted and negotiated according to the individual desires of the diners who frequented them.

Contemporary perspectives on eating out

Contemporary discourses on the catering trade, as well as on dining customs, revealed an underlying awareness of change, and an interest in restaurants as a historical phenomenon.[31] Guidebooks provided a typology of the various eating establishments available. Baedeker's guides to Paris listed restaurants, hotels, tables d'hôtes, prix fixes, bouillons, crèmeries and cafés. In London, there were restaurants, chophouses, taverns, dining rooms, confectioners and oyster houses. Where people ate out varied according to diverse factors, many of which were detailed in the pages of guidebooks and reviews. Reviews were not a very widely published genre in the nineteenth century, but some did exist. Guidebooks were more popular, and this was the age in which travelling, like eating out, was becoming increasingly open to the middle classes.[32] City guides offered contemporaries one way of gaining knowledge about the kinds of behaviour required in restaurants, and the range of possibilities for men and women who wished to eat out.

Business directories show that the number of restaurants increased significantly from 1850 to 1914 in both Paris and London. Looking at ten-yearly intervals, one can see how restaurants increased in London (table 1) and Paris (table 2). The London Post Office Directory had no listing for restaurants, instead having sections for

Table 1 Numbers of restaurants in London.

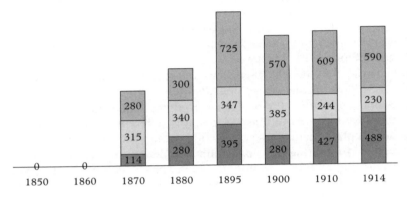

Table 2 Numbers of restaurants in Paris.

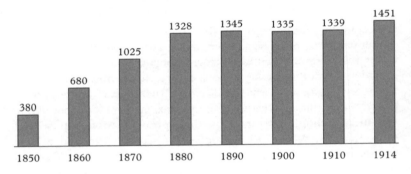

Refreshment Rooms, Hotels and Dining Rooms. Table 2 shows Parisian eating establishments listed under categories other than restaurants, namely Limonadier, Table d'hôte and Bouillon. These graphs and the numbers they represent show a clear, though not always steady, increase in the number of places to eat out in each city.

Writers in Paris and London, responding to different situations with respect to the availability of restaurants and other types of catering establishments, produced different discourses. The variety of places where people ate differed on either side of the Channel, but the restaurant itself, having been imported from Paris to London, was similar in both places. Parisian discourse on restaurants focused on the declining standards of cuisine, with only slight acknowledgement of positive changes. In London, the trade press and commercial publications provided readers with information about the wonderful changes occurring in the availability of eating out, while a disgruntled few wrote of their nostalgia for the eating places of the past. Whether embraced or decried, changes were occurring in the world of eating out in both London and Paris. In that context people had to learn how to behave and what to eat in new types of establishments, and this could be a daunting task. Restaurant-goers obtained little help from etiquette books, which, throughout the period, failed to respond to these new ways of dining. Only one of the etiquette books sampled advised readers on eating out, and this referred specifically to hotel table d'hôte. The advice focused on how to dress, advising: 'In dressing for hotel dinners, it is not in good taste to adopt a full evening costume, and to appear as if attired for a ball . . . such costumes should be reserved for evening parties. If worn at the table d'hôte, it may be suggested that you have no other place in which to display them. Your dress need not be more showy than you would wear when dining at a private house.'[33] Guidebooks, and later in the century restaurant reviews, were more helpful in informing would-be diners about the choices to make. Though significantly different from etiquette books, these genres of advice were equally prescriptive and fulfilled a similar role in providing guidelines to educate the bourgeoisie in matters of taste and knowledge.

While Paris may have been the capital of modernity, food writers there were suspicious of progress and tended to see restaurants as being in a period of decline.[34] Culinary historians argue that France created professional cooking, primarily through the introduction of rational, modern and efficient teamwork in restaurant kitchens. But humorous restaurant guide *Les Petits-Paris* earnestly protested that teamwork was killing the classic French restaurant, and that the time had come to bring back big-name chefs to French cuisine.[35] The view that restaurant cuisine in Paris was in serious decline was shared by many: 'I remember twenty years ago . . . culinary traditions were still respected . . . Today, the Parisian restaurant has reached an extreme, final, decisive point, and if an energetic reaction does not soon take place, it will be the end of the renowned establishments which were the sanctuaries of gastronomy,' wrote one culinary journalist.[36] Another stated that all one could hear in Paris was people complaining of the decline in restaurant cuisine.[37]

Both authors agreed that the blame lay not with the chefs themselves, but with the eating public. 'The gourmets of the past, by their expectations, could maintain the standards of the table . . . At present, apart from a few exceptions; it seems we no longer have the time to be gourmets.'[38] Blame was also attributed to the various new types of catering establishments which were challenging the supremacy of the first-class restaurants by providing food that was both more affordable and more accessible.[39] The general trend among culinary journalists was to mourn the passing of Paris's great traditional restaurateurs, such as Bignon and Brébant, and of the Café Procope, both for the food that they had served and for the ambiance and quality of people who had dined there.[40] Nostaliga for a 'golden age' of eating out was a common trope of food writing in London as much as in Paris, but there it was the passing of traditional inns and chophouses which elicited regret, while the innovations brought about by the importation of restaurants from France led many to take an optimistic view.[41]

As restaurants began to appear in London from the 1850s, there emerged a genre of food-related writing whose aim was to laud the changes occurring in the catering industry.[42]

> Until a very recent period . . . there could hardly be said to exist any restaurants at all in the capital – that is to say, restaurants in the Parisian sense of the term . . . within the last three or four years there has been opened in London a choice of restaurants resembling the palatial passenger saloons of American river steamers, and with chefs worthy of Delmonico's.[43]

This new genre of writing was a genuine recognition of actual change and progress in London's catering facilities, but also reflected the need of trade publications and promotional literature to find novelty wherever they could. Restaurants themselves contributed to the discourse on progress through advertising and celebratory booklets.[44] Lyons & Co., which was particularly successful at marketing itself, published a comparison of the dining situation of 1860 with the situation of 1900, to advertise the Trocadero, Lyons & Co.'s jewel in the crown. The booklet claimed that the quality of both food and surroundings in restaurants had vastly improved during the last forty years of the century: 'At the modern restaurant there is nothing to offend the eye . . . It was not so in the old days. An over-laden plate full of hunks of badly-cut food would destroy the appetite of the most ravenous man, whilst a dirty waiter would disgust the most fastidious epicure.'[45] The Trocadero also claimed that it was the modern restaurant that was responsible for the emancipation of women: 'The new table d'hôte, the new restaurant, the new hotel coffee rooms and dining rooms, where men and women mix freely together, have had a great deal to do with the social emancipation of women, who . . . enjoy their lives very much more than they did thirty or forty years ago.'[46]

Not all English writing on restaurants celebrated the changes that they observed. A prolific minority of elite upper-middle-class men lamented that French restaurants were destroying traditional city eating-places.[47] However, in spite of the fears of such writers, these traditional establishments continued to exist alongside Parisian-style restaurants well into the twentieth century. The nostalgia expressed by patrons of city taverns and chophouses was, like the Parisian discourse of nostalgia, an expression of longing for both the food and the general ambience. Great men had frequented the city taverns, and the food served was imagined as integral to a certain brand of masculine identity. As public spaces open to women and even children, restaurants were welcomed by a large proportion of the bourgeoisie. But to men like 'One of the Old Brigade': 'The Guildhall Tavern, The Albion and Simpson's long reigned supreme as places where saddles and sirloins, marrow-bones and welsh rarebits were to be obtained in perfection; but all have now disappeared, except in name.'[48]

Where to eat out

One eats in Paris in an incommensurable number of restaurants, large, medium and small, à la carte or prix-fixe, always open, very expensive or very cheap, very luxurious or very simple; not to mention hotel table d'hôte, cafés and brasseries where food is served, and creameries: there is an embarrassment of choices.[49]

In both Paris and London the growing number of places to eat each claimed to offer something special. Some were elegant and fashionable, others casual, while some were very cheap, with food to match the prices. Some places specialised in a particular dish and others in the foods of a specific region. Some restaurants chose a theme – waiters in costume or a specific genre of decor – to attract new customers, while other offered free gifts or other enticements.[50] Some places had been in existence for many years, and served food based on long-standing traditions. Others were new, innovative and modern. In Paris, the birthplace of the modern restaurant, it was rare for people to choose to eat in hotel dining rooms. In London, the big railway hotels had been partially responsible for introducing restaurants, and hotel restaurants continued to be popular with the dining public, even as other options were introduced.[51] Not all members of the middle classes ate out, but for those who did the choice of where to eat was varied, and something could be found to suit everybody's budget, cultural aspirations and appetites.

In the half century following London's Great Exhibition of 1851, both cities hosted a succession of exhibitions that proved to be a catalyst for change and growth in the catering trade.[52] These attracted huge crowds into the city centre, from the suburbs, the rest of the country and abroad, all of whom would need to eat during their visit.[53] International exhibitions embodied the twin themes of industrialisation and modernity and many expected catering provisions to reflect this.[54] In 1861, an English author commented, 'We should not think highly of any acquaintance of ours who went to the Exhibition with the deliberate purpose of giving up so much of his or her time as is demanded by a set dinner.'[55] Full, lengthy dinners were traditional, and modern people needed something different. A system of set-priced meals was therefore suggested, along the model already popular in France.[56] In 1889, a French writer concluded from the speed with which the Eiffel Tower had been erected that it was now speed that was the order of the day, which meant that visitors to the exhibition wanted fast meal options.[57]

But exhibitions brought more than speed and innovation. Owing to the need for temporary restaurants on the sites of the various exhibitions, it was necessary for those in charge to consider the requirements of visitors. The organisers of the Paris exhibition of 1867 divided catering establishments into four broad categories: Restaurant and Buffet; cafés-limonadiers and cafés-glaciers; cafés-brasseries; and restaurant-bouillon and restaurant *à bon-marché* (affordable).[58] Once they had received applications they decided on the following numbers:

Restaurant et Buffet: 24
Cafés-glacier: 12[59]
Cafés-brasserie: 10[60]
Restaurant à bon-marché ou bouillon: 5[61]
Débits et dépôt de vins et liqueurs: 11[62]
Débits d'eau gazeuse: 3[63]
Pâtissier, debits de pains d'epices: 3[64]
Confiseries: 2[65]
Débits de café ou chocolat à la tasse: 2[66]
Débits de fruits à l'état frais: 1[67]

Without the business records of these concessions, there is no way to know whether the number of each category of establishment actually fulfilled visitor needs. But the strict distinctions made between the various types of establishments are significant, and are part of the general desire for systematic classification present in all areas of bourgeois life. Catering establishments, just like the rooms in a private home, could be given a label that designated a precise and specific function.[68] How such facilities were eventually used by the public is another matter and one that is far more difficult to assess.

Baedeker's advised visitors to Paris that the city was 'the cradle of high culinary art' and that to get an idea of the 'extent to which this art is carried' it was necessary to eat at one of the city's first-class restaurants. These were expensive, with prices for a full dinner ranging from 15 to 20 francs.[69] For diners who felt such prices were prohibitive, the alternative was a less fashionably situated restaurant, where high quality food might be available at a lower price. In fact, the author of Baedeker's guide to Paris considered the restaurants of that city to be of such a high standard that 'wherever the traveller may chance to take up his abode, he may depend on obtaining a tolerable breakfast and dinner at some restaurant in the vicinity'.[70] Dinner time in Paris's restaurants was between 5 p.m. and 8 p.m.. However, restaurants were generally most crowded from 6 p.m. to 7 p.m., as this was the fashionable time to dine. Visitors were therefore advised to dine between 5 p.m. and 6 p.m. in order to avoid the crowds.[71]

Guidebooks assumed that tourists would not be participants in the wider cultural activities which took locals to restaurants, but that unlike locals, visitors would have no need to appear fashionable in their mealtimes. The story of Z***, from *L'Illustration* in

1875, suggested that tourists received different treatment than locals when eating out. The anecdote was of a man eating at one of the 'renowned cafes of the boulevards.' He looked at the clock to ensure he was not going to be late for a business meeting, and noticed it was seven o'clock – later than he had thought:

> The waiter, who knew Z*** to be a Parisian, leaned in and whispered in his ear:
>
> – Don't let yourself be influenced by the clock, sir.
> – Why, is there something wrong with it?
> – It tells the time of foreigners and provincials. You know that those travellers go to the theatre after dinner. In reality it is only six thirty.
>
> The explanation of this tactic is very simple: They wanted to have space and renew the public. Thus early comers had to be made to dine quickly. As soon as they had ordered their meals, the clock was mysteriously put forward by an hour, to make them hurry.[72]

Baedeker's advised diners on how to avoid the difficulty of reading an haute cuisine menu. *Diner à Prix Fixe* – dining rooms where set meals were available for a set price, usually including wine, were recommended to 'travellers who are not *au fait* at ordering a French dinner.'[73] Both the standard of cuisine and the price were lower at *prix fixe* than in restaurants. However, the difference in price could be misleading to diners in groups of two or more, as restaurant portions were significantly larger than the portions served at other types of establishments. *Prix fixes*, bouillons and brasseries served dishes in single portions but in restaurants portions were large so that whole parties could share the same meal. Thus, while a lone diner might find it more economical to avoid restaurants, groups of diners would save less by avoiding the first-class restaurants. The question of portion size was a potential trap for diners if they had not eaten out before, and might be one of the many ways in which an unknowing customer could be caught out.[74] Multiple-person portions may have been preferred as they allowed restaurant meals to mimic respectable dinner parties, at which all participants ate the same menu, as selected by the hosts. But as with the domestic dinner party, the restaurant meal could take many forms, and brasseries, bouillons and other forms of catering establishments offered other formulas for ordering dinner.

Restaurants were elite environments, difficult for the young, rural people, foreigners and even sometimes bourgeois Parisians to navigate. Newer establishments provided accessible eating out options for a wider range of people. A butcher by the name of Duval was behind the highly successful bouillons, where respectable people could eat out cheaply. His idea had been a shop where the working classes could consume bouillons (soups).[75] As figure 8 shows, the

Figure 8 Les serveuses d'un 'Bouillon Duval', restaurant économique ouvert à Paris par le boucher Duval (1811–70).

respectability of Duval's establishment was enhanced by clean, respectably uniformed waitresses. In London, Lyon's teahouses took a similar approach, with their uniformed waitresses, referred to as 'nippies'. While male waiters might indicate a more elite environment, women were seen as less intimidating to diners who might feel uncomfortable in more elegant surroundings.

The bouillon was a successful genre and was copied by many others, so that in Paris, by the end of the nineteenth century, there were several other chains of bouillons, as well as independent ones. Though the bouillon had started off as a working-class catering establishment, some late nineteenth-century manifestations were remarkably elegant. They grew increasingly successful, and gained popularity with the bourgeoisie. It became fashionable to eat at a bouillon, something the restaurant purists found difficult to accept.[76] Another option was the brasserie, based on an Alsatian model, serving the food and beer of that region. Unlike restaurants, brasseries offered food throughout the day and late into the night. The dishes served comprised individual portions, making them economical for solitary diners. They also offered an informal atmosphere, which, according to one French journalist, was their principal appeal. He claimed, in 1895, that their clientele was new and varied, but was not the same as the clientele of traditional restaurants, and did not therefore pose a threat to restaurants:

> Third-rate bookmakers and gamblers, lovers of sauerkraut and tête de veau, provincials raised with the classic terror of restaurants, ministers of the next boat or young people from the last living the highlife in these noisy, smoky rooms, where it is not unusual to see a German officer, a civil servant from the Quai D'Orsay, a cycling champion, a deputy or senator and a waiter from the café next door all seated together.[77]

While Paris was widely regarded as the capital of fine dining, London's position was more contested. According to *Baedeker's*, 'English cookery . . . has at least the merit of simplicity, so that the quality of the food one is eating is not so apt to be disguised as it is on the continent.'[78] However, it also had its fashionable and expensive restaurants. At these the food was generally French.[79] As in Paris, there were alternatives to first-class restaurants, at which a reasonable meal could be procured.[80] Dinner was served in London restaurants between 4 p.m. and 8 p.m..[81] Many places closed after 8 p.m., whereas in Paris, many restaurants stayed open late for supper.

In London there were a greater number of alternatives to restaurants than in Paris. As to the quality of the food, in the 1850s, French author Francis Wey observed that it was 'really a city for married life . . . the bachelor is not catered for at all.'[82] Yet many English writers felt that the traditional chophouses, inns, establishments specialising in fish ordinaries, and other places referred to simply as dining rooms and eating-houses were superior to foreign restaurants, and English food superior to French. One writer went so far as to argue that the paucity of foreign restaurants was an indication that visitors to London preferred English food to their own: 'They come here abusing our cooks and cookery, and end in finding that, as a whole, it suits them better than the watery fare on which they have been reared.'[83] English specialities, including mutton chops, steak, roast beef, fish and various types of pies may have been part of the appeal, but London's most famous eateries were renowned for their ambiance and traditions.

London saw many new catering venue open and thrive through the 1880s and 1890s. Among these were the immensely popular Lyons teahouses and corner houses, which remained a recognisable feature of London's busy streets well into the 1960s. Here key features of French restaurants, such as fixed prices, pleasant decor and separate tables were combined with a more English style of cuisine, which made ordering and eating accessible to a wider range of people. At the same time, prices were high enough to limit the clientele to what was considered respectably middle-class. While providing elegant surroundings, this new genre of restaurant made eating out appear respectable and safe, in the sense of familiar. Diners in Lyons teahouses or corner houses, like at the Savoy under Escoffier, did not need to fear ridicule for inappropriate behaviour, and did not need to confront foreign – French – dining customs, which might have been intimidating.

The best known places to eat in London had grown up around traditions of masculine sociability similar to those which evolved into the gentlemen's clubs of Pall Mall. Thus men sat side by side with strangers, all bound together by their understanding of the rules of the place and their desire to belong. For middle-class women this level of contact with strangers could seem inappropriate, whereas for men it was in keeping with coffeehouse and club sociability. At Simpson's dinner was served between 1 p.m. and 2 p.m., allying it with eighteenth-century mealtimes and customs. The men dining may have been having their lunch, but by calling it dinner, they were staking their claim to a tradition pre-dating either 'lunch' or 'restaurants'. Unlike the modern restaurant, Simpson's did not have an extensive menu. A chairman presided over dinner and personally served each diner from large dishes which were placed in front of him. While restaurant dinners resembled the modern practice of dining à la russe, at Simpson's the older tradition of dining à la française was maintained. At the end of dinner, a large cheese was brought to the table. Each diner was then given the opportunity to 'guess the cheese' – that is its height, weight and girth. If anyone managed to guess all three correctly, then everyone present was served a complimentary glass of champagne.[84] Simpson's did not admit women until about 1910.[85] After that date, it still continued to serve more men than women, because the style of dining it offered was part of a very masculine eating tradition.[86]

The Cheshire Cheese, like Simpson's had the appeal of history, and was frequented by men eager to indulge in a sense of nostalgia, and who enjoyed ritual and tradition. Colonel Newnham-Davies wrote fondly of it:

> I was a little late. The man who loves the Cheshire Cheese pudding is in his place at table a few minutes before the pudding is brought in at 6:30 pm, a surging billow of creamy white bulging out of a great brown bowl, and then when the host begins to carve – and there is a certain amount of solemnity about the opening of this great pudding – the early guest gets the best helping.[87]

Also like Simpson's, there was a host, serving each man his meal. Claiming to have served such eminent British men as Dr Johnson, Dickens and Thackeray meant that the Cheshire Cheese represented a certain strand of middle-class masculinity which it conferred on to those who dined there. To feel at ease, patrons had to know the customs of the place. This club-like atmosphere was an important element in the appeal for the men who are there. And like the club, dinner at the Cheshire Cheese provided a home-like quality, in uniting diners around a head of table who, like the pater familias, carved and served everyone their portion. But modern restaurants offered the possibility that anyone passing on the street, if they could read a menu, could order dinner.

Assumptions about the different foods enjoyed by men and women led to assumptions about the kinds of venues in which each sex might appropriately be catered for. While men went to places which served steak, roast beef and meaty pies, women were supposed to prefer lighter and sweeter foods, which they ate at confectioners, pastrycooks and coffee shops. Confectioners' shops were used for snacks and light midday meals, either by women who worked in town or by those who went into town on shopping trips. In 1878, *The Caterer* reported that American women were ruining their health by eating light, fluffy and sweet foods, finishing with a complaint that the same problem was occurring in England:

> Englishwomen are often addicted to the same practice, for when upon shopping excursions (those sweet fictions of the female mind) there are scarcely any refreshment-rooms save the pastry-cook's shop open to them. Light and airy ham sandwiches . . . and still more airy and indigestible puffs and tarts, constitute the only refreshment that the shopping excursionist can as a rule obtain; and these dainties are eaten with an accompaniment of fiery sherry that brings tears into the eyes of the fair ones.[88]

The attack on women's frivolity as shoppers gained strength when combined with such harsh criticism of their diet. Since diet was believed to directly shape character and morals, eating light and airy foods could have seriously bad consequences.

'A lady's café in Paris! . . . It would be forced to close within six months. People would talk too much to consume enough!'[89] Thus exclaimed a writer in *La Salle à Manger* in 1890 in an article about a group of Berlin women's demand for a women-only café to get refreshments when they were 'forced' to be out for several hours because 'the presence of a lone woman in a public establishment [was considered] unsuitable'. In spite of this clear message that women were not suited to café culture, it was unusual to find negative comments concerning women's use of catering establishments in Paris. Unlike in London, the respectability of eating out as an activity for women was generally unquestioned. From their origins as places in which to seek a cure for the ailments of the sensitive soul, restaurants in Paris had aimed to attract eaters of both sexes. The London press contained far more controversy surrounding women's use of commercial catering venues, but in both cities women as well as men were regular restaurant-goers.

A month after the article on the impossibility of a women-only café was published, a description appeared of exactly the sort of place deemed impossible, which was already doing a brisk trade right in the heart of Paris. *Le Tea-Room*, a supposedly English-style tea house, was at that moment the place for the fashionable ladies of Paris to see and to be seen. This was described as: 'A soberly painted boutique, set off by large mirrors and adorned with cream coloured blinds, a few discreet golden nets inside, a perfume of high elegance and of perfect respectability', where women went to chat. But mostly they went to show themselves off, 'because they know that the eyes of friends and strangers watch, from the corners of tables, the least incorrectness of their dress; because they know Le Tea-Room has become the most select place for the launching of new fashions'.[90] There was no suggestion that women eating out were risking their reputations. In fact, if they were dressed in the latest fashions, public appearances could enhance their social position. But the message that women were incapable of appreciating the pleasures of the table, which had been a long-held belief, was evident. An article in *L'Illustration*, from 1895, suggested that women not only did not understand fine food, but were in fact ruining haute cuisine for their men, stating that the decline of the great Parisian restaurants was due to husbands having to cut back on their restaurant expenditures in order to pay their wives' dressmakers' bills.[91]

The London press viewed women who ate out with suspicion. From this, some historians have inferred that middle-class women did not frequent restaurants. Richard Sennett's assertion that 'in the restaurants of the nineteenth century, a lone, respectable woman dining with a group of men, even if her husband was present, would cause a sensation' has often been repeated.[92] However, the evidence suggests that women were far more present in the commercial sphere than might be assumed from the evidence of the press.[93] A humorous article in *The Caterer*, from 1882, revealed another side to how women diners were viewed, while at the same time confirming that it was not uncommon or shocking for a waiter to serve a woman in a restaurant:

'When a lady comes into the restaurant,' said the waiter, 'she always sits down as if terrapin and turtles were nothing to her. . . . She always asks for the bill of fare, and reads the figures first. Men, you know, say, 'Do they cook oysters decent?' but she always says, 'what do they cost?' Then she talks, and to her friend, and she says 'Do you like vermicelli soup?' 'Oh,' says the other, 'don't let's have soup, it's so hot.' 'I don't want soup,' says she, 'and I hate vermicelli, don't you?' 'Yes,' says she, 'but what shall we have? They have splendid chicken patties at Maillard's, in New York, I wonder if they are good here?' 'I don't know says the other, 'I had sheep's head here once, and it was very good.' 'Well, let's have that.' 'No,' says she, 'don't let's have the same thing. You have the sheep's head and I'll have the chicken,' 'No, have you rare beef?' – to me – 'Yes, miss.' I say. 'You have shad?' says the other. 'No, it is too late, and don't let us both have fish. I wish they had Vienna coffee, or that lovely rose sherbet from the Turkish Bazaar. Let us go over there.' 'Oh, no, it's too hot.' 'Well, what are we going to have?' Then they ask if we have fried chicken, and all sorts of other things not on the bill, and if we had – as we haven't – what would it cost? [94]

The implication, which would have been obvious to contemporaries, was that women did not appreciate fine food or fine dining. Newnham-Davis described a conversation with Joseph, the maître d'hôtel at the Savoy in London, during which he has ordered a very grand meal for that evening:

> I ended by saying that I had invited a lady to dine with me. 'A lady!' said Joseph, in a rather startled tone; but I assured him that the good angel who was to be my guest knew as much of good cooking as any male gourmet, and was aware that there are some culinary works of art in the presence of which conversation is an impertinence. [95]

Women had already become participants in the eating-out culture, and the debate that surrounded this for many years would do nothing to change that fact.

The main issue of contention surrounding women eating out was not whether they should, or should not, do so, but rather whether or not they should do so alone and in single sex groups. In the company of husbands, fathers or brothers, there was rarely any question of the propriety of women appearing in the modern restaurants of London and Paris. However, if they were in public without a male companion, women were believed by some to be risking their reputation. The principal perceived danger was based on the belief that women were weak, and could easily be corrupted when faced with sensual pleasures. Restaurants, as well as offering fine foods, also served alcohol, which might cause women to mis-behave. Patriarchal notions of women as belonging to their fathers or husbands were evidently being renegotiated in this period. While some commentator expressed concern over women appearing to enjoy themselves in restaurants, a growing population of women employed as clerks, and women fulfilling their duties as consumers, filled the tables of many catering establishments.

In his memoirs, Félix Mornand recounted a story which was supposed to have occurred in Paris in around 1859, and acted as a warning to *crémeries* owners to be on their guard when 'little ladies' entered their premises. He told the story of a woman, Amélie Ramon, who entered a *crémerie* and ordered soup and a small piece of bread. While she ate, several or her friends entered the restaurant, one at a time. In response to their arrival, Ramon ordered a full dinner of *gigot*, wine, dessert and coffee, which lasted several hours. The bill finally came to 13fr. 80c., which the woman refused to pay: 'She laughed gently in my face [said the owner] . . . saying: "Don't you know that a pretty lady never pays for these things, my dear? Its obviously you've only just arrived in Paris." '[96] Like the contemporary panic over shoplifting studied by Elaine Abelson, this story signalled men's anxieties about women's lack of control, their inability to manage money, and the fear that in a male-dominated economy it was men who had to pay the price for women's irrational behaviour.[97]

The staff at London's elegant Trocadero received explicit instructions about how to receive women into the restaurant. These reflected concerns over women misbehaving in restaurants, while simultaneously revealing that many women were regular customers of one of London's finest restaurants, with or without male companions. The instructions stated that 'no Strange Lady or Ladies in couples (that is to say ladies who you know are not regular customers) are to be permitted to take tables on the Balcony for either Luncheon, Dinner or Supper; under no circumstance is Table 88 on Balcony to be let to Two Ladies.'[98] This implied a distinction between new female customers and those who are already known to the staff as regular eaters. The term 'strange ladies' is ambiguous, as it might imply that these ladies were prostitutes or in some other way undesirable. However, the acknowledgement that 'strange ladies' might be mistaken for regular customers indicates that they could simply be women who appeared respectable but were unknown to the staff:

> Should there be any doubt in your minds as to the respectability of a Lady or Ladies asking for tables & who you know to be new customers, you must ask them to take a seat in the Vestibule on the

pretence that you will see if any Tables are vacant, and immediately send for one of the Directors or Chief Superintendent. Under no circumstances must you use your own discretion in this matter.[99]

In cases when strange ladies were admitted to the restaurant, special precautions were taken in seating them: 'Strange Ladies to be placed at small tables round the Restaurant, the object being that in case of misbehaviour we can screen the <u>table</u> off.'[100] Judith Walkowitz and Lynda Nead have both argued about the ambivalence expressed towards women who chose to appear unaccompanied in public. Though each has argued that there was some possibility that such women being mistaken for prostitutes, their research makes it clear that women did, in fact often walk alone or in pairs and that there were men who defended their right to do so.[101] The possibility of screening off a table to protect respectable clients from women behaving badly indicates a level of ambivalence regarding the position of women in the public. However, it is not an assertion that any unaccompanied women were instantaneously surrounded by screens and hidden from view to protect the reputation of the restaurant, and in no way suggests that women were unusual customers in the restaurant.

Women and men were viewed differently as customers. General observers, as well as restaurant owners, revealed an awareness of the difficulty of accommodating women – especially when they were not in male company – in the world of public, commercial eating. Women eating in the public gaze ran the risk of being mistaken for prostitutes. At the same time, anxieties about respectable women's weakness in the face of temptation meant that unlike a male patron, they might create a nuisance by behaving inappropriately. While women and men did not experience restaurants in the same way in the second half of the nineteenth century, it is clear that in both London and Paris, both sexes availed themselves of the opportunity to eat out, for pleasure, out of necessity, and as a way of making an impression.

Manners and class: constructing cultural capital

In 1882, when Molly Hughes made her first visit to a restaurant, she was sixteen years old. She had had other experiences of eating out, as a child, but none that compared to dining at the Criterion with her brothers.[102]

Mother had put me into my nearest approach to an evening dress
. . . so I was not too shy when I sat in the dress circle, and walked
into the grill-room after the play. This was full of cheery people and
a pleasant hum of enjoyment and hurrying waiters. I felt it to be like
something in the Arabian Nights. We had hardly been bowed to our
seats when Tom and Charles walked in and joined us. A low-toned
chat with the waiter followed, while I looked with amazement at the
wide array of knives and forks by our places.

'What can these be for?' I asked Charles.

'You'll see. I'll tell you which to use as we go on; and remember
you needn't finish everything up; it's the thing to leave something on
your plate.'

Such a meal as I had never dreamt of was then brought along in
easy stages. Never had I been treated so obsequiously as by that
waiter. When wine was served I began to wonder what mother would
think. It gave that touch of diablerie to the whole evening that was
the main charm.[103]

The Hughes family was undeniably middle class. They were neither
rich nor poor, though Hughes remembered periods of relative
prosperity and relative deprivation during her childhood. Hughes's
father worked as a stockbroker, and went through periods of success, but also suffered downturns. Her mother was a respectable
wife who stayed home and raised her four children with the help
of a single servant. Like most middle-class families, the Hugheses
would not have considered eating out as something they could
afford to do regularly. However, Hughes had, in her childhood
and youth, experienced eating out at family picnics and at inns
during family excursions, but the way she recollected her meal at
the Criterion highlights the fact that restaurant dining was seen as
a significantly different activity from other forms of eating out. It
offered different possibilities for enjoyment but also required the
acquisition of new knowledge.

That eating out was a vehicle for displaying taste – or being
exposed to ridicule – is most easily seen in humorous or satiric
texts. Men and women who were comfortable in restaurants left
few recollections of their experiences but the presence of humorous
anecdotes in the press about people who failed to learn the rules of
good ordering reveals an underlying awareness of the importance
of understanding restaurant menus. Like many leisure activities,
eating out was an activity in which participants were judged by
one another on the extent to which they appeared at ease in their

surroundings and knowledgeable about what was required of them. Concern over displaying the correct manners and knowledge focused on the various types of people who were seen as not belonging in urban restaurants, as in the joke about the 'ruralist' which appeared in an English trade paper in 1881:

> A ruralist seated himself in a restaurant the other day, and began on the bill of fare. After employing three waiters nearly half an hour in bringing dishes to him, he heaved a sigh, and whispered, as he put his finger on the bill of fare: 'Mister, I've et to thar;' and moving his finger to the bottom of the bill: 'Ef it isn't agin the rule, I'd like to skip from thar to thar.'[104]

Restaurants remained a largely urban phenomenon throughout the nineteenth century, making rural people, who were stereotypically imagined as simpler than their urban counterparts, ideal targets for this type of humour.[105] Newlyweds were targeted by another trade paper, at around the same time: 'One of the most interesting studies of the hotel coffee room is the newly married couple who try to pass for veterans.'[106] The belief that newly married couples knew little about ordering food was widespread, and covered more than their potential behaviour in restaurants. It was a typical formula of etiquette and domestic advice literature to present advice as being aimed at the young married couple offering their first dinner party. Thus restaurant discourse expanded on a familiar theme to reinforce the point that ordering food in public was a special skill which needed to be acquired.

The French newspaper *L'Illustration* published the story of an eccentric writer who went under the pseudonym Timothy Trimm, who discredited himself by misunderstanding the nature and meaning of a good dinner. Having once heard that twenty-five francs was the minimum that any self-respecting man should spend on his lunch, Trimm decided that he would spend fifty. He chose the Café D'Orsay as his venue, wanting to impress 'the gallery' of fellow diners there. He ordered a poorly conceived meal, include eggs on a silver plate, not realising that eggs tarnish silver, and chose to wash it all down with Lacryma Christie, described by the writer as 'an awful wine, but very expensive'.[107] The story did not have a happy ending. When the war came, Trimm was ruined, having spent all his money on foolish luxuries and pretensions. This story could be read as a warning to anyone attempting to

appear knowledgeable about eating out when they were not ade-
quately aware of what was good rather than simply expensive. It
also indicated the extent to which restaurant eating was a performance, with diners at other tables, referred to here as the 'gallery',
as its audience.[108]

Restaurant reviewer Newnham-Davies recognised the difficulties
satirised by various writers. To him, the problem was knowing
what to order when faced with a list of unfamiliar foods, and he
believed that 'bravery' was needed to ask questions, rather than
allowing oneself to be urged on by a waiter to order 'very much
the dinner that he would have eaten in his suburban home had
he been dining there that night.'[109] Newnham-Davies saw that if
restaurant-goers did not educate themselves about the types of
foods that they were likely to encounter on restaurant menus, they
risked missing out on an essential element of the experience, which
was to eat foods that were different from what they would have
at home. Those who were very knowledgeable, and particularly
those who ordered their meal earlier in the day, could order without even looking at the menu, since all chefs were expected to be
adept at producing various standard recipes. According to the
authors of the humorous *Petit-Paris* restaurant guide 'You are lost
if you consult a menu at dinner time. It is like a poet who has
recourse to a rhyming dictionary to write verse.'[110] However, knowledgeable restaurant patrons who were serious about what they ate
were also aware of the specialities of the various restaurants they
frequented.

Ordering in restaurants was a man's job. In the early modern
period it was the man of the house who had been the principal host
of any dinner party. With the feminisation of the domestic sphere,
the duty of hosting came to rest on the mistress of the house,
while the restaurant meal replaced the dinner party as the occasion
for the male host to feed his guests, at the same time revealing his
knowledge of fine food and wine. Problems arose, however, if the
man lacked the knowledge, or cultural capital, to act the part of
host. Jean-Paul Aron stresses the importance of the restaurant in
bourgeois nineteenth-century Paris as the place for men to make
their reputations.[111] Restaurant menus were a greater source of
anxiety to Londoners than to Parisians in the mid-nineteenth century
since restaurants typically served French food and presented diners
with menus in French. As the century progressed, menus in English

became more common in London's eating places, and the food on offer was often simplified, as restaurant owners adapted to the extension of their clientele from a wealthy elite to the wider bourgeois public.[112]

In restaurants, masculinity was articulated through knowledge of food and drink, as it would have been in aristocratic homes of the eighteenth century, and as it also was in nineteenth-century clubs. In order to live up to the expectations of his critics, a man needed to be able to compose an excellent meal in which no expense was spared, but in which he was also seen to get value for money. He also had to choose appropriate wines to accompany this meal. Ordering such a meal could convey a variety of messages. A French newspaper told the story of a man who invited a group of friends to a restaurant to spend some money he had just inherited from an uncle. The friends were surprised that though the wine was of the best quality, the food ordered was very plain. He explained that this was the food that had kept his uncle alive for many years, and that if it was good enough for the uncle than it was good enough for them.[113] In this instance, the ordering of the meal acted as a memorial to the uncle who had passed away. Food carried messages, intended or otherwise, of extravagance, generosity, frugality, elegance or vulgarity.

Men in France valued their reputations as gourmets or gastronomes. To be invited for a cheap meal, or be tricked into eating inferior products, were not taken lightly.[114] A story in *L'Art Culinaire* from 1866 described writer Charles Monselet's despair at being exposed as a culinary fraud. A fellow writer, Eugene Chavette, had long been determined to undermine Monselet's gastronomic reputation. One day, he invited a group of literary friends to dine at Chez Brébant, one of Paris's best known restaurants. He had a superb meal served to them, with which Monselet was delighted. He praised each course in glowing terms. When the meal was over, Chavette revealed that none of the courses had been as they appeared, and that in fact each one was of some inferior food, disguised as a something more expensive and refined; the same was true for the wines. Monselet knew he had been deceived, and ended by imploring everyone present not to reveal his humiliation.[115] The authors emphasised Monselet's concern that the story should not become publicly known. There was humour in this, since Monselet already had a reputation as a writer, and did not need to rely on his gastronomic knowledge. However, his overall public reputation as a gentleman depended in part on his knowledge of good food and drink.

Successful bourgeois men found in the modern restaurant a stage on which reputations could be won or lost. As in the home, host and guests gathered around a shared meal in order to demonstrate their good manners, self-control and respectability, alongside their wealth and taste. But restaurants, unlike dinner parties, took this performance into the public sphere, where it could be played out in front of a wider audience. Here, women found a new avenue for emerging from domesticity, and by the end of the nineteenth century, they were accepted as diners in all sorts of venues. But while public eating was enjoyed by men and women alike, there were still many venues which explicitly promoted homosocial dining. Principal among these were the clubs and banquets which form the subject of Chapter 5.

Notes

1 A. Escoffier, *Memories of my Life*, trans. Laurence Escoffier (London: Van Nostrand Reinhold 1997) p. 90.

2 R. Spang, *The Invention of the Restaurant: Paris and Modern Gastronomic Culture* (London: Harvard University Press, 2000) pp. 34–63.

3 Spang, *The Invention of the Restaurant*, pp. 25–33; also S. Mennell, *All Manners of Food: Eating and Taste in England and France from the Middle Ages to the Present* (Oxford: Blackwell, 1985) pp. 135–6.

4 Spang, *The Invention of the Restaurant*, p. 235. Also D. J. Richardson, 'J. Lyons and c. Ltd: Caterers and Food Manufacturers, 1894 to 1939', in D. Oddy and D. Miller (eds), *The Making of the Modern British Diet* (London: Croom Helm, 1976) p. 162.

5 Mennell, *All Manners of Food*; J.-P. Aron, *The Art of Eating in France: Manners and Menus in the Nineteenth Century*, trans. N. Rootes (London: Owen, 1975) p. 29; J.-F. Revel, *Un Festin en paroles: histoire littéraire de la sensibilité gastronomique* (Paris: Pauvert, 1979) pp. 207–8; M. Toussaint-Samat, *History of Food*, trans. A. Bell (Oxford: Blackwell, 1992) pp. 731–4; J. Finklestein, *Dining Out: A Sociology of Modern Manners* (Cambridge: Polity Press, 1989) pp. 144–5.

6 J. W. Brown, *Fictional Meals and their Function in the French Novel, 1789–1848* (London: University of Toronto Press, 1984) pp. 5–7.

7 *The Caterer* (5 March 1881); *The Caterer* (15 Nov. 1881); P. D. S. Mrs. Tomkins in Town (London: W. Whiteley, 1882) p. 47.

8 Aron, *The Art of Eating in France*, pp. 219–20.

9 Finklestein, *Dining Out.*
10 A. de P. D1P4/892 Cadastre 1876, Restaurant Notta.
11 Anon., *Les Petits Paris, Paris-Restaurant* (Paris: A. Taride, 1854) pp. 73–4.
12 A de P. V.O11 2456 Permis de Construire.
13 LMA Building Case Files.
14 See, especially, E. Goffman, *The Presentation of Self in Everyday Life* (Harmondsworth: Penguin, 1974); and R. Sennett, *The Fall of Public Man* (New York: Knopf, 1977). On the sociology of restaurant dining in particular, see Finklestein, *Dining Out.* For a historical approach to the performative aspects of English middle-class life, see Simon Gunn, *The Public Culture of the Victorian Middle Class. Ritual and Authority in the English Industrial City 1840–1914* (Manchester: Manchester University Press, 2000).
15 Sennett, *The Fall of Public Man.*
16 Finklestein, *Dining Out,* pp. 2–3.
17 Mennell, *All Manners of Food,* p. 143.
18 R. Thorne, 'Places of Refreshment in the Nineteenth-Century City', in *Buildings and Society: Essays on the Social Development of the Built Environment,* ed. A. D. King (London: Routledge & Kegan Paul, 1980) p. 229; C. Reed (ed.), *Not at Home: The Suppression of Domesticity in Modern Art and Architecture* (London: Thames & Hudson, 1996) p. 7.
19 S. Freeman, *Mutton and Oysters: The Victorians and their Food* (London: Victor Gollancz, 1989) p. 271. Also U. Bloom, *Sixty Years of Home* (London: Hurst & Blackett, 1960).
20 E. Yates, *His Recollections and Experiences* (London: R. Bentley & Son, 1884) pp. 118–19.
21 A. Bennett, *Journals of Arnold Bennett,* Vol. I, ed. N. Flower (London: Cassell, 1933) p. 42.
22 Fond Montorgueil AN 428AP/2.
23 *The Lady* (27 Sept. 1888).
24 S. Beale, *Recollections of a Spinster Aunt* (London: William Heinemann, 1908) pp. 215–7, in a letter to her cousin Mary, Paris, May 1869.
25 Brame, *Le Journal intime de Caroline B.* ed. G. Ribeill and M. Perrot (Paris: Montalba, 1985) p. 96.
26 C. de Tours, *Vingt jours à Paris pendant l'exposition universelle 1889* (Paris: Quantin, 1889) p. 168. *Guinguettes* were dance halls just outside the city, where dinner and live music could be had for the whole family on a Saturday or Sunday afternoon. Several of them still exist, though their heyday was in the early twentieth century.
27 D. Shaw (pseud. One of the Old Brigade) *London in the Sixties* (London: Everett, 1908) pp. 33–4.
28 Yates, *His Recollections and Experiences,* p. 119.

29 'Journal d'une étrangère', *L'Illustration* (28 Jan. 1905).
30 G. Claudin, *Mes souvenirs, les boulevards de 1840–1870* (Paris: C. Lévy, 1884) p. 293.
31 *L'Art Culinaire* (15 Aug. 1892).
32 The impact of the railway on tourism is discussed by various historians. See for example: J. A. R. Pimlott, *The Englishman's Holiday: A Social History* (Hassocks: Harvester Press, 1976); M. Morgan, *National Identities and Travel in Victorian Britain* (Basingstoke: Palgrave, 2001) pp. 13–15, and on the rise of restaurants as a result of increasing tourism, p. 140.
33 Anon., *How to Dine; or, etiquette of the Dinner Table* (London: Ward, Lock and Tyler, 1879) p. 67.
34 See for example: F. Mornand, *L'Année anecdotique: petits mémoires du temps* (Paris: E. Dentu, 1860) p. 351; *L'Illustration* (9 Jan. 1875); 'Restaurant et Brasserie', *L'Illustration* (9 Feb. 1895); *L'Illustration* (5 May 1900).
35 Anon., *Les Petits Paris, Paris-Restaurant*, p. 26.
36 *Le Progrès du Cuisiner* (15 Jan. 1887).
37 *L'Art Culinaire* (Feb. 1889).
38 *L'Art Culinaire* (Feb. 1889). Also, *L'Art Culinaire* (15 June 1889).
39 'Un Restaurant Parisien', *L'Art Culinaire* (15 Aug. 1888); 'Restaurant et Brasserie', *L'Illustration* (9 Feb. 1895).
40 See for example: *L'Illustration* (27 June 1885); *L'Art Culinaire* (15 Aug. 1888) *L'Art Culinare* (15 Aug. 1890) *La Salle à Manger* (Oct. 1890) Anon., *Les Petits Paris, Paris-Restaurant*, pp. 65–8.
41 Food writing in England was a new genre in the nineteenth century. In France it had already been well established since at least the eighteenth century. E. Ehrman '19th Century', in *London Eats Out: 500 Years of Capital Dining* (Museum of London, 1999) p. 69.
42 See for example Yates, *His Recollections and Experiences*, Vol. I, p. 152.
43 *The Caterer* (3 Aug. 1878).
44 Parisian restaurant advertising also emphasised positive change and novelties. See for example A. de P. D17Z/1, A de P D17Z/2, A. de P. D17Z/4, A. de P. 6AZ/1139/4, which all contain various advertisements for restaurants in Paris, in particular the small neighbourhood restaurants. However, as the emphasis on the positive rarely appeared in other written sources, it seems to have been a less important aspect of the general discourse on eating out.
45 C. W. Scott, *How they Dined us in 1860 and How They Dine us Now* (A souvenir booklet issued by the Trocadero Restaurant, London, 1900) p. 20. Also, T. P. O'Connor (MP) *Trocadero: The Old and the New*, n.d. Lyons Archive AC 3572/232.
46 Scott, *How they Dined us in 1860*, p. 12.

47 See for example: Shaw, *London in the Sixties*.
48 Shaw, *London in the Sixties*, pp. 169–70.
49 Tours, *Vingt jours à Paris pendant l'exposition universelle 1889*, p. 138.
50 The Caves Restaurant Trudaine, *c.*1880, offered a free bar of soap to every 'loyal customer.' (A. de P. D17Z/2); the Maison Maubert, *c.*1897, had an opening promotion which offered a free coffee to every diner for the first fifteen days (A. de P. D17Z/2); between 1890 and 1895, the Grand Restaurant de la Bourse ran an ad campaign which offered free oysters and coffee with every meal (A. de P. D17Z/2).
51 A. Escoffier, *Souvenirs inédits: 75 ans au service de l'art culinaire* (Marseille: J. Lafitte, 1985) pp. 18–19, 83–4, 100–1.
52 *L'Illustration* (27 Jan. 1855); *L'Illustration* (16 June 1855).
53 *L'Illustration* (7 April 1855); *L'Illustration* (26 May 1855).
54 *L'Illustration* (23 June 1900).
55 *The Queen* (26 Oct 1861).
56 *The Queen* (26 Oct 1861).
57 *L'Art Culinaire*, Special Issue 'Le Gourmand à L'Exposition', 1889.
58 AN F/12/11902.
59 There are no exact translations for these terms, but approximate ones can be made. Café-glacier is a café which also serves ices.
60 A *Café-brasserie* is a café which also acts as a brasserie, meaning that beer and food are served there. Brasseries dervide from the Alsatian tradition of establishments which served local foods and beers.
61 *Bon-marché* means inexpensive.
62 *Débits et dépôt de vins et liqueurs* are wine and spirit merchants.
63 *Débits d'eau gazeuse* sell carbonated water.
64 *Pâtissier, debits de pains d'epices* can be translated as pastry shops and gingerbread merchants.
65 Confectioners.
66 These sold coffee and chocolate by the cup.
67 These sold fresh fruit.
68 See also AN F[7] 3025, a survey carried out by the French government in 1851 to determine the number of catering establishments in each departement. It requested that establishments be listed according to the following categories: '*hôteliers ou aubergistes, cabaretier, cafetiers, restauranteurs*'. The greater number of categories proposed in 1867 suggests an expansion in the types of catering facilities generally available.
69 Prices did not vary greatly from year to year. The Baedeker's guide from 1865 lists the price of a first-rate dinner at 10–15 francs, p. 6; in 1875 it is listed at 10–15 francs, p. 8, and in 1888 it is 10–15 francs, though the price is now without wine, p. 8.
70 K. Baedeker, *Paris and its Environs* (Leipzig: Karl Baedeker, 1888) p. 2.

71 K. Baedeker's *Paris and its Environs* (Leipzig: Karl Baedeker, 1865) p. 8; also 1874, p. 10; also 1888, p. 9.

72 *L'Illustration* (19 June 1875).

73 Baedeker, *Paris*, 1874, pp. 10–11; also 1888, p. 12. This statement was not included in the 1865 guide, which simply stated that the *Diner à Prix-Fixe* 'have within the last few years come into vogue'.

74 According to Baedeker's guide to London, London's finest restaurants also served portions large enough for two or more people. However, this was not commented on in any other source.

75 Baedeker, *Paris*, 1874, p. 16; 1888, p. 16. *L'Illustration* (4 June 1870); *La Salle à Manger* (July 1890); *L'Art Culinaire* (30 April 1892).

76 *The Caterer* (1 June 1878); *The Travellers' Journal* (17 April 1880).

77 'Restaurant et Brasserie', *L'Illustration* (9 Feb. 1895).

78 Baedeker, *London and its Environs* (Leipzig: Karl Baedeker, 1881) p. 11; also, 1889 p. 11; also 1898 p. 13.

79 Baedeker, *London*, 1881 p. 11; also, 1889 p. 11; also 1898 p. 13.

80 Baedeker, *London*, 1881 p. 11; also, 1889 p. 11; also 1898 p. 13.

81 The rush caused in restaurants by the need of all customers to dine at precisely the same hour for the sake of fashion attracted some criticism: *The Restaurant* (Oct. 1909).

82 F. Wey, *A Frenchman Sees the English in the Fifties*, trans. and ed. V. Pirie (London: Sidgwick & Jackson, 1935) p. 37.

83 *The Caterer* (1 June 1873).

84 Simpson's Restaurant, *Two Hundred Years* (*A souvenir*) (London: St Mary Press, 1923) p. xii.

85 Simpson's Restaurant, *Two Hundred Years*, p. xv.

86 M. V. Hughes, *London at Home* (London: W. Morrow & Co, 1931) p. 77.

87 Lieut.-Col. Newnham-Davis, *Dinners and Diners: Where and How to Dine in London* (London: Grant Richards, 1899) p. 10.

88 *The Caterer* (7 Dec. 1978) p. 142.

89 *La Salle à Manger* (Nov. 1890).

90 *La Salle à Manger* (Dec. 1890).

91 *L'Illustration* (9 Feb. 1895).

92 Sennett, *The Fall of Public Man*, p. 23.

93 See for example W. Hardman, *A Mid Victorian Pepys*, ed. S. M. Ellis (London: Cecil Palmer, 1923–25), p. 308; A. Schlueter, *A Lady's Maid in Downing Street*. ed. M. Duncan (London: T. Fisher Unwin, 1922), pp. 52 and 130; Newnham-Davis, *Dinners and Diners*, pp. 15, 18.

94 *The Caterer* (15 July 1882) p. 150.

95 Newnham-Davis, *Dinners and Diners*, p. 83.

96 Mornand, *L'Année anecdotique: petits mémoires du temps*, pp. 312–13.

97 E. S. Abelson, *When Ladies Go A-Thieving: Middle-Class Shoplifters in the Victorian Department Store*. (Oxford: Oxford University Press, 1989).

98 'Regulations re Ladies' LMA ACC3527/186.

99 'Regulations re Ladies' LMA ACC3527/186.

100 'Regulations re Ladies' LMA ACC3527/186.

101 J. Walkowitz, 'Going Public: Shopping, Street Harassment and Streetwalking in Late Victorian London', *Representations* 0:62 (Spring 1998) 1–30. L. Nead, *Victorian Babylon People, Streets and Images in Nineteenth-Century London* (London: Yale University Press, 2005).

102 M. V. Hughes, *A London Child of the 1870s* (Oxford: Oxford University Press, 1977) pp. 15, 48, 139.

103 M. V. Hughes, *A London Girl of the 1880s* (Oxford: Oxford University Press, 1978) p. 16.

104 *The Caterer*, 1881.

105 *The Caterer* (5 July 1879).

106 *The Hotel Gazette* (7 Feb. 1880).

107 *L'Illustration* (1 May 1875).

108 Some commentators referred to observation of the occupants of neighbouring tables as one of the pleasures of eating out: Mornand, *L'Année anecdotique: petits mémoires du temps* Dec. 1851, p. 1, Dec. 1858, p. 6; *L'Illustration* (28 Jan. 1905).

109 Newnham-Davis, *Dinners and Diners*, pp. xvii–xviii.

110 Anon., *Les Petits Paris, Paris-Restaurant*, p. 26.

111 Aron, *The Art of Eating in France*, p. 30.

112 *The Hotel Gazette* (3 Jan. 1880); *The Hotel Gazette* (17 Jan. 1880); *The Travellers Journal* (22 May 1880).

113 *L'Illustration* (13 March 1875).

114 Aron, *The Art of Eating in France*, pp. 139–40.

115 *L'Art Culinaire* (Oct. 1888).

5

Members and subscribers only: clubs and banquets

> Every Parisian of note belongs to one, two, or a dozen dinners, where colleagues, friends, or persons who are indifferent to each other meet once a fortnight or once a month, to exchange ideas, to gossip, and to keep up those bonds of good-fellowship, or *camaraderie*, without which success in Paris is almost impossible.[1]

R. J. Morris argues that associations were one of the ways in which middle-class identity was created in the nineteenth century.[2] Club membership allowed bourgeois Londoners and Parisians to forge and foster the connections necessary for business, politics and sociability. Many clubs were purely social, but some, like Les Chemins de Fer in Paris, were explicit in their intention of bringing together a community of people with common interest. At Les Chemins de Fer's monthly dinners, each member invited a guest in order to create bonds within the railway industry.[3] Whatever the reason for coming together, when men or women associated in this way, some of what they did was to take part in the performative element which historians have identified as a central one of bourgeois culture.[4] Like dinner parties, public dinners – be they in clubs or at banquets – brought together people united in the culture of respectability. Unlike in restaurants, the ability to pay for dinner was not sufficient. In clubs and at banquets a further selection process – invitation, balloting, professional or political affiliation – decided who could share in the meal. The subject of this chapter, being the delicate act of creating a highly exclusive situation within the public sphere and the public gaze, brings together a variety of distinct types of meals. All were performed in similar ways, and all also allow us to glimpse the changing nature of gender relations and the extent to which a once exclusively male privilege was gradually claimed by women in the final decades of the century.

The majority of clubs, *dîners* and banquets were exclusively male. Women's identities, constructed along familial lines, offered fewer opportunities for establishing connections based on professions, interests or hobbies. To say that bourgeois women were less involved in public dining is not to say that they were excluded altogether. As with restaurants, a dominant discourse, which conveyed the message that club and banquet dining was men-only hid a more complex reality in which both men and women were involved in a variety of clubs, associations and public banquets.

While London and Paris were similar in offering a range of opportunities for dining in public yet exclusive settings, the forms such meals took differed significantly between the two cities. Civic banquets were important ritual occasions in both London and Paris. In both cities, it was the upper bourgeoisie and the gentry who were primarily involved. Paris also had a banqueting culture that dated back to the political banquets of the French Revolution and, even more so, those of 1848. While political banquets ceased after 1848, the tradition of organising banquets to mark important occasions persisted. The frequent references to private banquets in the Parisian press were not replicated in London. Clubs were a primarily English, and especially London, phenomenon, which grew out of eighteenth-century coffeehouses. By the second half of the nineteenth century there were several well-established clubs in London, mostly located in or around Pall Mall. Because 'clubs' were banned in France, until the laws governing the rights of associations were loosened in 1901, *cercle* was used to convey a meaning similar to that denoted by club in England.[5] Like clubs, *cercles* grew out of coffeehouses, as the men who socialised there sought greater exclusivity. *Cercles* first appeared in the provinces, but by the second half of the nineteenth century there were several important *cercles* in Paris, most of which drew members from the aristocracy and the upper ranks of the bourgeoisie. While *cercles* fulfilled many of the same roles for Parisians as clubs did for Londoners, contemporaries often saw them as an English phenomenon which had been imported and adapted by the French.

Historians of the middle classes have argued for the important role played by clubs and associations in the creation of bourgeois identity.[6] Clubs were central to sociability, the construction of identity, and for forging bonds.[7] Jane Rendell has looked at club architecture to argue that clubs provided a space for both public display and private pursuits. These private pursuits ranged from respectable sociability to hidden vice, particularly in the form of gambling – a point also made by Mike Huggins in his examination of the hidden leisure pursuits of elite Victorian men. More recently, Amy Milne-Smith has argued that clubs provided an alternative domestic sphere in which men could escape from female-dominated domiciles while continuing to enjoy the comforts of home. This confirms an earlier argument from John Tosh, that in the later Victorian period men emerging from the homosocial public school environment were less comfortable in the family sphere than their fathers and grandfathers had been earlier in the century.

While clubs have been thought of both in terms of masculine identity and sociability, the particular role of food has never been examined. Parisian *cercles*, though very similar to clubs, have attracted far less attention. Maurice Agulhon's study of the role of the *cercles* in French bourgeois life was concerned more with the provinces than with Paris. Furthermore, his focus on the Restoration and July Monarchy meant that the prominent place of *cercles* in Paris during the second half of the nineteenth century has been largely neglected.[8] Women's clubs were far fewer in number than men's, though from the 1880s they gained some popularity in London. With the notable exception of Erika Rappaport's work, where women's clubs are linked to the rise of female access to the West End of London for shopping and leisure, women's participation in club sociability has been largely ignored.[9]

The need for exclusivity

If you didn't have the *cercle*, you would have its coarse parodies: the *tripot*, the café, the *estaminet*, and the brasserie . . . vulgar places where people find each other accidentally, where they meet without joining, where one feels responsibility neither for one's own actions nor for those of others.[10]

By 1885, Léon La Brière could argue that *cercles* were a necessity of modern life in Paris. They created a congenial space in which to socialise and, he argued, helped to create a bond between the upper and the middle classes. This was done by annexing the wealthier and more intelligent members of the bourgeoisie to the nobility, whom they encountered at the *cercle*.[11] Clubs and *cercles* provided well-regulated environments and membership procedures, which permitted social mixing among the gentry and upper middle classes, allowing for social mobility and useful business connections. However, in London, where a greater number of clubs existed, and where membership was more central to respectable masculinity, there were also numerous clubs whose members were drawn solely from the mid- to lower ranks of the middle classes.

For its members a club was a retreat and a place to relax among a group of equals. Jane Rendell as argued that clubs must be understood as patriarchal and fratriarchal masculine spaces, from which men excluded women as well as other groups of men, based on class, political or national boundaries.[12] Clubs were indeed exclusive, yet among members there is evidence for a great degree of toleration of, for example, political difference. Socially, membership could be an asset, as it offered men the opportunity to entertain guests away from the various anxieties associated with female company, domestic dinner parties and restaurant outings. London's Baedeker guides claimed that dining was one of the principal activities for which members used clubs.[13] Similarly an article in *Pot-au-Feu* in March 1908 regarded dining as the main reason for the formation of most Parisian *cercles*:

> From the first day that a number of gentlemen and wealthy bourgeois united to form a *cercle*, the matter of the table was raised before them as a very important one. In truth, more than one Parisian *cercle* was created only with a view to offering very good dinners, at reasonable prices, which is a difficult problem to resolve either at home or in restaurants.[14]

The large number of clubs in London meant that each middle-class man could hope to find one that suited him. They ranged in price and in social composition, but in all cases there were measures in place to control access. Yates recollected that when he first encountered 'clubland' in 1848, there were 23 clubs. Each club had its own set of members:

> The Alfred, a great place for superior government clerks . . . the Westminster, established by the leading London tradesmen, where the dinners were excellent and the play was high; the Coventry, known as the 'Velvet Cushion,' a very 'smart' place on Piccadilly hill.[15]

Brooks's was a Tory club with many aristocratic members. The Reform was liberal, and had a far greater proportion of upper-middle-class members, and a preponderance of MPs in its ranks.

The private archives of these two clubs form the basis of much the analysis of London clubs that follows.

Though various clubs were known to have particular political or professional affiliations, these were not necessarily the true criteria for membership. In 1851, the General Committee of the Reform Club received a letter from a member stating that 'six members of the club had been held up to reprobation at a public dinner given in the club last summer for votes which they had given in Parliament'.[16] The writer, Mr Cobden, requested that members' political affiliations should be respected, since 'a great difference of opinion may exist on public questions amongst members of the club'.[17] The same was true in 1913 when a letter was received from a member who asked whether 'in view of a change in his political opinions, he was under any obligation to resign his membership'.[18] The reply to this was that the club had no rule about this, and that it was left to the members' discretion.[19] In Paris, where politics was seen as both divisive and dangerous, as well as harmful to digestion, all *cercles* had regulations forbidding political discussions.[20] Throughout the period, clubs and *cercles* cohered around shared beliefs, but the question of political affiliation was less crucial than a commonly held moral and behavioural standard.

As Jane Rendell has argued, clubs, like homes, were governed in large part by routinised behaviour.[21] Each club had rules which all members were expected to follow. The extent to which they did so is difficult to determine, though club correspondence indicates that there were always some people who took the rules seriously. Club rules tended to be similar from one establishment to another, and the rules at Brooks's were typical. They specified the maximum number of members (550), the annual subscription (11 guineas), as well as procedures for electing new members (by ballot, after the name had been posted in the morning and evening rooms).[22] It was also stipulated that each new member should sign the rulebook, in order to indicate he accepted its content.[23] Several rules also referred specifically to meals served in the club, for example at Brooks's where, 'A dinner for six members, at fifteen shillings per head, including waiters and dessert; to be furnished daily, during the sitting of parliament; the dinner to be on the table at seven o'clock precisely.'[24]

Members intending to eat at this dinner had to sign up by five o'clock or, if they signed up late, pay a penalty of 5s. There was also a rule requiring that a supper 'consisting of hot and cold dishes, fish excepted' was to be provided on request every night during the sitting of Parliament.[25] At Gresham's, a smaller and less elite London club, the rules were similar to Brooks's in stipulating fees, membership requirements, and procedures for the upkeep of the club (by committee). But they did not include any rules specifically about the provision of meals.[26] Food was available at all clubs, but the importance placed on it depended on the character, history and membership of the club.

The *cercles* of Paris were also formed around shared identities.[27] Members of the Jockey Club were interested in horse racing, and also tended to be Anglophiles. Many of the *cercles* had names such as *Cercle des Beaux Arts*, or *Cercle Littéraire et Artistique*, which united people involved in artistic and literary pursuits, but whose membership also included middle- and upper-class people interested in the arts.[28] La Brière provided a guide to the identities of the various *Grands Cercles* of Paris, as well as similar clubs in London, Madrid, Rome, Berlin, Brussels, St Petersburg, Vienna, Pest, Nice and Cannes.[29] To a lesser extent, Parisian clubs, such as the *Cercle de la Jeunesse Catholique*, could bring together people from the lower bourgeoisie for the purpose of sharing an interest, or, in this instance, a religious faith.[30]

Cercle rules were very similar to one another, as well as being similar to the club rules in England. According to Charles Yiarte, all the important Parisian *cercles* used the same blackballing method as employed by English clubs for voting in new members.[31] L'Union, one of the most prestigious of the Parisian *cercles* had rules about when and how members had to book for dinner, as well as clear procedures on how to register complaints.[32] The similarities were not accidental. The English gentlemen's club provided the model for similar establishments in other countries. Also, because clubs had relationships with one another, they tended towards similarity rather than difference. These relationships principally took the form of agreements that members could attend one another's clubs during periods of annual closure (which were necessary for maintenance and upgrading), or when travelling abroad.[33]

Club membership was a privilege which had continually to be paid for. An annual subscription fee allowing access to the clubs' facilities was just the beginning. Everything had to be paid for separately, with meals being one of the costliest amenities. Both

Amy Milne-Smith and Jane Rendell have highlighted the domesticity of clubs, in spite of their apparently public nature.[34] This intersection between the public and private was revealed in the tensions over the exchange of money for food. Though it was clear that membership had to be paid for, this was not interpreted as payment for a service received. Instead, the club premises was seen as a sort of home, and members' fees were simply their contribution to housekeeping, in the same way that all respectable men had to work in order to maintain their actual households. Correspondence between members and management committees of both Brooks's and the Reform indicate that the price of meals was a highly contested issue. Numerous rules in both clubs and *cercles* about how and when meal bills should be settled suggest how difficult this was to control. The matter was minuted in a meeting of Brooks's management committee in 1858:

> The attention of the managers having been called to the fact that upon occasions of Members not paying their coffee room accounts for some time, Bandaret and son were in the habit of making an extra charge thereon – the managers have come to the conclusion that that custom is not to be continued, and have resolved that the account of every member shall be presented to him before he leaves the room.[35]

A minute from a meeting in March 1881 once again stated that 'every member was to be presented with his account before leaving the coffee room – that accounts were to be supplied to members for breakfasts and luncheons as well as for dinners, and that all accounts were to be settled within one month'.[36] The need to revisit the problem of payment over two decades later is a clear indication of how difficult it was to get money from members. The issue arose again fifteen years later at an extraordinary general meeting when 'Lord Kensington drew attention to the large amount of unpaid house accounts', indicating that the problem was a persistent one.[37] Similar problems also occurred, and were taken very seriously, at the Reform. In 1851, one member was expelled for having left the country after paying for dinner with a cheque, 'which had been dishonoured'.[38] At the Jockey Club in Paris, the rule was that meals had to be paid for on the day they were consumed, but the next rule stated that failing payment on the day, a bill would be sent on the first of the month, and 'exclusion from the *cercle* . . . if on the first of the following month the sum of the expenses had not been paid'.[39] Clearly, the difficulty of getting money out of members was widely known.

Club dining was generally less flexible and consumer-oriented than restaurant dining. The areas of the club were divided, with some spaces designated for eating, and others in which food might not to be consumed. Furthermore, clubs maintained strict rules about the hours when food could be ordered and consumed, though these changed frequently.[40] Thus, in 1904, Brooks's added the following rules to the bill of fare for their set dinner:

(1) the hours, 7 to 9
(2) the vegetable of the day
(3) A notice that any dish not on the bill of fare would be charged extra[41]

These were not new rules; it was simply the first time they had been made clear to diners. Similarly, for the first time in 1901, Brooks's managers decided: 'To move the service clerk into the breakfast room during the luncheon and dinner hours so as to enable members who wish to pay cash to get their bills promptly.[42] After many years of problems in getting members to pay for their meals, it was only at the beginning of the twentieth century that such a simple solution was considered.

The exclusivity of club dining was tightly guarded according to club rules about where guests could go within the club, and specified that not all rooms were open to them. However, access was under continual negotiation, and new policies were frequently introduced. At Brooks's in 1914, attempts were made to increase the accessibility of the club to strangers. An instruction to the steward stated that: 'Strangers might be shown into the Ground Floor Smoking Room when arriving at the club to lunch or dine with a member.'[43] Two months later another instruction was added: 'The Back morning Room should be opened if there was a Stranger's Room Dinner for 3 ordered, and even if a dinner for 2 . . . if the member asked for it.'[44] In the case of Brooks's, as in that of the Reform, it is difficult to determine the extent to which rules were observed by members. However, the reiteration of rules on the same subject over several years implies problems about their enforcement. The question of members at Brooks's needing to obtain permission if they wished to host dinner parties of several guests within the club was frequently raised at meetings. This was the case in June 1885, in October 1886 and again in May 1896 and in May 1900.[45] In May 1900 it was decided: 'as a consequence of a dinner of more than 10 guests given by Sir Robert Finlay', that the by-law concerning this matter would henceforth be strictly enforced 'and no infraction of it permitted without the sanction of at least one member of the House Committee'.[46] This new enforcing of the rule may have been effective, since in June 1903 Mr R. E. Morris requested and was granted permission to host a dinner party, with a maximum of fifteen guests.[47]

Members sometimes requested that the committee make a change in the policy regarding guests and meals. In 1850, seventy-four members petitioned for a new rule to 'permit any member of the club to introduce one stranger for the purpose of dining only during the prorogation of Parliament'.[48] This rule was not introduced, as the managers of the club decided: 'That the proposed rule would not lead to the comfort and general satisfaction of the club.'[49] In 1893, however, the rule about strangers dining while Parliament was in session was finally amended, allowing up to ten strangers to dine in that period, 'but giving the Steward discretionary power to increase this number where not inconvenient'.[50] There were many members to accommodate, and at different times the club promoted different priorities about who should have the right to eat there. Just like families, clubs had to have permeable boundaries, but the extent to which a family or a club chose to open itself to the outside world depended on a combination of factors.

Members were responsible for their guests and had to pay for their guests' dinners, and also guard against their guests misbehaving.[51] Members did not always take kindly to being charged for the privilege of receiving guests, especially in cases like that of Mr Morris, who was charged £2 for a dinner guest who never appeared, though in that instance the committee decided to refund the £2.[52] Inviting guests into one's club seemed to be a frequent occurrence. The number of guests entertained can be seen in Brooks's 'Dinner Books', which exist for the period from 1881 onward. In the 1880s, the tendency was for members to bring in few guests at a time. However, by the early decades of the twentieth century, increasing numbers of dinner guests were being brought into the club. In 1906, Gerrard Wallop had fourteen guests on one occasion. In 1911, Sir John Fuller had twenty-one guests for dinner and in 1913 an MP whose name is difficult to make out had nineteen dinner guests.[53] This increase in the number of guests suggests that the usefulness of belonging to a club changed from mid-century, when it was a matter of personal comfort and a way of socialising with fellow members, to the end of the century, when clubs played a greater role in making an impression, providing a homosocial space in which to host dinner parties when domestic dining rooms had become highly feminised spaces. The new club rules outlined above, extending the areas of the club to which outsiders could have access, shows that clubs members were in some agreement about the desirability of being able to entertain large groups of non-members: the privilege of doing so was one of the advantages of belonging to a club.

Although the evidence suggests that many club members made frequent use of their clubs' dining facilities for themselves and their guests, club dining was not popular with all members. Many club and *cercle* dining rooms found it difficult to make a profit.[54] Numbers of diners were never as high as club management committees hoped. One reason for this was the existence of so many other dining options in both London and Paris. Restaurants, cafés, tea houses and brasseries all offered greater ordering flexibility, and were often less costly.[55] At Brooks's General Meeting of 1909, the chairman outlined the diminution of numbers for both luncheon and dinner. He stated that in 1907 there were 193 fewer dinners served than in 1906, though this was partially compensated for by an increase in lunches by 309. However, he went on to state that in the current year, dinners were down by 238 and lunches down by 269. These 'disastrous' numbers he attributed to: 'the fact that people in this twentieth century neither seem to eat nor drink . . . If they do, I suppose they go to restaurants or in their own homes.'[56] This, together with the frequent complaints about the quality of the food served at both Brooks's and the Reform, suggest that as restaurants came to dominant the London catering trade, the importance of club dining was threatened. Clubs were never entirely undermined by restaurants, but the constraints, which differentiated club meals from their restaurant equivalents, meant that men who sought variety and flexibility in their meals were likely to turn away from clubs.

The clubs of clubland, as well as the *Grands Cercles* of Paris, were establishments that opened every day, had their own premises, and ran for many years. They were not, however, the only kinds of clubs to which bourgeois men could belong or in which they could share meals with their peers. Dining clubs had a long history in London, as did the *dîners* of Paris. These were groups who met periodically but regularly to share a meal. Some altered their venues for each meeting, but most had a set location, and in the case of the famous Dîner Magny, the restaurant in which the dinner took place gave the group its name. Robert Baldrick was so fascinated with the witty literary conversations which took place at the regular dinners at Magny, which included the Goncourt brothers, George Sand, Saint-Beuve, and Balzac among others, that he made it the subject of a book.[57] Though dining clubs were less formal than clubs, they often also entailed conditions of membership and other rules, needed to maintain the exclusivity and the identity of the club.

Brooks's, in London, was home to the exclusive Fox's dining club. Not all members of Brooks's were members of Fox's, an even more exclusive grouping of men who met for dinner one Saturday of every month.[58] These monthly dinners were held in the strangers' room, and Brooks's members were informed that on the night of a Fox's dinner, they could not invite guests to dine, since the strangers' room was unavailable.[59] Fox's Club dinner menus were written in French and the food served was more luxurious than what was ordinarily served at Brooks's.[60] Most dining clubs were not linked to specific gentlemen's clubs, but met in restaurants. Whether these clubs had one or several venues, the dinner was a central feature of the clubs' identity, since members never gathered other than for a meal.

In London, one dining club's members chose the name 'the Thirteen', as they were brought together through a desire to combat superstition and were determined to prove that there was nothing unlucky about having thirteen people seated round the dinner table.[61] In 1862, William Hardman mentioned another in his diary, 'calling itself by the presumptuous title of "our club" '.[62] This was a dinner with about forty members, who met in a restaurant in Covent Garden, for 'a plain dinner – fish, boiled beef, pigeon pie, rump steak and marrow bones, with punch at a later part of the evening'.[63] Hardman himself was not a member, but was invited by Shirley Brooks, who was. The entertainment of the evening, as at most dinner parties, lay in conversation:

The drawing of the cloth was the signal for the fun of the evening, which consisted of constant fine badinage and good-humoured personality. From eight o'clock till eleven I laughed inextinguishably. I am given to understand that sometimes these meetings don't always go off amicably: occasionally thin-skinned men are riled, because the criticism of a man's books is very free.[64]

Edmund Yates described a similar dining club, called the Fielding Club, established in 1852.[65] French literary men, like Gustave Claudin, were frequently involved in one or more dining club, which they referred to simply as *dîners*.[66] The Goncourt brothers were known to participate in the Dîner Magny along with other artists and professionals of their generation.[67] Members of the public who were interested in the goings-on at these dinners could learn more in a volume written by Auguste Lepage, devoted entirely to describing the membership lists and conversation topics of all the prominent *dîners* of Paris.[68] He cited the 'Vilains Bonshommes', founded in 1866 at the Café de Fleurus: 'with its clienèle of painters, sculptors, some already famous, others on the way to becoming so',[69] Or the 'Rigobert', a *dîner* of artists held at a restaurant whose owner, Noël, preferred to exchange dinners for works of art rather than for money.[70] Participation in these meals was not limited to members of the artistic or literary professions. Political groups, for example, could organise similar associations: 'The *café-restaurant* Durand is where some of the members of the right have their meals. These gentlemen have created a set-price dinner and lunch, which they have named *le dîner de la Poule au Pot.*'[71]

Club management and the domestication of masculinity

The club and the *cercle* provided a men-only space for sociability, and for food consumption. However, by providing a home away from home in this way, the club actually succeeded in replacing traditional domesticity with a new and exclusively masculine variation on domestic comforts. Clubs were like families in that members had to maintain a certain level of respectability for the good of the group. In a family, each member's behaviour could reflect badly on the others' reputations and the same was true in clubs. Brooks's confirmed this in a decision taken by the management committee at their monthly meeting in May 1875. The new rule stated that any member whose behaviour was deemed 'injurious to the character and interests of the club' could be asked to resign. The judgement as to what could be deemed injurious was based on the opinion either of the managers or of thirty club members. And this rule was concerned with behaviour not only within the club, but also with the way that club members behaved outside it.[72]

Clubs struggled to maintain their respectability by controlling the behaviour of their members. While many of the men who belonged to the big West End clubs may have been content to comply with club rules, and some were even instrumental in creating and maintaining them, the rules were made because they were needed. As with any family, some members had their own ideas as to what use to make of their own and the club's time and space. If rules were made to be broken, then this minute from November 1882 is a case in point:

> It having been reported that a member of the club had been in the habit for some years of receiving visits from a lady, who was shewn [sic] into the lower dressing room by his directions, and there supplied with refreshments; a letter was drawn up, which the secretary was instructed to send, requesting that this practice might be at once discontinued.[73]

In spite of complexities such as financial arrangements and the applications of a multitude of rules and regulations covering every aspect of members' actions and behaviour, clubs were essentially intended to provide comfort and a sense of belonging. Like private homes, clubs had boundaries, they had rooms with specific functions, and they had timetables for various activities. Also like homes, the running of clubs entailed a great deal of work, most of it of a mundane and domestic nature. The work of provisioning, cleaning, washing, cooking and hiring and firing servants was as much a part of the running of a club as of a domestic establishment.

Restaurants provided the middle classes with an opportunity to emulate aristocratic dinner parties without requiring the service of a large household staff and the same was true of clubs. When Francis Wey visited the Reform Club in London, he perceived it as such:

> We went into the coffee-room, a large high room giving on to a charming garden. Twenty servants in dress clothes wait on a number of small tables noiselessly and with extreme promptitude. They tread with felt soles on the thick pile of expensive carpets; plates and dishes, instead of being piled on top of one another, are brought and

removed singly. The sound of footsteps, creaky shoes, the clatter
of crockery and knives and forks are vexations unknown to the
fortunate mortals who dine in clubs. This quietude may account for
the excessive complacency of their digestions.[74]

Unlike at home, the hierarchy of decision making within the club
was unclear and open to negotiation. Within the nuclear family,
in theory at least, there was a clear pattern of privilege. The male
breadwinner was at the top, with his wife second. The wife might
have an ambiguous relationship of authority with relation to adult
sons, but a hierarchy existed in principle. In the club, all members
tended to be successful men who were used to having a degree of
decision-making power. This led to a continual need to renegotiate
club rules as each member had his own ideas about what constituted a comfortable 'home'. Club members could apply to the
management committee if they wanted a rule changed,[75] and in
theory, the committee had the final decision. In practice, however,
it must have been a difficult matter to decide whose comfort to
sacrifice, since no club could afford to lose many members.

At home, domestic tasks were the clear purview of the female
members of the household. Men might hold the purse strings,
provide authority, and offer opinions on a range of things, but
domestic work was carried out by women. Historians have emphasised the gendered aspect of consumption, pointing to the fact that
women were responsible for consumption while men looked after
production. But in clubland, there were no women, so men had to
make decisions about consumption and display, which they might
have considered beneath themselves in a domestic context. The
intended escape from the demands of the opposite sex led to an
unexpected 'domestic' situation in which men were at their most
domestic in the place that was supposed to remove them from
the constraints of the domestic sphere. Members of gentlemen's
clubs made up the management committees, charged with making
decisions about such mundane matters as when a butcher needed
to be replaced because he was not providing value for money,
or when table linens had become shabby enough to warrant the
cost of replacing them. They made these decisions in committees,
in official meetings, which were minuted for the club records.
However, though framed within public, official modes of operating,
these decisions represented men involving themselves with what
were traditionally feminine concerns.

When a club member wanted to complain about a meal he had been served, the custom was for him to 'back' his dinner bill.[76] Backed bills were discussed at the monthly meetings of the management committee and each complaint received a response by letter.[77] It is difficult to know how seriously the management committee took backed bills, but none of them was ignored. A typical minute might be:

> A dinner bill, backed by P. Didley Esq. with a complaint, was produced by the Secretary who was instructed to inform Mr. Didley that the matter would be enquired into and the cook cautioned.[78]

All backed bills were considered by the committee, and often the cook was cautioned as a result.

Club members expressed dissatisfaction, at times, with everything from price, to quality, to cooking, to the manner in which food was presented and served in the club dining rooms. An example can be found in a Brooks's management committee meeting minute from June 1883. Based on complaints from several members, a decision was made: 'The secretary was instructed to speak to the Steward with regards to the carelessness and inattention of the waiters.'[79] Complaints could be about anything, but careless service was a frequent issue for members and managers to deal with. The complaints of club members reveal, perhaps more than any other sort, the extent to which men were, or considered themselves to be, knowledgeable about food preparation. A letter to the managers of Brooks's in 1866 was typical of the complaints written and received in all gentlemen's clubs: 'Mr. Lamont . . . suggest[s] . . . that as we have now got a new cook it might be advisable occasionally to vary the bill of fare – it having been almost invariably the same . . . for the seven years during which Mr. Lamont has had the honor [sic] of being a member.'[80]

The members at Brooks's commented frequently on the quality, quantity and cost of the food served at the club.[81] Many club members revealed themselves to be well versed in the arts of cookery and good housekeeping. Though they may never have had hands-on experience of such matters, they seemed to have opinions on a range of topics which, in the private sphere, were generally the concern of women. Thus, in 1881, the committee of Brooks's made several housekeeping decisions, based on comments from members. At the meeting in March, a complaint from the Hon. H.

Leeson about the quality of food was read out. A similar letter was received and read on the same date from the Hon. H. Brougham. Brougham recommended that the current chef be replaced by 'J. Copart, who lived with the late Sir R. Musgrave.'[82] On Brougham's recommendation, 'It was decided to engage Copart at a salary of £150 a year, and that notice be given to the present cook.'[83]

Though complaints about food were frequent in all years, in May 1881, Brooks's decided to look into the food choices they were offering. 'A sub-Committee, consisting of Lord Monson . . . and Sir Henry Tafton, was appointed to enquire into the bills of fare, and to make any alterations which might be deemed advisable.'[84] A sub-committee was again formed in 1883, for the purpose of enquiring into 'the question of the amount of meat supplied to the club, and whether it would be advisable to make any alterations in the prices on the bill of fare.'[85] The following month, the sub-committee's report was read to the management committee. A further decision was taken, to look into the amounts of foods consumed within the club. In particular, the sub-committee was asked to produce a weekly statement including information on the number of pounds of meat consumed and the average per head. The committee was also asked to look into the prices charged for fish and soup and into the diet of the clubs' servants.[86]

Invitations and subscriptions

Banquets, like club meals, highlight the importance of exclusivity and exclusion in the performance of bourgeois identity. In addition, the two forms of dining often overlapped in their practices, and with regard to the individuals who took part in each. Clubs were often the locales for banquets, and club members took the initiative of organising banquets to honour visiting dignitaries, or fellow club members who were also figures of national importance. Thus, in 1850, the managers of Brooks's received a letter from several members requesting that: 'the managers will allow the great room of the club to be used for the purpose of giving the proposed entertainment to Mr. Tufnell', to which the managers agreed.[87] And similar correspondence reveals a banquet in honour of Viscount Hampden, which was organised and hosted by Brooks's members in 1884.[88] Overall, clubs and banquets united respectable men over food, and allowed them to publicly perform their role as moral, political and financial authorities in venues that were exclusive in terms of class and gender.

In 1855, the prefect of Paris wrote to the mayors of all the *arrondissements*, stating that the Emperor had approved the organisation of a banquet for 20,000 diners at the *Palais de L'Industrie* in honour of the troops returning from Crimea. The banquet was to be hosted by 'the population of Paris', and the prefect wrote: 'This is why I invite you to open a subscription in your *arrondissement* in order to cover the costs.'[89] A banquet of 20,000 covers, offered by the whole population of Paris, was clearly not as exclusive as most banquets. Yet by asking for subscribers, the banquet provided the opportunity for participants to make a statement about their wealth, their patriotism, and their willingness to participate in the rituals of public dining.

As public events, banquets received attention from the press. They were also events to commemorate, and photographers like Fradelle and Young on Regent Street presented themselves as specialists in banquet photography, and included photos of banquets on their letterhead. Banquets promoted a form of exclusivity which was different from, but related to, that of the clubs and *cercles*. At banquets, generally organised by committees whose duty it was to determine who could be included, participants could only be present at the meal if they had been invited, or had paid a subscription for the privilege of attending.

There were various types of banquets, and many ways of determining guest lists. Civic banquets often honoured visiting dignitaries, or celebrated days or people of national importance.[90] Political banquets had been an important element of the French Revolution, and even more so for the revolution of 1848, and in 1870 one commentator stated: 'Political banquets are coming back into fashion, speckled with toasts and speeches.'[91] But they never took on the same significance as they had had in 1848. In London, the Speaker of the House gave an annual series of parliamentary dinners which were commented on in the press.[92] Private banquets could be organised by certain industries to honour their employees or for people with something in common such as having attended the same school, or come from the same region.[93] In Paris, there was also a custom of organising banquets in honour of prominent individuals.[94] In such cases, a committee would send invitations to friends and would-be friends of the individual in question, inviting them to pay a subscription and attend the banquet.

Victor Hugo, as France's most beloved literary figure in his own lifetime, was honoured at many banquets. In the 1880s, Hugo's birthdays were treated almost as national holidays, and there were banquets and celebrations in his honour in Paris and many other cities, whether or not Hugo himself could attend.[95] The toasts and speeches made at a banquet, together with the food and wine that were served, formed a tribute to the individual being honoured. While the food was not always at its best, by the time it was served to the large number of people who assembled at most banquets, the composition of the menu, the choice of what to serve and how to present it, were meant to flatter diners, especially the guest of honour. However great an accolade a banquet was, it nonetheless had to compete with more intimate dinners, and especially with family dinners. Hugo's birthdays may have prompted celebrations on a national scale, but they also highlighted these tensions. Hugo was admired as a literary figure, but also as a socialist and as a family man; on some of his birthdays, it was reported that while celebrations in his name took place throughout France, he remained at home in Paris and dined with his family.[96]

Hugo was not alone in preferring to dine intimately rather than in the huge and formal setting of a banquet. In Paris, in particular, where banquets were a significant part of the culinary culture, there was much criticism aimed at them. Banquets were criticised for serving bad food as well as for being uninteresting and impersonal.[97] In 1900, a writer in L'Illustration complained about the banality of banquets, and of the toasts and speeches made.[98] Another commented that Carnot, when he was president, had had to attend so many banquets at which mediocre food was served, that he had developed the ability to 'eat with his lips', which he went on to explain meant that Carnot would 'simulate chewing' while automatically moving his fork up and down, but without actually eating anything.[99] Food was a central feature of every banquet, but it was rarely good, and eating was not the principal reason to attend.

Exclusivity was a key feature in establishing the credentials of both clubs and banquets. The excluded 'other' was as important as the member or subscriber in giving meaning to the meal. But it was not enough to simply draw the boundaries – they had to be witnessed by the public in order to be given meaning. What is common to all the meals described in this chapter is that they were all to varying degrees carried out under the gaze of, and in some instances for the benefit of, the wider excluded public. Some banquets were announced in the press at the initial planning stage, in order to attract subscribers, or simply to advertise their imminence. *L'Illustration* in Paris published lists of upcoming banquets,[100] as well as notices of banquets being organised for specific interests.

> The annual banquet for the former students of the Lycée de Metz will take place on Wednesday 27 April next, at six thirty in the evening, at the Frères Provençaux, at the Palais-Royal. Please register one day in advance. (Subscription 15 francs).[101]

Just as information about banquets and the nature of their participants was considered to be of interest to the reading public, so club membership was often made public. In Paris, each *cercle* published an Annual containing the names and addresses of each member.[102] These were intended to be for the use of other members, and were a way of publicising the status of the club through the status of its members. Banquets were reported in the press, with toasts and speeches being reproduced in full, along with descriptions of the guest lists, surroundings and, sometimes, the food itself.[103]

Dîners were of interest to the public if they were made up of prominent literary, artistic or political personalities. The Dîner Magny has already been referred to. But Auguste Lepage published catalogues of the various *dîners* of Paris. These were in two separate volumes, one devoted to the artistic and literary and another to the political. To the diners, a *dîner* might be an occasion to share a delicious meal with friends. Restaurants were chosen which offered good food at a fair price. In France, the pleasures of the table were not taken lightly, and creating a *dîner* was about sharing food as well as conversation. But for the public what was interesting was the grouping of the people, and the types of discussion they might have; food was not mentioned in the pages of Lepage's books. His descriptions ran along different lines. A typical entry was the one for 'La Vrille', which met monthly at chez Brébant:

> This dinner was established in 1879, and the first meeting took place at chez Notta on April 22nd of that year. It has only forty members – like the *Académie Française* – and refers to itself as *young*. To become a member one has to be a painter, an engraver, a sculptor,

an architect, a man of letters or a musician; this is a condition which admits no exceptions.[104]

For the *dîner* with particularly notable members, Lepage provided extensive lists, as was the case with the '*Dîner de la société des gens de lettres*' at which literary men and women ate and socialised side by side:

> M Edourard de Montagne, editor of the *Memorial diplomatic* . . . M Felix Jahier . . . Edmond Gonzales, . . . Mme Raoul de Vavery, erudite historian and imaginative novelist . . . M. du Boisgobey . . . Mme George de Peyrebrune.[105]

Another notable *dîner* was 'Les Spartiates':

> The Goncourt brothers . . . have been part of the *dîner*, as well as Paul de Saint-Victor, Arsene Houssaye and his son Henry; Paul Lacroix . . . MM. Paul Dalloz, director of the *Moniteur Universelle*; Jules Valfrey; Francis Magnard, editor-in-chief of the *Figaro*; G. de Molinari et Joussemet, from the *Debats*; Rebert Mitchel, former editor-in-chief of the *Constitutionnel*; Jules Claretie, Chronicler from the *Temps*; Fortune de Boisgobery, one of our most prolific novelists.
>
> Military men, political men, diplomats are also part of the Spartiates.[106]

Lepage gave the reading public a glimpse of the world of semi-private dining, listing members but also hinting at the kinds of discussions they had the privilege of participating in. The Spartiates, for example, were described as serious men who discussed everything except serious matters.[107] Such descriptions put the diners in the public gaze, while at the same time tantalisingly augmenting their aura of exclusivity.

If the banquet was a spectacle carried out in the public eye, then the food served, and the composition of the menu, were aspects of display equal in importance to the space, the guest list, the toasts and speeches. Menus created a feast of words for the enjoyment of eaters and of the wider public. They were generally printed on beautifully decorated cards, and were intended to be kept as souvenirs. There is no evidence as to who precisely made decisions about the content of these menus. At home, in the second half of the nineteenth century, dinner party menus were composed by able housewives. In earlier periods, gentlemen had been expected to possess the knowledge required to put together impressive meals with many courses, and while cooking was considered as manual labour, composing a menu could be an aesthetic and intellectual feat. Banquets were a masculine meal, generally organised by men for other men. The composition of a banquet menu, as opposed to a domestic one, was a creation intended for the public sphere and was the responsibility of male organisers.

Large meals at the Hotel-de-Ville in Paris were often catered by Potel & Chabot. Details of the reception there for the Lord Mayor of London in 1895 has left evidence that menus were composed through a negotiation between the caterer and the organising committee. A first menu was proposed, but rejected, though it unclear why. A second menu was then marked 'adopted.'[108] The first menu proposed by Potel et Chabot contained the following dishes:

Hors d'Oeuvre variés
Kilkef Sprodi fumé
Olives, Saucisson, Beurre

———

Truite saumonée Sauce Indienne

———

Cuissot de Chevriel Chasseur
Poulet de Mans sautés aux fonds d'Artichauds
Cailles en Bellevue

———

Sorbets au Lunil
Spooms [*sic*] au Volky

———

Faisans et Perdreaux sur Croustade
Pains de foi gras Xérès

———

Salade Venitienne

———

Glasses Suerés
Gaufrettes

———

Corbeille de Fruit
Fours et fruits glacées

———

Café, Pains, Fromages
Glace[109]

This original proposal was very different from the menu which was eventually approved by the banquet organisers. The adopted menu contained dishes that were equal in luxury to those on the first menu, but were less exotic. A decision may have been made that the Lord Mayor and his party would not appreciate exotic fare, or perhaps that it would be better for the city of Paris to impress its English guests with genuine French delicacies. In either case, the decision to serve quite standard French banquet fare would convey the message that French food was a lavish compliment to pay on official guests to the capital:

Melons Glacé

———

Filets de Soles Granité Normandes

———

Selles de Pré-Salé aux Tomates
Perdreaux à la Bohémienne
Poulardes à l'Estragon

———

Granités au Vin de Samos
Punch à la Romaine

———

Faisans rôtis truffés
Fois Gras de Nancy, glacé

———

Salade
Fonds d'Artichauds Parisienne

———

Glace Nesselrode
Gaufrettes

———

Corbeille de Fruit
Fours et fruits glacées

———

Café, Pains, Fromages
Glace[110]

Dinner at a banquet was a feast of words more than of tastes. If cultural capital could be constructed on knowledge of food and drink, then banquets displayed the great wealth of the host or organising committee, for the consumption of guests and spectators alike. It was of no consequence that a meal served to, sometimes, as many as several hundred guests could be cold and tasteless by the time it travelled to the diners' mouths. What the banquet offered was the possibility of offering a written tribute to the excellent culinary taste of the honoured guest, and the extensive culinary knowledge of the hosts. It was the beautiful words on the beautifully printed menu cards that would form the lasting impression of the banquet. And it was this lasting impression which conveyed the banquets' importance as displays of status and authority. It was through banquets that the urban elite could demonstrate that the city was their home and that they were good hosts. Words on the menu spoke to the taste of the guests. They also sought to establish the identity of the host, or host institution. The Corporation of London had a signature dish, 'Barons of Beef', which appeared frequently though, not invariably, at its public meals throughout the period but with increasing frequency around the turn of the twentieth century. Beef had long been synonymous with Englishness in the eyes of the English, the French and the rest of the world. 'Barons of Beef' was not a typical restaurant or domestic menu item, and seems to have been one which the Corporation had either invented or adopted as its own. Its regular appearance on public menus lent it an air of importance, and associated the Corporation with a solid, long-standing aspect of English culture.

Menus for civic banquets were generally lavish. A typical banquet given by the Corporation of the City of London was the one in honour of the Prefect of the Seine, and the Mayors of British and Foreign Municipalities, in 1875:

Menu

Potages.
Tortue at Tortue Claire

Poisson.
Saumon   Turbot

Relevés.
Hanches de Venaison

Rôts.
Cailles   Bardés   Canetons

Entremets.
Gelées aux Fruits   Patisserie à la Française
Meringues à la Crême   Poudins à la Nesselrode

Dessert.
Peaches   Pines Hot-House Grapes
Greengages Apricots &c.

Wines.
East India Madeira Sherry (Duff Gordon) Amontillado

Champagne.
Piper, Carte D'Or 1868   Roeder, Carte Blanche 1868
Piper, 1863 Brut
Claret, Chateau Léoville Old Port

Liqueurs.
Maraschino Grande-Chartreuse Old Cognac[111]

This was a well chosen selection of fine foods and wines. The
menu was written mostly in French, indicating that the banquet
organisers were striving for the elegance associated with French
cuisine, which English cuisine lacked. Though this was a banquet
offered to a French dignitary, it was not unusual for English
banquet menus to contain some French, mixed with English terms,
as a way of conveying knowledge of the high culinary achievements
of France.

The menu served by The Corporation of London may have presented a menu in French to the Prefect of the Seine but the food
itself was very English. The central course, and therefore the most
important dish to be served, was venison. For the English there was
a long tradition which considered venison as a highly prized meat,
and one which conveyed a sense of luxury. Similarly, turtle soup at
the start of the meal placed the banquet firmly in the tradition of
English, rather than French, luxury. If we compare this menu to
the earlier one, which was presented to the Lord Mayor in Paris
two decades later, we can see how each capital city tried to present
its own version of luxury as a way of impressing visiting dignitaries
from across the Channel. While the English menu simply named
the meats that would be served, emphasising English pride in the
quality of the meat available in their country, the French menu
placed greater emphasis on recipes, listing each course in terms of
how the various meats were prepared. This was in line with French
pride in their culinary achievement, as opposed to the English
pride in the quality of raw ingredients.

While a banquet menu could impose an aspect of the identity
of the hosts in they eyes of the guests, it could also be a way of
paying tribute to this identity. We have already seen that a dinner
offered to the Prefect of the Seine by the Corporation of the City
of London used French language and French cuisine to create

an haute-cuisine menu. When a similar meal was hosted by the City of Paris for a delegation from the Corporation of London in 1906, the French menu contained several nods to British-inspired dishes. A dinner on 15 October offered, among several more typically French items, 'Jambons de Limerick Renaissance', 'Spooms [*sic*] de Whisky', 'Pains de Canetons Stuart' and 'Glaces Victoria', while a *déjeuner* on 17 October included 'Ballotines de Rameraux a L'Écossaise'.[112] A public banquet was a feast of words, and dishes which appeared on the menu were chosen with as much regard for issues of national or municipal identity as for culinary taste and knowledge.

Women and the world of public dining

Women's relationship with the world of clubs, banquets and public eating was more complex than that of men. Recent research has shown that concepts like separate spheres and the domestication of women are inadequate to explain the multiple interactions of men and women in modern urban environments. In light of this new understanding of women's more varied opportunities in Victorian London and Paris, it is nonetheless important to highlight the fact that women's access to different kinds of meals continued to be limited. There was a small number of women-only clubs in London, and an even smaller number in Paris. There were also, as we have seen, a certain number of opportunities for mixed public dinners. In addition, women could sometimes have access to clubs and banquets in the role of visitor and observer.

In 1850, there were no opportunities for women to dine in clubs of any sort. But like restaurants, once clubs became increasingly widespread and were incorporated into the lives of growing numbers of people, women's access widened. As it was for gentlemen's clubs, the goal of clubs for ladies was to provide a space in town for women to be comfortable, to socialise, eat and, in many cases, stay overnight. However, the legitimacy of women having access to such spaces evoked concern in some corners, as did all aspects of women's access to public urban spaces. Sophia Beale complained in a letter written in the 1860s about women's lack of access to the benefits of club life: 'The camaraderie of the club; when will that be supplied? Shall we ever have clubs after the manner of the man's club?'[113] And a commentator in a successful Parisian women's periodical wrote, in 1871:

> You may have believed that we were finished with emancipated women . . . and other varieties of females, infinitely less interesting than monkeys . . . you were mistaken – These LADIES are busy renting a huge room . . . to create a *cercle*. There, until the government of the country assigns women a place in politics and administration . . . worthy of their intelligence . . . they will deliberate, work . . . however the pleasant part of club life will not be neglected, there will be . . . *salons* for conversation, game room, smoking room, restaurant and café, for those who do not enjoy looking after the fastidious details of animal life.[114]

In spite of such sentiments about the inappropriate behaviour of women wanting to enjoy club life in the way their male counterparts did, by the end of the nineteenth century, clubs for women existed in both London and Paris.

Women's clubs were inferior in status to men's, they were fewer, and were viewed with suspicion by some observers. Also, while men's clubs provided members with luxurious surroundings to recreate the ambiance of an aristocratic home, women's clubs were more modest in scale and decor. For the women who used them, London clubs were less a luxury or comfort and more a requirement for maintaining respectability while gaining access to the male-dominated public sphere. While men might take for granted their entitlement to the privileges and pleasures of club life, for women, a club provided a safe places to eat or sleep in town when that was required, and meant that it was possible to socialise with fellow members and avoid the expense as well as the social inconveniences of dining alone in a restaurant. Yet what most distinguishes men's from women's clubs is the extend to which men's clubs became a widely recognised part of the urban landscape, one of many ways in which bourgeois masculine authority was displayed in the architecture of the period, while women's clubs have remained largely unknown and invisible.

The number of clubs in London in which women could enjoy the privilege of membership increased throughout the century. There is little evidence to suggest that the women of Paris possessed clubs like the ones of London, and they may have felt less need for clubs of their own. The restaurants of Paris had always welcomed women diners. Though café culture was seen by some to be exclusively masculine, eating out in restaurants was an acceptable leisure activity for both sexes, unlike in London, where women's participation in restaurant meals was a source of concern for some. Furthermore, as the pattern of suburbanisation was far less prevalent for the bourgeoisie of Paris that for their London counterparts, Parisian women were in less need of places to retire for a rest or some refreshments on a day out in town. However, Parisian women could participate in a number of *dîners*, while English dining clubs were most often exclusively male.[115]

Clubs gave women a place to eat and socialise away from the public gaze, while they pursued activities such as shopping and seeking amusement in town, which were quickly becoming respectable elements of bourgeois women's lives. The Lyceum, a prominent London women's club, set itself up as the social equal to the exclusive gentlemen's clubs of the West End, and sought to maintain a membership of independent and successful women. Its criteria for membership, as cited in *The Englishwoman's Yearbook*, was 'ladies who have published any original work in literature, journalism, science, art, or music; who have university qualifications, or are wives or daughters of distinguished men.'[116] According to Arnold Bennett, the Lyceum was very popular among the women of his acquaintance: 'All the women I know seem to have joined the N. Lyceum club, & they are all so proud of it that they are all asking me to lunch there.'[117] Other clubs were intended less for the bourgeois lady of leisure and more for the increasing numbers of young white-collar working women, who needed to live respectably in town while earning their livings in offices and shops.

In 1880, a new club was reported to have opened in London which made an exception to the general rule of excluding ladies: 'The "Salisbury" as it is called, has its head-quarters at No. 10, St James's Square . . . the principal attraction it offers in comparison with other clubs is the privilege which members will possess of introducing ladies as visitors.'[118] This did not, however, imply that women could move freely among the male members' spaces: 'Special rooms have been set apart for the reception of the members' wives, and also their "sisters, their cousins, and their aunts".'[119] Only specific women were allowed in, and only to specified areas: 'these rooms, although partially detached from the main building, in no way differ from the apartment forming the body of the club in the matter of comfortable and luxurious fittings'.[120] And not all women were allowed in. By specifying that it was female relatives who were to be allowed as club guests, the Salisbury maintained respectability while extending the boundaries of exclusivity.

Though it was rare for London clubs to accept women as members or even visitors, there were occasions on which clubland opened its doors to the ladies. Royal, or other public processions, were the principle events around which such occasions were based. In the 1860s and 1870s, both Brooks's and the Reform regularly hosted luncheons for members and female guests – again restricted to wives and relatives for the sake of respectability – so that the ladies could view various public processions.[121] By the end of the century, this custom was disappearing, and clubs became, for the next several decades, truly masculine fortresses.[122]

The decision to invite women into men's clubs on special occasions was taken very seriously. Allowing non-members into a club was always a matter upon which members had to agree. And there had to be measures in place to monitor who gained access, and to which spaces. When a royal or other important procession was to take place, it was the management committee of Brooks's or the Reform who met to decide whether ladies should be admitted. When the decision was in the affirmative, a fixed number of places would be allotted for women guests. There would then be a ballot to determine which male members could bring a lady.[123] Successful applicants would be issued tickets. These tickets could only be used to invite female relatives since inviting other women into the club would have risked the reputation of the whole establishment. Like clubs on procession days, the Corporation of London sometimes allowed guests to bring a female relative. Being allowed to invite a woman on special occasions could accord status. This is demonstrated by decisions such as that concerning a reception held in 1908 in honour of the French President. Aldermen were allowed to bring two female guests to this reception, while commoners were only allowed to invite one. Thus the number of spaces allotted to each person depended on their status. Moreover, the number of women to whom each man could provide this honour was an outward manifestation of his importance.[124]

Banquets exposed diners to the public gaze in entirely different, and far more overt, ways than clubs or dining clubs. While lists of club members might be available to the reading public, along with vague references to topics of conversation, the diners themselves were behind closed doors. Banquets, which were larger and often with an explicitly public – often political – agenda often took place in front of an audience, and illustrations sometimes appeared in newspapers and magazines as well. This public form of dining was exclusively male and, unlike the club, was never adopted by groups of women. When women were present at banquets, they were as members of the audience, seated in galleries above the dining area in order to gain a bird's eye view of the meal and its consumers. A description of a Royal Banquet in Scotland, from the *Hotel Review* of 1886, expressed the rarity of women being present at public dinners: 'The party . . . was brilliant and distinguished, and indeed, unique, in so far as it was graced by the presence of ladies at the table, a sight rarely witnessed at a public dinner in Edinburgh or elsewhere.'[125] Separate sphere, and middle-class notions of respectability tended to preclude women's participation, even in the 1880s, when many women were claiming their right to enter the public sphere and even, in some cases, rejecting their traditional role of wife and mother.

At banquets, as in clubs, there were criteria established for who could sit down at the dinner table. Mechanisms were put in place to judge would-be eaters, and financial constraints, either in membership fees or subscriptions, further ensured that only those with enough money were included. Like all the meals described in the preceding chapters, club dinners and banquets required that participants be aware of certain basic rules of polite sociability. But like in the other examples, these rules were fluid and open to interpretation. While masculinity was enhanced though participation in homosocial rituals, men also became aware of domestic matters through their participation in management committees. And though women were excluded from some forms of public dining in mid-century, by the 1890s, there were increasing numbers of ways for women to take part in public mealtime sociability. In both France and England, meals were the principal element in bourgeois social life, and this social life was a crucial element for bringing people together, be it to form marriages, business deals or political alliances.

Notes

1 *The Caterer* (15 March 1882).

2 R. J. Morris, *Class Sect and Party: The Making of the British Middle Class, Leeds, 1820–1950* (Manchester: Manchester University Press, 1990).

3 C. Yriarte, *Les Cercles de Paris, 1828–1864* (Paris: Librairie Parisienne, 1864) p. 286.

4 S. Gunn, *The Public Culture of the Victorian Middle Class*, Manchester: Manchester University Press, 2000); D. Z. Davidson, *France after Revolution: Urban Life, Gender and the New Social Order* (London: Harvard University Press, 2007).

5 On the law of 1901, see C. Grumbach, *Loi du 1er juillet* (Paris, 1904) p. 6. According to the new law, *cercles* were defined as: 'associations . . . whose object is to provide to its members, at shared costs, distractions and intellectual or material advantages such as rooms for conversation, reading, games, consumption, etc.' p. 64.

6 See, for example: M. Agulhon, *Le Cercle dans la vie bourgeoise* (Paris: A. Colin, 1977); Morris, *Class Sect and Party*; Gunn, *The Public Culture of the Victorian Middle Class*; C. E. Harrison, *The Bourgeois Citizen in Nineteenth-Century France: Gender, Sociability and the Uses of Emulation* (Oxford: Oxford University Press, 1999).

7 Agulhon, *Le Cercle dans la vie bourgeoise*; P. Clarke, *British Clubs and Associations 1580–1800: The Origins of an Associational World* (Oxford: Oxford University Press, 2000); S-L Hoffman, 'Civility, Male Friendship and Masonic Sociability in Nineteenth-Century Germany', *Gender & History* 13:2 (2001) 224–48, O. Heilbronner, 'The German Bourgeois Club as a Political and Social Structure in the Late Nineteenth and Early Twentieth Centuries', *Continuity and Change* 13:3 (1998) 443–73; T. W. Margadant, 'Primary Schools and Youth Groups in Pre-War Paris: Les "Petits A's"', *Journal of Contemporary History* 13:2 (1978) 323–36.

8 Agulhon, *Le Cercle dans la vie bourgeoise*, pp. 31–2.

9 E. Rappaport, *Shopping for Pleasure: Women in the Making of London's West End* (Oxford: Princeton University Press, 2000) pp. 75–94.

10 L. Leroy de La Brière, *Au Cercle* (Paris: C. Lévy, 1885) pp. x–xi.

11 La Brière, *Au Cercle*, p. xi.

12 J. Rendell, 'The Clubs of St. James's: places of public patriarchy – exclusivity, domesticity and secrecy', *The Journal of Architecture*, 4:2 (1999) p. 168.

13 Baedeker, *London and its Environs* (Leipzig: Karl Baedeker, 1881) p. 70. Also 1889, pp. 73–4 and 1898, pp. 100–1.

14 'La Cuisine dans les cercles,' *Le Pot-au-Feu* (21 March 1908).

15 E. Yates, *His Recollections and Experiences*, Vol II (London: R. Bentley & Son, 1884) pp. 1–2.

16 Reform Club, General Committee, Minutes, 2 May 1851.
17 Reform Club, General Committee, Minutes, 2 May 1851.
18 Reform Club, General Committee, Minutes, 4 Dec. 1913.
19 Reform Club, General Committee, Minutes, 4 Dec. 1913.
20 See for example Cercle Artistique et Littéraire, *Annuaire*, 1882, Jockey Club, *Annuaire*, 1866, art. 23, p. 14.
21 Rendell, 'The Clubs of St. James's', p. 173.
22 ACC/2371/BC/04/103: Brooks's Club rules 1822–55. Cercle Artistique et Littéraire, *Annuaire*, 1882 and Cercle de Dauville, *Annuaire*, 1883, had similar rules, though nothing about dining.
23 ACC/2371/BC/04/103: Brooks's Club rules 1822–55.
24 ACC/2371/BC/04/103: Brooks's Club rules 1822–55, Similarly, L'Union in Paris set out specific rules about dining. See also Yriartes, *Les Cercles de Paris, 1828–1864*, p. 35.
25 ACC/2371/BC/04/103: Brooks's Club rules 1822–55.
26 Gresham Club, 18th Annual Meeting, 1861.
27 For example, the Cercle Saint-Simon was founded to bring together people with and interest in history, La Brière, *Au Cercle*, p. 169.
28 La Brière, *Au Cercle*, p. 151. This was also true of the Marmite Republicaine, which published illustrations created for the cercle by its artist members. Anon. *La Marmite en 1900* (Paris: Braun, Clément et Cie, 1901).
29 La Brière, *Au Cercle*.
30 Cercle de la Jeunesse, *Annuaire*, Paris, 1877.
31 Yiartes, *Les Cercles de Paris, 1828–1864*, pp. 47, 62, 233.
32 Yiartes, *Les Cercles de Paris, 1828–1864*, pp. 35–6.
33 See, for example: AC/2371/BC/02/006 Minute Book. Meeting of 11/04/1867; AC/2371/BC/02/006 Minute Book. Meeting of 12/07/1878.
34 A. Milne-Smith, 'A Flight to Domesticity? Making a Home in the Gentlemen's Clubs of London, 1880–1914', *Journal of British Studies*, 45 (2006) 796–818; Jane Rendell, 'The Clubs of St James's'.
35 ACC/2371/BC/02/006: Minute Book.
36 ACC/2371/BC/02/007: Minute Book.
37 ACC/2371/BC/02/008: Minute Book.
38 Reform Club, General Committee, Minutes, 14 Feb. 1851.
38 Jockey Club, *Annuaire*, 1900, art. 26, pp. 16–17.
40 Yriarte, *Les Cercles de Paris, 1828–1864*, p. 195.
41 ACC/2371/BC/02/008.
42 ACC/2371/BC/02/008.
43 ACC/2371/BC05/016: Standing Orders. Steward's Copy 1910–1919 (note 28, 30/4/1914).
44 ACC/2371/BC/05/016: Standing Orders. Steward's Copy 1910–1919 (note 31, 11/6/1914).

45 ACC/2371/BC/02/007: Minute Book and ACC/2371/BC/02/008: Minute Book.

46 ACC/2371/BC/02/008: Minute Book.

47 ACC/2371/BC/02/008: Minute Book.

48 ACC/2371/BC/02/006: Minute Book.

49 ACC/2371/BC/02/006: Minute Book.

50 ACC/2371/BC/02/007: Minute Book. See also ACC/2371/BC/02/008: Minute Book. 12 June 1895, discussion about admitting strangers to lunch.

51 ACC/2371/BC/02/008: Minute Book, see for example, 15 Dec. 1904.

52 ACC/2371/BC/02/008: Minute Book, 19 Nov. 1903.

53 ACC/2371/BC/04/077, ACC/2371/BC/04/078, ACC/2371/BC/04/079.

54 For Brooks's see, for example: ACC/2371/BC/02/008 (extraordinary general meeting, March 1896 and meeting Dec. 1896), ACC/2371/BC/02/002/01: Minutes, meeting reports 1909–28 (annual general meeting, 1911).

55 Cercle Agricole, *Annuaire*, 1863, only 58 people dined in the whole month of September, pp. 80–81. Jockey Club, Annuaire, 1914, dinners were reported to have declined by 162.

56 ACC/2371/BC/02/002/01: Minutes, meeting reports 1909–28.

57 R. Baldrick, *Dinner at Magny's* (Harmondsworth: Penguin, 1973).

58 ACC/2371/FC/01/008.

59 ACC/2371/BC/02/008.

60 ACC/2371/FC/01/009.

61 *L'Art Culinaire* (Feb. 1890).

62 W. Hardman, *A Mid Victorian Pepys*, ed. S. M. Ellis (London: Cecil Palmer, 1923–25) p. 200.

63 Hardman, *A Mid Victorian Pepys*, p. 200.

64 Hardman, *A Mid-Victorian Pepys*, Nov. 8, 1862, p. 200.

65 Yates, *His Recollections and Experiences*, pp. 235–6.

66 G. Claudin, *Mes souvenirs, les boulevards de 1840–1870* (Paris: C. Lévy, 1884) pp. 276–7.

67 Baldrick, *Dinner at Magny's*.

68 A. Lepage, *Les dîners artistiques et littéraires de Paris* (Paris: Bibliothèque des Deux-mondes, 1884).

69 Lepage, *Diners Littéraires et Artistiques de Paris*, p. 157.

70 Lepage, *Diners Littéraires et Artistiques de Paris*, p. 183.

71 *L'Art Culinaire* (May 1888).

72 AC/2371/BC/02/006 Minute Book. Meeting of 6 May 1875. See also *Le Journal Illustré*, 25 June 1865.

73 AC/2371/BC/02/007 Minute Book. Meeting of 8 Nov. 1882.

74 F. Wey, *A Frenchman Sees the English in the Fifties*, trans. and ed. V. Pirie (London: Sidgwick & Jackson, 1935) p. 54.

75 AC/2371/BC/02/006 Minute Book. Meeting of 27 Jul. 1859.

76 This is still the custom in London clubs to this day.

77 There are too many references to backed bills to provide an extensive list, since at least one was mentioned at almost every monthly meeting of both Brooks's and the Reform. See for example AC/2371/BC/02/007 Minute Book. Meeting of 4/05/1881; AC/2371/BC/02/007 Minute Book. Meeting of 13 Jun. 1883; AC/2371/BC/02/007 Minute Book. Meeting of 16 Nov. 1888.

78 AC/2371/BC/02/007 Minute Book. Meeting of 30 May 1881.

79 AC/2371/BC/02/007 Minute Book. Meeting of 13 Jun. 1883.

80 AC/2371/BC/02/006 Minute Book. Meeting of 21 Apr. 1866.

81 See for example: AC/2371/BC/02/007 Minute Book. Meeting of 16 Mar. 1888; AC/2371/BC/02/007 Minute Book. Meeting of 9/05/1888; AC/2371/BC/02/007 Minute Book. Meeting of 8 May 1889.

82 AC/2371/BC/02/007 Minute Book. Meeting of 2 Mar. 1881.

83 AC/2371/BC/02/007 Minute Book. Meeting of 2 Mar. 1881. See also AC/2371/BC/02/007 Minute Book. Meetings of 28 Mar. 1888 and 9 May 1888; AC/2371/BC/02/007 Minute Book. Meeting of 10/07/1889; AC/2371/BC/02/007 Minute Book. Meeting of 24 Oct. 1889.

84 AC/2371/BC/02/007 Minute Book. Meeting of 4 May 1881.

85 AC/2371/BC/02/007 Minute Book. Meeting of 10 Jan. 1883.

86 AC/2371/BC/02/007 Minute Book. Meeting of 14 Feb. 1883.

87 ACC/2371/BC/03/124 Brooks's Correspondence. Letter dated 4 Jul. 1850.

88 ACC/2371/BC/03/130 Correspondence 1884–85.

89 A. de P. VK3 75, 11 Dec. 1855.

90 Both the A. de P. and the Corporation of London Record office contain numerous examples of these kinds of banquets. See for example: A. de P: VK3 162, Diner offert aux colleges echevins de Bruxelles at d'Anvers, 15 Jul. 1910, VK3 162 Reception to the King and Queen of Belgium, 15 Jul. 1910, VK3 89 Diner at the Hotel de Ville, 11 May 1889, VK3 81, Inaugural Banquet at the Hotel de Ville, 13 Jul. 1882, VK3 170, Dejeuner in honour of the mayor and representatives of the city of Sophia, 29 Feb. 1912, VK3 87, Banquet for the centenary of the Dauphinois Revolution, 9 Jun. 1888, VK3 133, Reception for the members of parliament of Denmark, Sweden and Norway, 29 Nov. 1904.

91 'Courrier de Paris, 'L'Illustration (5 Feb. 1870).

92 The Hotel Gazette (14 Feb. 1880).

93 See for example A de P D13Z/1 which contains an invitation from the railway concession holders of the Exposition of 1889 to a banquet in honour of the railway employees. Also The Travellers Journal, 17 April 1880, p. 5 which contains a list of banquets hosted by Spiers

and Pond for: 'the Army pay department . . . the 95th regiment . . . the Indian Navy . . . the 74th Highlanders . . . the 49th Regiment . . . the 8th Regiment . . . the 18th regiment . . . and the Buffs'. Also: *Le Progrès Culinaire* (March 1886), *The Hotel Review* (Sept. 1886).

94 See for example: AN 428AP/2, Fond Montorgeuil, letter of 4 Nov. 1903, also 428/AP/3, two letters *c.*190?; Also: A de P D13Z/2, 1804, and D14Z/1, 1906; Reform Club archive, B101, Garibaldi Breakfast, 1864; Anon., *La Marmite en 1900*, p. 138; *L'Illustration* (2 March 1895).

95 Maison Victor Hugo. There is a box of material pertaining to Victor Hugo's birthdays in this period but the material is not formally catalogued.

96 Maison Victor Hugo.

97 See for example: *L'Illustration* (28 April 1900); Claudin, *Mes Souvenirs*, pp. 193–4 ; P. Boitard, *Guide Manuel de la bonne companie.* (Paris: Passard, 1851) p. 297; S. Beale, *Recollections of a Spinster Aunt* (London: William Heinemann, 1908) pp. 63–4.

98 *L'Illustration* (24 Feb. 1900); See also *L'Illustration* (13 May 1905).

99 *L'Illustration* (16 June 1900).

100 See *L'Illustration*, weekly, 1895–1900.

101 *L'Illustration* (23 April 1870). See also for example *L'Illustration* (1 April 1865).

102 See also, Bon de Tully, *Annuaire des Grands cercles et du grand monde* (Paris, 1901). The *Annuaire* for La Marmite, in 1900, published the names of members along with their occupations.

103 See, for example: *L'Illustration* (17 March 1860); *Le Journal Illustré* (14 Feb. 1864).

104 Lepage, *Les dîners artistiques et littéraires de Paris*, p. 73.

105 Lapage, *Les dîners artistiques et littéraires de Paris*, pp. 5–7.

106 Lepage, *Les dîners artistiques et littéraires de Paris*, pp. 44–5.

107 Lepage, *Les dîners artistiques et littéraires de Paris*, p. 46.

108 A. de P. VK3 102.

109 A. de P. VK3 102. Reception du Lord Mayor de Londres 15 Sept. 1895.

110 A. de P. VK3 102. Reception du Lord Mayor de Londres 15 Sept. 1895.

111 Corporation of London records Office. Entertainments. Banquet given by the Corporation of the City of London to the Prefect of the Seine and the Mayors of British and Foreign municipalities, in the Guildhall, Thursday 29 July 1875.

112 Corporation of London records Office. Entertainments. Visit of the Corporation to Paris, October 1906.

113 Beale, *Recollections of a Spinster Aunt*, p. 141. This was written in a letter to her cousin Mary, probably in the early 1860s.

114 E. de Mursen, 'Le Cercle des femmes,' *La Mode de Paris* (Dec. 1871).

115 See, for example, Lepage, *Diners Littéraires et Artistiques de Paris*, p. 207.

116 L.M.H. *The Englishwoman's Yearbook* (London: Hatchards, 1905). See also yearbooks for 1906–13.

117 A. Bennett, *The Letters of Arnold Bennett*, Vol. II. ed. J. Hepburn (Oxford: Oxford University Press, 1968) p. 191. This is from a letter written to Edith Evors on 18 August 1904.

118 *Traveller's Journal* (28 Feb. 1880)

119 *Traveller's Journal* (28 Feb. 1880).

120 *Traveller's Journal* (28 Feb. 1880).

121 See for example: AC/2371/BC/02/006 Minute Book. Meeting of 18 Feb. 1863; AC/2371/BC/02/006; Minute Book. Meeting of 3 Mar. 1863; AC/2371/BC/02/007 Minute Book. Meeting of 1 Jun. 1887; AC/2371/BC/02/007 Minute Book. Meeting of 15 Jun. 1887; AC/2371/BC/02/007 Minute Book. Meeting of 14 Jun. 1893.

122 See for example: AC/2371/BC/02/008 Minute Book. Meeting of 19 Oct. 1900; AC/2371/BC/02/008 Minute Book. Meeting of 19 Dec. 1900; AC/2371/BC/02/008 Minute Book. Meeting of 16 Jan. 1901; AC/2371/BC/02/008 Minute Book. Meeting of 28 Jan. 1901.

123 See for example: AC/2371/BC/02/006 Minute Book. Meeting of 10 Nov. 1852 and 16 Nov. 1852.

124 CLRO 27 May 1908.

125 *The Hotel Review* (Sept. 1886). Similarly, *L'Illustration* on 22 April 1865 reported on a banquet where women were, surprisingly, present.

Conclusion

James Vernon's recent study on hunger in modern Britain challenges historians to think about food in history in a new light.[1] Looking at the politics of hunger, and at the changing concepts of its causes, consequences and cures in modern Britain, Vernon has allowed us to think of food as more than just sustenance. Through his analysis, it becomes clear that nutrition is a social issue, involving both the state and the public. Hunger, Vernon argues, is about more than lack of food. It is about deficiencies in nutrition as well as about the lack of a public voice for the hungry. This book has looked at the social role of food from the opposite end of the social spectrum, focusing not on hunger but rather on those who had too much and were continually in a position to make choices about where, when and with whom to eat. Yet the questions this provokes makes it similar in some ways to Vernon's work, in historicising the need to confront a new situation in which abundance of food is present, but is not used to eradicate social division. Thus while Vernon has found a newly emerging set of ideas and projects for eradicating hunger, the ways in which the bourgeoisie wrote and thought about food suggest that food was an important marker of distinction, and that class divisions that people clung to were predicated on, among other things, having access to different (as well as better and more abundant) food than was available to those in the classes below.

The middle classes of London and Paris were a diverse constituency brought together by their ability to make choices beyond subsistence, and by the boundaries within which they elected to make those choices. Their wealth, and the modern, capitalist cities they inhabited, changed the way that people eat. Nourishment was an important reason to sit down to a meal, but for the men and women living in London and Paris in the nineteenth century, other reasons became almost as important. The meals could be occasions for training children to become well-behaved adults, a time for interacting with old friends and for making new ones, for showing oneself in public or for demonstrating belonging to a particular group or social environment.

Between 1850 and 1914, there were continuities as well as changes in how, what and where people ate. Some of the changes were ongoing, with their origins in the eighteenth and early nineteenth centuries. Chief among these were the change from midday to early evening dinner time, along with the introduction of lunch as the midday meal, the fashion for tea as a drink and social occasion, and the gradual move from à la française service to à la russe. Each of these was linked to the growth of the middle class, and to how this class placed its mark on the daily rituals of European life. Changes in mealtimes were, at least in part, an outcome of changes in working and living patterns, involving long workdays and the separation of home and work. Similarly, afternoon tea, which brought leisured women together during their men's workdays were also a cultural outcome of the gendered division of labour and the separation of home and work. Changes in the style of meal services reflected a democratisation of who could afford to entertain, as an à la russe meal required fewer dishes and a smaller domestic staff than did the older style à la française.

Even more notable changes occurred in the world of public dining. Though clubs were not new to this period, the last decades of the nineteenth century have been identified as a time when men showed more inclination for homosocial institutions than for the comforts of home or the company of women. Though clubs are more usually identified with British masculinity, and have not been widely studied in their French guise as cercles, there is ample evidence to suggest that in both Paris and London the opportunity to belong held great appeal, and one of the reasons for this was the possibility it gave to have a meal in a congenial venue where one could feel at home without feeling the constraints of home. Banquets had been a long-standing tradition in French masculine and political life, which was not paralleled in England. Yet after 1848, French banquets became less political and were, instead, adapted by the bourgeois mainstream as a way to combine socialising with a public display of belonging to an exclusive group. In both

London and Paris, civic banquets were a feature when receiving official visits, and an obvious way to show hospitality while, at the same time, showing off the host city's taste and culture.

Restaurants, first in Paris and then elsewhere, caused the biggest changes in eating habits by opening up the possibility of fine dining to the widest possible audience. Membership did not need to be applied for and, unlike at home, no domestic staff was needed. Indeed the only explicit requirement was the ability to pay for the meal. Restaurants were on the whole democratic, yet they did not do away with class distinctions. On the contrary, restaurants conformed to, and found ways to reinforce, existing social hierarchies. While restaurants extended the concept of eating as leisure, and brought meals into public view, there were gradations of restaurant based on cost and location. There was also a body of knowledge to be acquired in order to succeed at eating out, principally in terms of how to read and order from a menu. Because restaurants were French in origin, and because French persisted as the language of haute cuisine throughout the period, learning how to eat out was a greater challenge in London than it was in Paris. But, through the period, change can be observed not only in terms of the increase in the number of restaurants; there was also a clear extension in the range of restaurant types, many of which created more acceptable ways for people from the middle classes to enjoy eating out.

As well as change, continuities are also clearly evident in the way people ate. Though the scarcity of meat during the siege of Paris gave rise to the French taste for horse meat, in general, people's tastes in food did not alter. Likewise, the concept of the family dining room as the heart of the home, both for intimate family gatherings and the cementing of bonds of friendship, persisted unchanged. So too did table manners, which were repeated decade after decade in the pages of etiquette books, whose authors often plagiarised earlier works, with little regard for changes occurring in the society they addressed. Yet there were important changes in the availability of food, brought about by improved transportation and preservation technologies, which meant that though national cuisines did not change, diets did become increasingly detached from seasons and regions.

Comparing Paris and London has suggested interesting differences and even more interesting similarities. Discourse surrounding each city tended to highlight different features. In Paris, these features can be grouped into two areas. The first is tied to the history of political upheaval, which characterised the French experience from 1789 onward. This led to the banning of the term 'club', yet clubs existed under other names, though with explicit rules forbidding politics as a topic of conversation. It also led to medical and etiquette writers' deep and persistent suspicion of political discussions at dinner, which were argued to have a deleterious effect on both social standing and the digestive process. The second set of features characterising Parisian discourses centres on Paris's role as the culinary and aesthetic capital. Men ranging from the celebrity chef Auguste Escoffier to the politician and art critic Charles Blanc, to the prefect of the Seine Baron Haussmann, all participated in putting Paris at the forefront on judgements of good taste in all walks of life.

Victorian London appears in a different light, with Britain's role as industrial and economic superpower, along with its 'Victorian values' tending to be paramount. London also appears to us as a city of contrast, with extremes of wealth and poverty, plenty and deprivation. People like Henry Mayhew and Charles Booth brought the plight of impoverished Londoners to the attention of the middle classes. Yet when one looks into the social and cultural practices, and especially the rounds of dinner parties and evening entertainments that seem to occupy much of their time, one can almost be forgiven for falling back on clichés about the well-off bourgeoisie as a class of heedless oppressors. And in both cities, we can easily see where tensions arise between the uprightness of the moderate bourgeoisie and their need to carve a path in urban environments which were often portrayed as depraved, crime-ridden and frighteningly unknowable. Generally, in their daily lives, and especially at mealtimes, the bourgeoisie of Paris and London shrouded themselves in the rules of polite behaviour while enjoying the worryingly large quantities of food and wine they could afford.

But London and Paris were both centres of consumption, watching each other's developments and quickly adopting or adapting new forums for spending money and leisure time. The restaurant and, some time later, the department store were pioneered in Paris but went on to find equal success in London. In each city there was an appetite for new and interesting foods, consistent with a more general appetite for novelty, which was fed by department store merchandise and also by events like the Great Exhibition and its successors, which brought the world to the doorsteps of London and Paris. The desire for novelty, part of the overarching capitalist environment that fuelled the bourgeois way of living, gave rise to multitudes of catering venues and to new ways of offering up what – once it was on the plate – was recognisably a meal just like any other.

London and Paris resembled each other in other ways, beyond their similarities as capitals of culture and consumption. When we begin to think in more detail about the bourgeoisie and what their eating habits reveal about their sense of themselves and of the world around them, what emerges is a class which is transnational and has more in common with fellow bourgeois in other cities than with members of other classes in their own country or city. Through their eating habits, the middle classes reveal the ambivalences that come with the social middle ground: neither greed nor extreme abstemiousness were to be tolerated and good manners – mostly concerning the need for self-control – were presented as the key to entry into good society. At the same time, individuals' stories, where they can be found, show a flexible approach to manners, and an openness to mealtime sociability of all kinds. Most British and European historians continue to focus on the national state as the meaningful boundary within which to look for historical change, even at a time when the idea of the nation state has been called into question. Yet comparative histories like this one can offer the opportunity of gaining a greater understanding of how factors such as wealth and cultural aspiration combined, in a period of great advances in transportation and communication, to facilitate the emergence of ideals and behaviours that transcended national borders. It is to be hoped that more research into the ways in which cultural ideals are formed and disseminated will encourage historians to look beyond national borders and, perhaps, use comparative methods to enhance our understanding of how factors such as national and regional identity interacted with class and gender in shaping individual experiences in daily life.

By looking at a series of discourses and locations, this book has highlighted some significant ways in which class and gender identities were shaped by meals. Yet many avenues of research were thrown up in the course of this study, which could not be pursued, owing to constraints of time and space. This book has looked at the middle classes of London and Paris. Living in the great cities of the age, these men and women had access to choices and to spaces which were not paralleled in the provincial cities and towns of France or England. In her groundbreaking study of French restaurants, Rebecca Spang uncovered a document which suggests that, as late as 1851, outside of Paris, no mayor in France, when asked to list the restaurants in his locality, was willing to give a single establishment that name. By the end of the century, as the careers of Ritz and Escoffier make clear, restaurants had spread through France, England and the rest of Europe. Yet, very little is known about the relationship between metropolitan and provincial eating habits. This is true of restaurant dining as much as of other forms of mealtime sociability. While Amélie Weiler, a doctor's daughter from Strasbourg, learned similar domestic arts – and described them in similar ways – from her mother in the 1840s as M. V. Hughes did in London in the 1870s, it would be worth knowing more about how class-based practices such as hosting dinner parties and dining out were experienced in smaller towns, where there was less aristocrat influence and also a less international population.

The international characters of both London and Paris, each with its overseas empire, each a centre for increasingly global trade and commerce, each hosting a series of exhibitions throughout the period, is another area for further study. There have already been several studies of food and Empire, but there is more to learn about the impact of foreign food on the domestic and public meals of the metropolises. By the end of the nineteenth century, London had a number of Italian restaurants, and the influence of India was being felt in both home cooked and restaurant food, with Lyons' introducing a curry night in their chain of Cornerhouse restaurants. Paris had some English and American restaurants, but too little is known about French cuisine beyond our assumption that the immense part played by French haute cuisine in shaping national identity must have largely precluded any French interest in foreign delicacies.

From 1850 to 1914, bourgeois identities were consolidated. In their metropolitan context, these identities were shaped by the urban environment, as city centres were increasingly experienced as spaces of leisure and consumption. Conflicts over who could inhabit the public sphere were played out via anxious discourse over women's access to clubs and restaurants and the temptations they placed at the disposal of anyone with money to spend. At home, boundaries between private and public, and men and women, were marked by flexible approaches to commensality, while men also found a new form of domesticity within the confines of the private club. Yet this world of respectability, in which etiquette presented clearly articulated rules for recognising who belonged, thereby protecting class boundaries, was about to be challenged, and eventually altered beyond recognition, starting with the Great War of 1914 to 1918. But the middle classes and their mores did not vanish in the twentieth century. And indeed, even today, many of our assumptions and attitudes towards our bodies and what we eat can be traced back to the nineteenth century.

Note

1 J. Vernon, *Hunger: A Modern History* (London: Harvard University Press, 2007).

Bibliography

Primary sources

Books

Agogos. *Hints on Etiquette and the Usages of Polite Society: With a Glance at Bad Habits*, 26th edn (London: Longman & Co., 1849).

Alq, Mme Louise D'. *Le Maître et la maîtresse de maison*, 2nd edn (Paris: Bureau des Causerie Familiaire, 1875).

Anon. *Album général ameublement Parisien* (Paris: Camis, 1891).

Anon. *Annuaire du Jockey Club* (Paris, 1866).

Anon. *Annuaire du Jockey Club* (Paris, 1889).

Anon. *Annuaire du Jockey Club* (Paris, 1900).

Anon. *Annuaire du Jockey Club* (Paris, 1911).

Anon. *L'Art de plaire et de briller en société.* (Paris, 1879).

Anon. *Le Banquet des Egaux* (Paris: C. Joubert, 1851).

Anon. *Cassell's People's Physician: A Book of Medicine and of Health for Everybody*, 5 vols (London: Cassell & Co., 1900–15).

Anon. *The Etiquette of Courtship and Matrimony: with a complete guide to the forms of a wedding* (London, 1865).

Anon. *The Family Physician: A Manual of Domestic Medicine. By physicians and surgeons of the principal London hospitals*, 2nd edn (London: Cassell & Co., 1879).

Anon. *How to Dine; or, etiquette of the Dinner Table* (London: Ward, Lock and Tyler, 1879).

Anon. *How to Entertain; or etiquette for Visitor* (London: Ward, Lock and Tyler, 1876).

Anon. *The Lady's Manual of Modern Etiquette* (London, 1864).

Anon. *La Marmite en 1900.* (Paris: Braun, Clément et Cie, 1901).

Anon. *Les Petits Paris, Paris-Restaurant* (Paris: A. Taride, 1854).

Anon. *Salle à manger de bon goût dans les styles Louis XVI, Directoire et moderne par un comité de dessinateurs* (Paris: C. Moreau, n.d.).

Anon. *Table Etiquette, Domestic Cookery and Confectionary* (London, 1854).

Baedeker, Karl. *London and its Environs* (Leipzig: Karl Baedeker, 1881).

Baedeker, Karl. *London and its Environs* (Leipzig: Karl Baedeker, 1889).

Baedeker, Karl. *London and its Environs* (Leipzig: Karl Baedeker, 1989).

Baedeker, Karl. *Paris and its Environs* (Leipzig: Karl Baedeker, 1865).

Baedeker, Karl. *Paris and its Environs* (Leipzig: Karl Baedeker, 1874).

Baedeker, Karl. *Paris and its Environs* (Leipzig: Karl Baedeker, 1888).

Banting, William. *Letter on Corpulence*, 3rd edn (London: Harrison, 1864).

Bargny, Jeanne de. *Code de la Femme du Monde, Journal d'une américaine* (Paris: aux bureaux de 'la Mode pour tous', 1890).

Bassanville, Mme la Comtesse de. *Code du cérémonial guide des gens du monde dans toutes les circonstances de la vie*, 4th edn (Paris: Lebigre-Duquesne frères, 1868).

Beale, Sophia S. *Recollections of a Spinster Aunt* (London: William Heinemann, 1908).

Beeton, Isabella. *Mrs Beeton's Book of Household Management* (London: S. O. Beeton Publishing, 1861).

Bennett, Arnold. *Journals of Arnold Bennett*, Vol I, ed. N. Flower (London: Cassell, 1933).

Bennett, Arnold. *The Letters of Arnold Bennett*, Vol. II. ed. J. Hepburn (Oxford: Oxford University Press, 1968).

Blanc, Charles. *Grammaire des arts décoratifs, décoration intérieur de la maison* (Paris: Librairie Renouard, 1870).

Bloom, Ursula. *Sixty Years of Home* (London: Hurst & Blackett, 1960).

Boitard, Pierre. *Guide Manuel de la bonne companie* (Paris: Passard, 1851).

Booth, Lorenzo. *A Series of Original Design for Decorative Furniture* (London: Houlston and Wright, 1864).

Bourdeau, Louis. *Histoire de l'alimentation* (Paris: Alcan, 1894).

Boursin, Eugène. *Le Livre de la femme au XIXème siècle* (Paris, 1865).

Brame, Caroline. *Le Journal intime de Caroline B.* ed. Georges Ribeill and Michelle Perrot (Paris: Montalba, 1985).

Cercle Agricole. *Annuaire* (Paris, 1863).

Cercle de la Jeunesse. *Annuaire* (Paris, 1877).

Chapus, Eugene. *Manuel de l'homme et de la femme comme il faut* (Paris: A. Bourdilliat, 1861).

Cheadle, Eliza. *Manners in Modern Society: Being a Book of Etiquette* (London, 1872).

Cheyne, Geroge. *The English Malady* (London: G. Strahan, 1733).

Claudin, Gustave. *Mes souvenirs, les boulevards de 1840–1870* (Paris: C. Lévy, 1884).

Cloquet, L. *Traité d'architecture* (Paris: Baudry, 1898).

Coppée, François. *Souvenirs d'un parisien* (Paris: A. Lemerre, 1910).

Crichton-Brown, Sir James. *Delusions in Diet: or, Parsimony in Nutrition* (London: Funk and Wagnalls Company, 1910).

Curtis, John Harrison. *Advice on the Care of the Health* (London: Whittaker, 1845).

Daly Cèsar. *L'Architecture privée au XIXe siècle* (Paris: Ducher & Cie, 1870).

Davidson, W. *A Treatise on Diet, Comprising the Natural History, Properties, Composition, Adulterisations and uses of Vegetables, Animals, Fishes & c. used as Food* (Glasgow: Blackie, 1846).

Dobell, Horace. *On Diet and Regimen in Sickness and Health*, 5th edn (London: H. K. Lewis, 1872).

Douglas, A. E. *The Etiquette of Fashionable Life* (London: Easingwold, 1849).

Drohojowska, Comtesse. *De la Politesse et du bon ton, ou devoir d'une femme chrétienne dans le monde*, 7th edn (Paris: V. Sarlit, 1878).

Dufaux, Ermance. *Le savoir-vivre dans la vie ordinaire et dans les cérémonies civiles et religieuses* (Paris: Garnier frères, 1883).

Eastlake, Charles Locke. *Hints on Household Taste in Furniture, upholstery and other details*, 2nd edn, revised (London: Longmans, Green and Co., 1868).

Edis, Robert. *Decoration and Furniture of Town Houses* (London: C. Kegan Paul & Co., 1881).

Escoffier, Auguste. *Memories of my Life*, trans. Laurence Escoffier (London: Van Nostrand Reinhold, 1997).

Escoffier, Auguste. *Souvenirs inédits: 75 ans au service de l'art culinaire* (Marseille: J. Lafitte, 1985).

Fonssagrives, J.-B. *Hygiène alimentaire des malades, des convalescents et des valétudinaire, ou, Du régime envisagé comme moyen thérapeutique*. 3rd edn (Paris: J.-B. Baillière et fils, 1881).

Foote, Edward B. *Dr. Foote's Home Cyclopedia of Popular Medicine, Social and Sexual Science* (London: L. N. Fowler, 1906).

Forsyth, J. S. *The Natural and Medical Dieteticon* (London: Sherwood, Gilbert and Piper, 1824).

Fréminville, Bernard de. *Marthe: Recueil de lettres extraites d'une correspondance familiale, 1892–1902* (Paris: Seuil, 1981).

Gaultier, Armand. *L'Alimentation et le régime chez l'homme sain et chez les malades* (Paris: Masson, 1904).

Gencé, Comtesse de. *Madame est servie ou l'art de recevoir à sa table* (Paris, 1910).

Green and Stansby. *No. 21, Old Bond Street. Important and early sale, removed from Regent's Park, and St. John's Wood . . . A catalogue of a valuable assemblage of capital nearly new modern furniture . . . which will be sold . . . by Messrs. Green and Stansby . . . May 13 and 14, 1858, etc.* (Lambeth: H. Kemshead, 1858).

Gresham Club. *18th Annual Meeting* (London, 1861).

Grumbach, Charles. *Loi du 1er juillet* (Paris, 1904).

Guadet, J. *Éléments et théorie de l'architecture* (Paris: Librairie de la Construction Moderne, 1902).

Guichard, Edouard. *De l'ameublement et de la décoration intérieure de nos appartements* (Paris: E. Rouvergre, 1880).

Haig, Alexander. *Diet and Food in Relation to Strength and Power of Endurance, Training and Athletics* (London: Churchill, 1902).

Hardman, Sir William. *A Mid Victorian Pepys.* 2 vols, ed. S. M. Ellis (London: Cecil Palmer, 1923–25).

Hayward, Abraham. *The Art of Dining* (London: Murray, 1852).

Hughes, M. V. *A London Child of the 1870s* (Oxford: Oxford University Press, 1977).

Hughes, M. V. *A London girl of the 1880s* (Oxford: Oxford University Press, 1978).

Hughes, M. V. *A London Home in the 1890s* (Oxford: Oxford University Press, 1978).

Hughes, M. V. *London at Home* (London: W. Morrow & Co., 1931).

James, Emily. *The Englishwoman's Yearbook and Directory* (London: Hatchards, 1900).

James, Emily. *The Englishwoman's Yearbook and Directory* (London: Hatchards, 1904).

James, E. *The Englishwoman's Yearbook and Directory* (London: Hatchards, 1905).

James, E. *The Englishwoman's Yearbook and Directory* (London: Hatchards, 1906).

James, E. *The Englishwoman's Yearbook and Directory* (London: Hatchards, 1911).

James, E. *The Englishwoman's Yearbook and Directory* (London: Hatchards, 1913).

Kerr, R. *The Gentleman's House; or, how to plan English Residences from the Parsonage to the Palace; with tables of accommodation and cost,* 3rd edn, revised (London: John Murray, 1871).

L. M. H. [Hubbard] *The Englishwoman's Yearbook* (London: Hatchards, 1882).

L. M. H. *The Englishwoman's Yearbook* (London: Hatchards, 1905).

La Brière, L. L. de. *Au Cercle* (Paris: C. Lévy. 1885).

Lambert, T. *Meubles de salle à manger modernes* (Paris: Tous les libraires, c.1905).

Lasègue, E. C. 'De l'anorexie hystérique', *Archives générales de médecine* 21 (1873) 385–403.

Lepage, A. *Les dîners artistiques et littéraires de Paris* (Paris: Bibliothèque des Deux-mondes, 1884).

Le Verrier, L. *Journal d'une jeune fille Second Empire: 1866–1878.* ed. Lionel Mirisch (Paris: Cadeilhan, 1994).

Linière, Alice de. *Faites Ceci Dites Cela: guide pratique du savoir vivre et des usages mondains* (Paris: Librairie, 1913).

Loftie, Mrs M. J. *The Dining Room*, Art at Home Series (London: Macmillan and Co., 1876).

Lovett, William. *Elementary Anatomy and Physiology, for schools and private instruction: with lessons on diet, intoxicating drinks, tobacco and disease* (London: Darton, 1851).

Marianne, Mlle. *La Bonne Cuisine pour tout le monde de la ville et de la campagne* (Paris: C. Douniol, 1862).

M. H. E. *A Manual of Etiquette for Ladies and Gentlemen* (London: George Routledge & Sons, 1907).

Macfadden, Bernard Adolphus. *The Power and Beauty of Superb Womanhood. How they are lost and how they may be regained* (London: Macfadden Physical Development, 1901).

Macqueen-Pope, W. *Goodbye Piccadilly* (London: Joseph, 1960).

Maincent, E. *La Disposition des appartements. Intérieurs complet* (Paris: Librairie du Garde-meuble, 1883).

Marcé, Louis-Victor. 'Note on a form of Hypochondriacal Delusion Consecutive to the Dyspepsias and Principally Characterized by the Refusal of Food', trans. Andrew Blewett and Alain Bottéro [first published 1860]. *History of Psychiatry* 5 (1994) 273–83.

Marriott, T. *Female Conduct, Being an Essay on the Art of Pleasing* (London, 1759).

Mayo, Herbert. *The Philosophy of Living*, 3rd edn (London: John W. Parker, 1851).

Monin, Erneste. *L'Hygiène de l'estomac* (Paris: O. Doin, 1888).

Mornand, Félix. *L'Annee anecdotique: petits mémoires du temps* (Paris: E. Dentu, 1860).

Morris, Thomas. *A House for the Suburbs, Socially and Architecturally sketched* (London: Simpkin, Marshall, 1870).

Murray, J. Alan. *The Economy of Food: A Popular Treatise on Nutrition, Food and Diet* (London: Constable, 1911).

Newnham-Davis, Lieut.-Col. *Dinners and Diners: Where and How to Dine in London* (London: Grant Richards, 1899).

O'Connor, T. P. (MP) *Trocadero: The Old and the New* (n.d.) (Lyons Archive AC 3572/232).

P. D. S. *Mrs. Tomkins in Town* (London: W. Whiteley, 1882).

Parisienne, Une. *Les Usages du siècle: lettres, conseils pratiques, savoir vivre* (Paris, 1908).

Parr, Catherine. *L'usage et le bon ton de nos jours* (Paris: Rueff, 1892).

Parry, T. *On Diet, with its Influence on Man* (London: S. & J. Bentley, Wilson and Fley, 1844).

Raymond, E. *La Civilité non puérile, mais honnête* (Paris: Firmin-Didot frères, 1865).

Remon, George. *Intérieurs modernes* (Paris: Librairie de l'art ancien et moderne, 1907).

Rossetti, W. M. *The Diary of W. M. Rossetti, 1870–1873.*, ed. O. Bornand (Oxford: Clarendon Press, 1977).

Routledge, George. *Routledge's Etiquette for Gentlemen* (London: Routledge, 1864).

Routledge, George. *Routledge's Etiquette for Ladies* (London: Routledge, 1864).

Saverny, Marie de *Le Femme chez elle* (Paris: bureaux de la 'Revue de la Mode', 1876).

Savory, John. *A Compendium of Domestic Medicine and Companion to the Medicine Chest* (London: John Churchill, 1852).

Schlueter, August. *A Lady's Maid in Downing Street.* ed. M. Duncan (London: T. Fisher Unwin, 1922).

Scott, Clement William. *How they Dined us in 1860 and How They Dine us Now* (a souvenir booklet issued by the Trocadero Restaurant) (London, 1900).

Shaw, Donald (pseud. One of the Old Brigade). *London in the Sixties* (London: Everett, 1908).

Simoneton, Adrien. *La Décoration intérieur* (Paris: Aulanier, 1893).

Simpson's Restaurant, *Two Hundred Years (A souvenir)* (London: St Mary Press, 1923).

Stanhope, Philip Donmer, Fourth Earl of Chesterfield, *Encyclopædia of Manners and Etiquette* (London: H. G. Bohn, 1850).

Stevenson, J. J. *House Architecture.* Vol. II. *House-Planning* (London: Macmillan, 1880).

Thompson, Sir H. *Diet in Relation to Age and Activity, with Hints Concerning Habits Conductive to Longevity* (London: Frederick Warne, 1902).

Timbs, John *Clubs and Club life in London, with anecdotes of its famous coffee houses, hostelries and taverns, from the seventeenth century to the present time* (London: Richard Bentley, 1872).

Tours, Constant de. *Vingt jours à Paris pendant l'exposition universelle 1889* (Paris: Quantin, 1889).

Trusler, John. *The Honour of the Table, or Rules for Behaviour During Meals; with the whole art of carving* (London: Literary-Press, 1791).

Tully, Bon de. *Annuaire des Grands Cercles et du grand monde* (Paris, 1901).

Villeneuve, Théodore. *Intérieurs d'appartements de haut style vus en perspectives d'après les travaux des frères Guéret* (Paris: A. Guérinet, *c.*1895).

Warren, Mrs. E. *How I Managed my House on two hundred pounds a year* (London, 1864).

Weiler, Amélie *Journal d'une jeune fille mal dans son siècle,* ed. N. Stroskopf (Strasbourg: La Nuée bleu, 1994).

Wey, Francis. *A Frenchman sees the English in the Fifties.* trans. and ed. Valérie Pirie (London: Sidgwick & Jackson, 1935).

Wheeler, Gervase. *The Choice of a Dwelling: A Practical Handbook of Useful Information* (London: John Murray, 1872).

Yates, Edmund. *His Recollections and Experiences* (London: R. Bentley & Son, 1884).

Yriarte, Charles. *Les Cercles de Paris, 1828–1864* (Paris: Librairie parisienne, 1864).

Periodicals

L'Art Culinaire.

The Caterer and Refreshment Contractors Gazette.

Cornhill Magazine.

La Cuisine française et étrangère.

Le Figaro

The Hotel and Tavern Advertiser.

The Hotel Gazette.

The Hotel News.

The Hotel Review and Catering and Food Trades Gazette.

The Hotel World.

L'Illustration.

L'Illustrateur des Dames.

The Lady.

La Mode de Paris.

La Petite revue illustrée littéraire, artistique et gastronomique.

Le Petit Journal illustré.

Le Pot-au-feu.

Le Progrès du cuisiner.

The Queen.

The Restaurant.

La Salle à Manger.

The Travellers Journal and Hotel Gazette.

Manuscripts and archives

Archives de Paris, Fonds Privée Famille Labaty (DE1/11/120).

Archives de Paris, Administration Communale, VK3 75.

Archives de Paris, Administration Communale, VK3 76.

Archives de Paris, Administration Communale, VK3 87.

Archives de Paris, Administration Communale, VK3 102.

Archives Nationales de France, Fonds Georges Montorgueil, 428AP.

Archives Nationales de France, Relevé par département des débitants de boisson, hôteliers, restaurateurs, etc. 1851–1852. F7 3025.1/216p.

Archives Nationales de France, Exposition universelle 1867. Concessions restaurants. F12 11902.

Archives Nationales de France, Exposition universelle 1889. Restaurant, cafés, brasseries. F12 3771.

Archives Nationales de France, Exposition universelle 1889. Concession divers. F12 3836.

Archives Nationales de France, Exposition universelle 1900. Banquet des maires. F12 4094.

Archives Nationales de France, Etudes de Notaires, Inventaires après décès. Etude VI.

Archives Nationales de France, Etudes de Notaires, Inventaires après décès. Etude XV.

Archives Nationales de France, Etudes de Notaires, Inventaires après décès. Etude XXXIII.

Archives Nationales de France, Etudes de Notaires, Inventaires après décès. Etude XXXIV.

Bibliothèque Historique de la Ville de Paris, Service Actualité.

Corporation of London Record Office, Hospitality Files.

Guildhall London, Greshams Club, The Eighteenth Annual Meeting of the Club Held May 2nd, 1861. Broadside 20.54.

London Metropolitan Archive, Brooks's Club Archives, ACC/2371/BC/01/011 File of Correspondence of Henry Bandret, 1854–1872.

London Metropolitan Archive, Brooks's Club Archives, ACC/2371/BC/02/002/01 Minutes, proceedings, reports 1909–1928.

London Metropolitan Archive, Brooks's Club Archives, ACC/2371/BC/02/006 Minute Book, 1850–1880.

London Metropolitan Archive, Brooks's Club Archives, ACC/2371/BC/02/007 Minute Book 1880–1894.

London Metropolitan Archive, Brooks's Club Archives, ACC/2371/BC/02/008 Minute Book 1894–1909.

London Metropolitan Archive, Brooks's Club Archives, ACC/2371/BC/02/017/A Minutes of House Committee Meetings 1893–1901.

London Metropolitan Archive, Brooks's Club Archives, ACC/2371/BC/02/026 Minutes of House Committee Meetings 1901–1915.

London Metropolitan Archive, Brooks's Club Archives, ACC/2371/BC/03/124 Correspondence 1846–1855.

London Metropolitan Archive, Brooks's Club Archives, ACC/2371/BC/03/126 Correspondence 1860–1869.

London Metropolitan Archive, Brooks's Club Archives, ACC/2371/BC/03/130 Correspondence 1884–1885.

London Metropolitan Archive, Brooks's Club Archives, ACC/2371/BC/03/131 Correspondence 1886.

London Metropolitan Archive, Brooks's Club Archives, ACC/2371/BC/03/133 Correspondence 1890.

London Metropolitan Archive, Brooks's Club Archives, ACC/2371/BC/03/134 Correspondence 1891–1892.

London Metropolitan Archive, Brooks's Club Archives, ACC/2371/BC/03/148 Correspondence 1913–1914.

London Metropolitan Archive, Brooks's Club Archives, ACC/2371/ BC/04/077 Dinner Book 1881–1898.

London Metropolitan Archive, Brooks's Club Archives, ACC/2371/BC/ 04/078 Dinner Book 1898–1907.

London Metropolitan Archive, Brooks's Club Archives, ACC/2371/BC/ 04/079 Dinner Book 1907–1915.

London Metropolitan Archive, Brooks's Club Archives, ACC/2371/ BC/04/103 Club Rules 1822–1855.

London Metropolitan Archive, Brooks's Club Archives, ACC/2371/BC/ 04/106 Members remark book 1861–1880.

London Metropolitan Archive, Brooks's Club Archives, ACC/2371/BC/ 05/016 Standing Orders 1910–1914.

London Metropolitan Archive, Brooks's Club Archives, ACC/2371/BC/ 07/056 Plans of Club, Ground Floor and Larder 1903.

London Metropolitan Archive, Building Act Case Files. GLC/AR/BR/19.

London Metropolitan Archive, Fox's Club Archives, ACC/2371/FC/01/001 Candidates Proposed and Results 1841–1853.

London Metropolitan Archive, Fox's Club Archives, ACC/2371/FC/01/002 List of the Fox Club 1844–1855.

London Metropolitan Archive, Fox's Club Archives, ACC/2371/FC/01/003 Subscription Book 1851–1860.

London Metropolitan Archive, Fox's Club Archives, ACC/2371/FC/01/004 Subscription Book 1877–1937.

London Metropolitan Archive, Fox's Club Archives, ACC/2371/FC/01/008 List of Members and Accounts 1843–1871.

London Metropolitan Archive, Fox's Club Archives, ACC/2371/ FC/01/009 Members Dinner Menus.

London Metropolitan Archive, Fox's Club Archives, ACC/2371/FC/03/001 General Correspondence 1859–1952.

London Metropolitan Archive, Lyons and Co. Archives.

Maison Victor Hugo, Paris, Archives.

Reform Club, London, Archives.

Wellcome Trust Library for the History of Medicine. Elizabeth Pease and others, Collection of cookery, MS 3824.

Wellcome Trust Library for the History of Medicine. Hannah Sheppard, Collection of cookery receipts, MS 4520.

Wellcome Trust Library for the History of Medicine. Mrs M. H. Turnbull, Collection of culinarym household and medicinal remedies. MS 5853.

Wellcome Trust Library for the History of Medicine. Charlotte Hobhouse, medical recipe book, MS 6826.

Wellcome Trust Library for the History of Medicine. Lady Julia Lockwood and others, Collection of medical, cookery and household receipts, MS 3318.

Wellcome Trust Library for the History of Medicine. Mrs L. N. White and others, Collection of medical cookery and other receipts. MS 4995.
Wellcome Trust Library for the History of Medicine. Mary Susan Selby Lowndes, Medical receipt book MS 3339.
Wellcome Trust Library for the History of Medicine, Sarah Alice Ede, Collection of cookery receipts MS 2280.

Secondary sources

Abelson, E. *When Ladies Go A-Thieving: Middle Class Shoplifters and the Victorian Department Store* (Oxford: Oxford University Press, 1989).
Adams, A. *Architecture in the Family Way: Doctors, Houses and Women, 1870–1900* (Montreal: McGill-Queens University Press, 1996).
Adamson, J. (ed.). *The Princely Courts of Europe: Ritual, Politics and Culture under the Ancien Regime, 1500–1750* (London: Weidenfeld & Nicolson, 1999).
Agulon, M. *Le Cercle dans la vie bourgeoise* (Paris: A. Colin, 1977).
Albala, K. *Eating Right in the Renaissance* (Berkeley: University of California Press, 2002).
Allen, R. I. *The Clubs of Augustan London* (London: Harvard University Press, 1966).
Andrieu, P. *Fine Bouche: A History of the Restaurant in France*, trans A. L. Hayward (London: Cassell & Co., 1956).
Ariès, P. *Centuries of Childhood*, trans. Robert Baldrick (London: Cape, 1962).
Ariès, P.and G. Duby (eds). *A History of Private Life. Vol. 4: From the Fires of Revolution to the Great War* (London: Belknap Press, 1990).
Armstrong, N. and L. Tennenhouse (eds). *The Ideology of Conduct: Essays in Literature and the History of Sexuality* (London: Methuen, 1987).
Aron, J.-P. *The Art of Eating in France: Manners and Menus in the Nineteenth Century*, trans. Nina Rootes (London: Owen, 1975).
Attar, D. *A Bibliography of Household Books Published in Britain, 1800–1914* (London: Prospect, 1987).
Auslander, L. *Taste and Power: Furnishing Modern France* (Berkeley: University of California Press, 1996).
Baldrick, R. *Dinner at Magny's* (Harmondsworth: Penguin, 1973).
Barker-Benfield, G. J. *The Culture of Sensibility: Sex and Society in Eighteenth-Century Britain* (London: University of Chicago Press, 1992).
Barry, J. and C. Brooks (eds). *The Middling Sort of People: Culture, Society and Politics in England, 1500–1800* (Basingstoke: Macmillan, 1994).
Barthes, R. 'Towards a Psychosociology of Contemporary Consumption'. in E. and R. Forster (eds), *European Diet from Pre-Industrial to Modern Times* (New York: Harper Torchbooks, 1975).

Beardsworth, A. and T. Keil. *Sociology on the Menu: An Invitation to the Study of Food and Society* (London: Routledge, 1997).

Bell, D. and G. Valentine. *Consuming Geographies: We are Where we Eat* (London: Routledge, 1997).

Bell, R. M. *Holy Anorexia* (Chicago: Chicago University Press, 1985).

Benson, J. *The Rise of Consumer Society in Britain, 1880–1980* (London: Longman, 1994).

Best, G. *Mid-Victorian Britain, 1851–75* (London: Fontana Press, 1979) p. 25.

Biasin, G.-P. *The Flavours of Modernity: Food and the Novel* (Princeton: Princeton University Press, 1991).

Bickham, T. 'Eating the Empire: Intersections of Food, Cookery and Imperialism in Eighteenth-Century Britain', *Past & Present* 198:1 (2008) 71–109.

Blackbourn, D. and R. J. Evans (eds). *The German Bourgeoisie* (London: Routledge, 1991).

Blumin, S. M. 'The Hypothesis of Middle-Class Formation in Nineteenth-Century America: A Critique and Some Proposals', *The American Historical Review* 90:2 (1985) 299–338.

Bourdieu, P. *Distinction: A Social Critique of the Judgement of Taste*, trans. R. Nice (London: Harvard University Press, 1984).

Bourgeat, J. *Les Plaisires de la table en France des gaulous à nos jours* (Paris: Hachette, 1963).

Boutaud, J.-J. (ed.). *L'Imaginare de la table: convivialité, commensalité et communication* (Paris: L'Harmattan, 2004).

Bouton, C. A. *The Flour War: Gender, Class and Community in Late Ancien Régime French Society* (Pennsylvania: Pennsylvania State University Press, 1993).

Bowlby, R. *Carried Away: The Invention of Modern Shopping* (New York: Columbia University Press, 2001).

Branca, P. *Silent Sisterhood: Middle-Class Women in the Victorian Home* (London: Croom Helm, 1975).

Breward, C. *The Hidden Consumer: Masculinities, Fashion and City Life 1860–1914* (Manchester: Manchester University Press, 1999).

Brewer, J. and R. Porter (eds). *Consumption and the World of Goods* (London: Routledge, 1993).

Briggs, A. *Victorian Things* (London: Chicago University Press, 1988).

Bruegel, M. and B. Laurioux (eds). *Histoire et identiés alimentaires en Enrope* (Paris: Hachette, 2002).

Brumberg, J. J. *Fasting Girls: the Emergence of Anorexia Nervosa as a Modern Disease* (London: Harvard University Press, 1988).

Bryson, A. *From Courtesy to Civility: Changing Codes of Conduct in Early Modern England* (Oxford: Oxford University Press, 1998).

Burnett, J. *England Eats Out: A Social History of Eating Out in England from 1830 to the Present* (London: Pearson, 2004).

Burnett, J. *Plenty and Want: A Social History of Diet in England from 1815 to the Present Day* (London: Nelson, 1966).

Brown, J. W. *Fictional Meals and their Function in the French Novel, 1789–1848* (London: University of Toronto Press, 1984).

Camporesi, P. *The Magic Harvest: Food, Folklore and Society*, trans. J. K. Hall (Cambridge: Polity Press, 1993).

Certeau, M. de, L. Giard and P. Mayol. *The Practice of Everyday Life Vol II: Living and Cooking*, trans. Timothy J. Tomasik (London: University of California Press, 1988).

Charles, N. and M. Kerr. *Women, Food and Families* (Manchester: Manchester University Press, 1988).

Châtelet, N. *A Table!* (Paris: Edition du May, 1992).

Châtelet, N. *Le corps à corps culinaire* (Paris: Edition du Seuil, 1977).

Chelminski, R. *The French at Table: Why the French know how to eat better than any people on earth and how they have gone about it, from the Gauls to Bocuse* (New York: William Morrow & Co., 1985).

Cherbonneau, B. *Un Festin pour Tantale: nourriture et société industrielle* (Paris: Sang de la Terre, 1997).

Chernin, K. *Womansize: The Tyranny of Slenderness* (London: Women's Press, 1983).

Clarke, P. *British Clubs and Associations 1580–1800: The Origins of an Associational World* (Oxford: Oxford University Press, 2000).

Counihan, C. M. *The Anthropology of Food and Body: Gender, Meaning and Power* (London: Routledge, 1999).

Counihan, C. and P. Van Esterik. *Food and Culture: A Reader* (London: Routledge, 1997).

Courtine, R. *Géographie gourmande de Paris* (Marseille: Edition Jeanne Lafitte, 1983).

Courtine, R. *Le Ventre de Paris: de la Bastille à l'Etoile . . . de siècles d'appétit* (Paris: Libraire Académique Perrin, 1985).

Courtine, R. *La Vie parisienne: cafés et restaurants des boulevards, 1814–1914* (Paris: Libraire Académique Perrin, 1984).

Coveney, J. *Food, Morals and Meaning: The Pleasure and Anxiety of Eating* (London: Routledge, 2000).

Cowan, B. 'What was Masculine about the Public Sphere? Gender and the Coffeehouse Milieu in Post-Restoration London', *History Workshop Journal* 51 (2001) 127–48.

Cressy, D. *Birth, Marriage, and Death: Ritual, Religion, and the Life-cycle in Tudor and Stuart England* (Oxford: Oxford University Press, 1997).

Crisp, A. 'Ambivalence towards Fatness and it Origins', *British Medical Journal* 315 (1997) 1703.

Crossick, G. and H.-G. Haupt. *The Petite Bourgeoisie in Europe 1780–1914: Enterprise, Family and Independence* (London: Routledge, 1995).

Crossick, G. and S. Jaumain (eds). *Cathedrals of Consumption: the European Department Store, 1850–1939* (Aldershot: Ashgate, 1998).

Curtin, Michael. 'A Question of Manners: Status and Gender in Etiquette and Courtesy', *Journal of Modern History* 57 (1985) 61–81.

Daumard, Adeline. *La Bourgeoisie Parisienne de 1815 à 1848* (Paris: SEVPEN, 1963).

Daumard, A. *Les Bourgeois et la bourgeoise en France depuis 1815* (Paris: Flammarion, 1991).

Davidoff, Leonore *The Best Circles* (London: Croom Helm, 1973).

Davidoff, Leonore and Catherine Hall. *Family Fortunes: Men and Women of the English Middle Class 1780–1850* (London: Hutchinson, 1988).

Davidson, Denise Z. *France after Revolution: Urban Life, Gender and the New Social Order* (London: Harvard University Press, 2007).

Davin, Anna. *Growing Up Poor: Home, School and Street in London, 1870–1914* (London: Rivers Oram Press, 1996).

Denvir, Bernard, *The Late Victorians: Art, Design and Society, 1852–1910* (Harlow: Longman, 1986).

Diprose, Rosalyn. *The Bodies of Women: Ethics, Embodiement and Sexual Difference* (London: Routledge, 1994).

Dixon, Roger and Stefan Muthesius, *Victorian Architecture* (London: Thames & Hudson 1978).

Donald, M. 'Tranquil Havens? Critiquing the Idea of Home as the Middle-Class Sanctuary', in I. Bryden and J. Floyd (eds), *Domestic Space: Reading the Nineteenth-Century Interior* (Manchester: Manchester University Press, 1999).

Döring, T. M. Heide and S. Mühleisen. *Eating Culture: The Poetics and Politics of Food* (Heidelberg: C. Winter, 2003).

Douglas, M. 'Deciphering a Meal', *Daedalus* 101 (1972) 61–81.

Douglas, M. *Purity and Danger: An Analysis of the Concepts of Pollution and Taboo* (London, Routledge & Kegan Paul, 1966).

Drummond, J. C. and A. Wilbraham. *The Englishman's Food: Five Centuries of English Diet* (London: Pimlico, 1991).

Earle, P. *The Making of the English Middle Class* (London: Methuen, 1989).

Ehrenreich, B. and D. English. *For Her Own Good: 150 Years of Experts' Advice to Women* (Garden City, NY: Anchor Books, 1978).

Ehrman, E. '19th Century', in *London Eats Out: 500 Years of Capital Dining* (London, 1999).

Eleb-Vidal, M. *Architecture de la vie privée [1]: maisons et mentalités XVIIè–XIXè siècle* (Bruxelles: Archives d'architecture moderne, 1989).

Eleb-Vidal, M. et A. Debarre. *L'Invention de l'habitation moderne: Paris 1880–1914: Architecture de la vie privée* (Paris: Hazan, 1995).

Elias, N. *The Civilizing Process: The History of Manners*, trans. E. Jephcott (Oxford: Blackwell, 1994).

Ennès, P., P. Thiebaut and G. Mabille. *Histoire de la table: les arts de la table des origines à nos jours* (Paris: Flammarion, 1994).

Evans, R. J. 'Family and Class in the Hamburg grand bourgeoisie 1815–1914', in D. Blackburn and R. J. Evans, *The German Bourgeoisie* (London: Routledge, 1991).

Evans Braziel, J. and K. LeBesco (eds). *Bodies out of Bounds: Fatness and Transgression* (Berkeley: University of California Press, 2001).

Farb, P. and G. Armelagos. *Consuming Passions: The Anthropology of Eating* (Boston: Houghton Mifflin, 1980).

Faucheux, M. *Fêtes de table* (Paris: P Lebaud, 1997).

Faure, Olivier, *Les Français et leur médecine au XIXe siècle* (Paris: Belin, 1993).

Featherstone, Mike. 'Body in Consumer Culture', *Theory, Culture and Society* 1:2 (1982) 18–32.

Featherstone, Mike, M. Hepworth and B. S. Turner (eds). *The Body: Social Processes and Cultural Theory* (London: Sage, 1991).

Fenton, Alexander and Ester Kisban (eds). *Food in Change: Eating Habits from the Middle Ages to the Present Day* (Edinburgh: John Donald, 1986).

Feild, Rachael. *Irons in the Fire: A History of Cooking Equipment* (Ramsbury, Wiltshire: Crowood Press, 1984).

Finklestein, Joanna. *Dining Out: A Sociology of Modern Manners* (Cambridge: Polity Press, 1989).

Finn, Margot. 'Sex in the City: Metropolitan Modernities in English History', *Victorian Studies* 44:1 (2001) 26–32.

Forth, Christopher and Ana Carden-Coyne (eds). *Cultures of the Abdomen: Diet, Digestion and Fat in the Modern World* (New York: Palgrave Macmillan, 2004).

Freeman, Sarah. *Mutton and Oysters: The Victorians and their Food* (London: Victor Gollancz, 1989).

Frykman, Jonas and Orvar Löfgren. *Culture Builders: A Historical Anthropology of Middle-Class Life* trans. Alan Crozier (London: Rutgers University Press, 1987).

Garrison, Fielding H. 'Medicine in the *Tatler*, *Spectator* and *Guardian*', *Bulletin of the History of Medicine* II (1934) 477–503.

Gay, Peter. *The Bourgeois Experience: Victoria to Freud, Vol. II The Tender Passion* (Oxford: Oxford University Press, 19860.

Geisser, Catherine and Derek Oddy (eds). *Food, Diet and Economic Change Past and Present* (Leicester: Leicester University Press, 1993).

Gillet, Philippe. *Soyons français à table!: petit manuel de la civilité nouvelle* (Paris: Edition Payot et Rivages, 1994).

Gillis, John R. *A World of their Own Making: Myth, Ritual and the Quest for Family Values* (New York: Basic Books, 1996).

Girard, A. R. 'Le Triomph de "La Cuisinière bourgeoise": Livres culinaires, cuisine et société en France aux XVIIe et XVIIIe siècles', *Revue d'Histoire moderne et contemporaine* 24 (1977) 497–523.

Glants, Musya and Joyce Toomre. *Food in Russian History and Culture* (Bloomington: Indiana University Press, 1997).

Goffman, Erving. *The Presentation of Self in Everyday Life* (Harmondsworth: Penguin, 1974).

Goody, Jack. *Cooking, Cuisine and Class* (Cambridge: Cambridge University Press, 1982).

Gottschalk, Alfred. *Histoire de l'alimentation et de la gastronomie, depuis la préhistoire jusqu'à nos jours*, 2 vols (Paris: Editions Hippocrate, 1948).

Grazia, Victoria de and E. Furlough (eds). *The Sex of Things: Gender and Consumption in Historical Perspective* (London: University of California Press, 1996).

Gunn, S. *The Public Culture of the Victorian Middle Class. Ritual and Authority in the English Industrial City 1840–1914* (Manchester: Manchester University Press, 2000).

Gunn, S. and R. J. Morris (eds). *Identities in Space: Contested Terrains in the Western City since 1850* (Aldershot: Ashgate, 2001).

Gutton, J. P. *Domestique et serviteurs dans la France de l'ancien régime* (Paris: Aubier Montaigne, 1981).

Guy, C. *La Vie quotidienne de la société gourmande au XIXe siècle* (Paris: Hachette, 1971).

Hall, C. *White, Male and Middle Class: Explorations in Feminism and History* (Cambridge: Routledge, 1992).

Harrison, C. E. *The Bourgeois Citizen in Nineteenth-Century France: Gender, Sociability and the Uses of Emulation* (Oxford: Oxford University Press, 1999).

Harvey, D. *Paris: Capital of Modernity* (London: Routledge, 2006).

Heilbronner, O. 'The German Bourgeois Club as a Political and Social Structure in the Late Nineteenth and Early Twentieth Centuries', *Continuity and Change* 13:3 (1998) 443–73.

Helmlow, J. 'Fanny Burney and the Courtesy Books', *PMLA* 65 (1950) 732–61.

Hemphill, C. D. *Bowing to Necessities: A History of Manners in America, 1620–1860* (Oxford: Oxford University Press, 1999).

Henson, L. '"Half Believing, Half Incredulous": Elizabeth Gaskell, Superstition and the Victorian Mind', *Nineteenth-Century Contexts* 24:3 (2002) 251–69.

Higonnet, P. *Paris: Capital of the World*, trans. A Goldhammer (London: Harvard University Press, 2002).

Higgs, E. *Domestic Servants and Households in Rochdale 1851–1871* (London: Garland, 1986).

Hindle, S. 'The Growth of Social Stability in Restoration England', *European Legacy* 5:4 (2000) 563–76.

Hoffman, S-L. 'Civility, Male Friendship and Masonic Sociability in Nineteenth-Century Germany', *Gender & History* 13:2 (2001) 224–48.

Houston, Gail Turley. *Consuming Fictions: Gender, Class and Hunger in Dickens's Novels* (Carbondale: Southern Illinois University Press, 1994).

Hunt, M. R. *The Middling Sort: Commerce, Gender, and the Family in England, 1680–1780* (Berkeley: University of California Press, 1996).

Kamminga, H. and A. Cunningham. *The Science and Culture of Nutrition, 1840–1940* (Amsterdam: Rodopi, 1995).

Kelly, C. *Refining Russia: Advice Literature, Polite Culture, and Gender from Catherine to Yeltsin* (Oxford: Oxford University Press, 2001).

Kidd, A. and D. Nicholls. *Gender, Civic Culture and Consumerism: Middle-Class Identity in Britain 1800–1940* (Manchester: Manchester University Press, 1999).

King, H. *The Disease of Virgins: Greensickness, Chlorosis and the Problems of Puberty* (London: Routledge, 2004).

Kocka, J. 'The Middle Classes in Europe', *The Journal of Modern History* 67:4 (1995) 783–806.

Kocka, J. and A. Mitchell (eds). *Bourgeois Society in Nineteenth Century Europe* (Oxford: Berg, 1993).

Koshar, R. (ed.). *History of Leisure* (Oxford: Berg, 2002).

Kuchta, D. *The Three-Piece Suit and Modern Masculinity: England, 1550–1850* (London: University of California Press, 2002).

Lane, M. *Jane Austen and Food*. London: Hambledon Press, 1995.

Lange, F. *Manger, ou les jeux et les creux du plat* (Paris, Editions du Seuil, 1975).

Lawrence, C. J. 'William Buchan: Medicine Laid Bare', *Medical History* 19 (1975) 20–35.

Lees-Maffei, G. 'From Service to Self-Service: Advice Literature as Design Discourse, 1920–1970', *Journal of Design History* 14:3 (2001) 187–206.

Lévi-Strauss, C. *The Origin of Table Manners* (New York: Harper & Row, 1978).

Lewis, J. ed. *Labour and Love: Women's Experience of Home and Family, 1850–1940*. Oxford: Blackwell, 1986.

Long, H. *The Edwardian House: The Middle-Class Home in Britain, 1880–1914* (Manchester: Manchester University Press, 1993).

Loudon, I. 'The Disease called Chlorosis', *Psychological Medicine* 14 (1984) 27–66.

MacBeth, H. (ed.). *Food Preferences and Tastes: Continuity and Change* (Oxford: Barghahn Books, 1997).

MacKaman, D. *Leisure Settings: Bourgeois Culture, Medicine and the Spa in Modern France* (Chicago: Chicago University Press, 1998).

MacLeod, D. S. *Art and the Victorian Middle Class: Money and the Making of Identity* (Cambridge: Cambridge University Press, 1996).

Marcus, S. *Apartment Stories: City and Home in Nineteenth-Century London and Paris* (London, University of California Press, 1999).

Marenco, C. *Manière de table, modèle de moeurs: 17e–20e siècles* (Cachan: Edition de l'ENS-Cachan, 1992).

Margadant, T. W. 'Primary Schools and Youth Groups in Pre-War Paris: Les "Petits A's" ', *History Journal of Contemporary History* 13:2 (1978) 323–36.

Martin-Fugier, A. *La Bourgeoise: femme au temps de Paul Bourget* (Paris: B. Grasset, 1983).

Mayer, A. J. 'The Lower Middle Class as Historical Problem.' *The Journal of Modern History* 47:3 (1975) 409–36.

McKendrick, N., J. Brewer and J. H. Plumb. *The Birth of a Consumer Society: The Commercialisation of Eighteenth-Century England* (London: Europa, 1982).

Mennell, S. *All Manners of Food: Eating and Taste in England and France from the Middle Ages to the Present* (Oxford: Blackwell, 1985).

Merchant, C. *The Death of Nature: Women, Ecology and the Scientific Revolution* (New York: HarperCollins, 1980).

Milne-Smith, A. 'A Flight to Domesticity? Making a Home in the Gentlemen's Clubs of London, 1880–1914', *Journal of British Studies* 45 (2006) 796–818.

Mintz, S. W. *Sweetness and Power: The Place of Sugar in Modern History* (Harmondsworth: Penguin, 1986).

Mintz, S. W. *Tasting Food, Tasting Freedom: Excursions into Eating, Culture and the Past* (Boston: Beacon Press, 1996).

Mitchell, B. R. *European Historical Statistics 1750–1975* (London: Macmillan, 1981) pp. 35, 79.

Montanari, M. *The Culture of Food*, trans. Carl Ipsen (Oxford: Blackwell, 1994).

Morales, E. *The Guinea Pig: Healing, Food, and Ritual in the Andes* (Tucson: University of Arizona Press, 1995).

Morgan, M. *National Identities and Travel in Victorian Britain* (Basingstoke: Palgrave, 2001).

Morris, R. J. *Class Sect and Party: The Making of the British Middle Class, Leeds, 1820–1950* (Manchester: Manchester University Press, 1990).

Moulin, L. *Les Liturgies de la table: une histoire culturelle du manger et du boire* (Anvers: Fonds Mercator, 1989).

Muir, E. *Ritual in Early Modern Europe* (Cambridge: Cambridge University Press, 1997).

Nead, L. *Victorian Babylon: People, Streets and Images in Nineteenth-Century London* (London: Yale University Press, 2005).

Nenadic, S. 'Businessmen, the Urban Middle Classes, and the "Dominance" of Manufacturers in Nineteenth-Century Britain', *The Economic History Review*, New Series, 44:1 (1991) 66–85.

Nenadic, S. 'Middle-Rank Consumers and Domestic Culture in Edinburgh and Glasgow 1720–1840', *Past and Present* 145 (1994) 122–56.

Neuman, R. 'French Domestic Architecture in the Early 18th Century: The Town Houses of Robert de Cotte', *The Journal of the Society of Architectural Historians*, 39:2 (1980) 128–44.

Neuschel, Kristen B. 'Noble Households in the Sixteenth Century: Material Settings and Human Communities.' *French Historical Studies* 15:4 (1988) 595–622.

Nicholls, David. 'The English Middle Class and the Ideological Significance of Radicalism, 1760–1886', *The Journal of British Studies* 24:4 (1985) 415–33.

Nicholson, Shirley. *A Victorian Household* (London: Barrie and Jenkins, 1988).

Nord, Philip. *The Republican Moment: Struggles for Democracy in Nineteenth-Century France* (London: Harvard University Press, 1995).

Oberlé, Gérard. *Les fastes de Bacchus et de Comus ou histoire de boire et de manger: en Europe, de l'antiquité à nos jours, à travers les livre* (Paris: Belfond, 1989).

Oddy, Derek and Derek Miller (eds). *Diet and Health in Modern Britain* (London: Croom Helm, 1985).

Oddy, Derek and Derek Miller (eds). *The Making of the Modern British Diet* (London: Croom Helm, 1976).

Oliver, Raymond. *The French at Table* (London: Wine and Food Society, 1967).

Pennell, S. 'The Material Culture of Food in Early Modern England, *c.*1650–1750', Oxford, DPhil thesis, 1997.

Perrot, Michelle (ed.). *A History of Private Life. Vol. IV. From the Fires of Revolution to the Great War*, trans. A. Goldhammer (London: Belknap Press, 1990).

Perrot, Philippe. *Fashioning the Bourgeoisie: A History of Clothing in the Nineteenth Century* (Princeton: Princeton University Press, 1994).

Peterson, Sarah T. *Acquired Taste: The French Origins of Modern Cooking* (London: Cornell University Press, 1994).

Pilbeam, Pamela. *The Middle Classes in Europe 1789–1914: France, Germany, Italy, Russia* (Basingstoke: Macmillan, 1990).

Pimlott, J. A. R. *The Englishman's Holiday: A Social History* (Hassocks: Harvester Press, 1976).

Pitte, Jean-Robert, *Gastronomie française: histoire et géographie d'une passion* (Paris: Fayard, 1991).

Ponsonby, M. 'Ideal, Reality and Meaning: Homemaking in England in the First Half of the Nineteenth Century', *Journal of Design History* 16:3 (2003) 201–14.

Porter, R. *Doctor and Society: Thomas Beddoes and the Sick Trade in Late-Enlightenment England* (London: Routledge, 1992).

Porter, R. (ed.). *Patients and Practitioners: Lay Perceptions of Medicine in Pre-Industrial Society* (Cambridge: Cambridge University Press, 1985).

Porter, R. and M. Mulvey (eds). *Pleasure in the Eighteenth Century* (Basingstoke: Macmillan, 1996).

Rappaport, E. *Shopping for Pleasure: Women in the Making of London's West End* (Oxford: Princeton University Press, 2000).

Reed, C. (ed.). *Not at Home: The Suppression of Domesticity in Modern Art and Architecture* (London: Thames & Hudson, 1996).

Rendell, J. 'The Clubs of St. James's: Places of Public Patriarchy – exclusivity, domesticity and secrecy', *The Journal of Architecture*, 4:2 (1999) 167–89.

Revel, J.-F. *Un Festin en paroles: histoire littéraire de la sensibilité gastronomique* (Paris: Pauvert, 1979).

Rich, R. 'Designing the Dinner Party: Advice on Dining and Décor in London and Paris, 1860–1914', *Journal of Design History*, 16:1 (2003) 49–61.

Ridgway, E. S. 'John Elliotson (1791–1868): A Bitter Enemy of Legitimate Medicine? Part 1: Earlier Years and the Introduction to Mesmerism', *Journal of Medical Biography* 1:4 (1993) 191–8.

Rogers, B. *Beef and Liberty: Roast Beef, John Bull and the English Patriots* (London, Chatto & Windus, 2003).

Rosenberg, C. E. 'Medical Text and Social Context: Explaining William Buchan's *Domestic Medicine*', *Bulletin of the History of Medicine* 57 (1983) 22–42.

Ross, E. *Love and Toil: Motherhood in Outcast London, 1870–1918* (New York: Oxford University Press, 1993).

Rotberg, R. I. and T. K. Rabb (eds). *Hunger and History: The Impact of Changing Food Production and Consumption Patterns on Society* (Cambridge, Cambridge University Press, 1985).

Salaman, R. N. *The History and Social Influence of the Potato: with a Chapter on Industrial Uses by W. G. Burton* (Cambridge: Cambridge University Press, 1949, revised edn 1985).

Satkowski, L. 'The Palazzo Pitti: Planning and Use in the Grand-Ducal Era', *The Journal of the Society of Architectural Historians* 42:4 (1983).

Scapp, R. and B. Seitz (eds). *Eating Culture*, Albany NY: SUNY Press, 1998.

Schivelbusch, W. *Disenchanted Night: The Industrialisation of Light in the Nineteenth Century*, trans. A Davies (London: University of California Press, 1995).

Scholliers, P. 'Culture et élite: les restaurants bruxellois de la belle époque', *Les cahiers de la fonderie* 18 (1995) 48–55.

Scholliers, P. (ed.). *Food, Drink and Identity: Cooking, Eating and Drinking in Europe since the Middle Ages* (Oxford: Berg, 2001).

Sennett, R. *The Fall of Public Man* (New York: Knopf, 1977).

Siegel, J. *Bohemian Paris: Culture, Politics and the Boundaries of Bourgeois Life, 1830–1930* (London: Johns Hopkins University Press, 1986).

Simmons, J. 'The Victorian Hotel'. The Sixth H. J. Dyos Memorial Lecture, 15 May 1984, Victorian Studies Centre, University of Leicester.

Sinha, M. 'Britishness, Clubbability, and the Colonial Public Sphere: The Genealogy of an Imperial Institution in Colonial India', *Journal of British Studies* 40:4 (2001) 489–521.

Sjögren- De Beauchaine, A. *The Bourgeoisie in the Dining-Room: Meal Ritual and Cultural Process in Parisian Families of Today* (Stockholm: Stockholm Universitet, 1988).

Smith, B. *Ladies of the Leisure Class: The Bourgeoises of Northern France in the Nineteenth Century* (Princeton: Princeton University Press, 1981).

Smith, L. 'Women's Health Care in England and France, 1650–1775', University of Essex, PhD Thesis, 2001.

Smith, L. W. 'Imagining Women's Fertility before Technology', *Journal of Medical Humanities* 31:1 (2010), 69–79.

Spang, R. *The Invention of the Restaurant: Paris and Modern Gastronomic Culture* (London: Harvard University Press, 2000).

St. George, A. *The Descent of Manners: Etiquette, Rules and the Victorians* (London: Random House, 1993).

Stearns, P. N. 'The Middle Class: Toward a Precise Definition', *Comparative Studies in Society and History* 21:3 (1979) 377–96.

Stine, J. 'Opening Closets: The Discovery of Household Medicine in Early Modern England', Stanford University, PhD dissertation, 1996.

Sussman, G. D. *Selling Mothers's Milk: The Wet-Nursing Business in France, 1715–1914* (Urbana: University of Illinois Press, 1982).

Tannahill, R. *Food in History* (New York: Three Rivers Press, 1988).

Teutberg, H. J. (ed.). *European Food History: A Research Review* (Leicester: Leicester University Press, 1992).

Thorne, R. 'Places of Refreshment in the Nineteenth-Century City.' in *Buildings and Society: Essays on the social development of the Built Environment*, ed. Anthony D. King (London: Routledge & Kegan Paul, 1980).

Tiersten, L. *Marianne in the Market: Envisioning Consumer Society in Fin-de-Siècle France* (Berkeley: University of California Press, 2001).

Tiersten, L. 'Redefining Consumer Culture: Recent Literature on Consumption and the Bourgeoisie in Western Europe', *Radical History Review* 57 (1993) 116–59.

Tosh, J. *A Man's Place: Masculinity and the Middle-Class Home in Victorian England* (London: Yale University Press, 1999).

Toussaint-Samat, M. *History of Food*, trans. Anthea Bell (Oxford: Blackwell, 1992).

Trentman, F. 'Gentleman and Players: The Leisure of British Modernity', *Contemporary Record* 7:3 (1993).

Trubek, A. B. *Haute Cuisine: How the French Invented the Culinary Profession* (Philadelphia: University if Pennsylvania Press, 2000).

Turner, V. W. *The Ritual Process: Structure and Anti-Structure* (London: Routledge & Kegan Paul, 1969).

Vandereychen, W. and R. van Deth. *From Fasting Saints to Anorexic Girls* (New York: New York University Press, 1994).

Vernon, J. *Hunger: A Modern History* (London: Harvard University Press, 2007).

Vicaire, G. *Bibliographia gastronomica: une bibliographie de la gastronomie et des sujets relatifs depuis le commencement de l'imprimerie à 1890* (London: Derek Verschoyle Academic & Bibliographical Publications, 1954).

Vickery, A. 'Golden Age to Separate Spheres? A Review of the Categories and Chronology of English Women's History', *Historical Journal* 36:2 (1993) 383–414.

Visser, M. *The Rituals of Dinner: The Origins, Evolution, Eccentricities and the Meaning of Table Manners* (London: Penguin, 1992).

Walker Bynum, C. *Holy Feast and Holy Fast: The Religious Significance of Food to Medieval Women* (London: University of California Press, 1987).

Walkowitz, J. 'Going Public: Shopping, Street Harassment and Street-walking in Late Victorian London', *Representations* 0:62 (1998).

Walter, J. and R. Schofield (eds). *Famine, Disease and the Social Order in Early Modern Society* (Cambridge: Cambridge University Press, 1989).

Warde, A. and L. Martens. *Eating Out: Social Differentiation, Consumption and Pleasur* (Cambridge: Cambridge University Press, 2000).

Wiessner, P. and W. Schiffenhövel (eds). *Food and the Status Quest* (Oxford: Berghahn Books, 1996).

Wilson, C. A. ed. *Food for the Community: Special Diets for Special Groups* (Edinburgh: Edinburgh University Press, 1993).

Wilson, S. *The Magical Universe: Everyday Ritual and Magic in Premodern Europe* (London: Hambledon and London, 2000).

Wood, R. C. *The Sociology of the Meal* (Edinburgh: Edinburgh University Press, 1995).

Young, G. M. (ed.). *Early Victorian England, 1830–1865* (London: Oxford University Press, 1934).

Index

abstemiousness 25
abstinence 37–8
advertisements 125
advice literature 24–6, 64, 68, 147, 163
  historical approaches to 29–30
  success of 28
à la carte 135–6
à la française 102, 104, 156, 208
à la russe 102, 111, 156, 208
Alq, Mme Louise D' 47–8, 68
anorexia nervosa 13, 33, 38
  and greensickness 37
  and medieval fasting girls 14, 37
appetite 10
architectural advice 25, 30, 46–8
aristocracy
  and club membership 173
  emulation of 12, 28, 31, 139
L'Art culinaire 88, 165

banquets 16, 102, 188–90, 208
  menu composition for 191–6
  presence of women at 196, 200
  see also civic banquets; political banquets; private banquets
Banting, William 35–6
  Letter on Corpulency 35
Bassanville, Comtesse de 29, 75, 106
Beale, Sophia 121–2, 144, 196–7
beef 43, 155, 157
Beeton, Mrs Isabella 34, 47, 68, 75, 81, 87, 102–4

Book of Household Management 61, 89
Bennett, Arnold 32, 87–8, 143, 198
Bignon, Chez 148
Bloom, Ursula 6, 32, 39, 69–70, 100
  mother's knowledge of cooking 83–4
body as machine 45
bouillon 145, 152, 154
  Duval 153–4
bourgeoisie
  and club membership 173–4
  as transnational class 1, 7, 26, 211
  boundaries of 11–12
  food choices of 207–8
Brame, Caroline 124, 144
brasserie 152
breastfeeding 41, 82
Brébant, Chez 148, 190
Brooks's Club 175–6, 178–81, 183, 186–7, 199

cabinets particulier 138
café 145
Café Procope 148
Café Riche 145
Caterer, The 29, 79, 157
cercles 173–5, 178, 190, 208
  membership procedure 177
Cercle des Beaux Arts 177
Cercle Littéraire et Artistique 177

Champs-Elysées 7, 144
Chatillon-Plessis 46, 89
Chavette, Eugene 165
chefs
    professionalisation of 135, 147
Cheshire Cheese, The 156
Cheyne, George 34
childhood 62–3
    and dinner 76
    and nursery 41
    and infant food 41, 82
    education of at mealtimes 64,
        208
    food for 41
chophouses 145, 149, 155
civic banquets 173, 194–6, 209
Claudin, Gustave 145, 183
clothing 11, 75
clubs 173–5, 208
    and backed bills 186
    and masculinity 175
    and receiving guests 179–81
    and vice 174
    as alternative to domestic sphere
        174, 183–4
    see also domesticity and clubs
    membership in 172
    see also women and club
        membership
    membership procedure 176
    payment of fees 177–8
    separation of space within 179,
        184–5
    timekeeping in 184
    women as guests in 199
coffeehouses 155, 173
confectioners' shops 157
conspicuous consumption 1, 13
consumption 7, 11
conversation 106, 111, 121–2
    topics harmful to digestion
        109–11
cookery books 61, 85
    see also manuscript cookbooks
corpulence 34
    see also obesity
crèmerie 145

Criterion, The 161–2
cultural capital 96, 101, 143
    see also display of

department stores 2, 13
desire 10
dessert 108
digestion 77
    theories of 45
digestive disorders 13, 44
    middle-class obsession with 32
dîners 182, 190–1
    see also dining clubs
    women at participants in 198
Dîner Magny 182–3, 190
dining clubs 182–3
dining room 100
    décor 69–70
    furniture 48–50
    gendering of 48, 50
display 113, 141, 162–3, 174
    of cultural capital 15, 136
domestic economy 28
    and women 67–8
domesticity 81–2, 89
    and clubs 178, 185
domestic sphere 174
    feminisation of 3, 164, 181

economy 1
embonpoint 35
    see also obesity
Escoffier, Auguste 1, 4, 135–6,
    155
etiquette books 24, 28
    see also advice literature
exhibition of 1867 (Paris)
    catering establishments for
        150–1

fashion 80
fathers
    as head of table 40, 63
formula milk 41–3
Franco-Prussian war 3
Frith, W. P. 63–5
Fox's dining club 182

gifts 109
  of food 83, 109
  handed out in restaurants 150
gluttony 1, 13, 25, 31–2, 33–5, 38
Goncourt Brothers 182–3, 191
  Goncourt, Edmond 2
Great Exhibition of 1851
      (London) 4, 150, 211
Gresham's Club 176
guests
  number of 102, 106
  role of 105, 109
  unexpected 125
guingettes 144
Gull, William 38

Hardman, Sir William 97–8, 122,
      182–3
haute cuisine 1, 7, 88, 135–6
homes
  as sanctuary 61
  compartmentalisation of 25,
      68–73
hosts
  role of 105–12, 139
  widows as 105
hotel restaurants 1, 135, 138–9,
      145, 150
Hotel Review 43, 200
Hughes, M. V. (Molly) 63, 74, 76,
      83, 125–6, 161–2, 212
  mother's knowledge of cooking
      84–5
Hugo, Victor 189
humoral system 39, 44

indulgence 37
industrialisation 45, 82, 150
  and food availability 4, 32
inns 142, 155
inventaires après décès 62, 70–2
invitations 97, 106
  received by George Montorgueil
      113–20
  self invitations 119–20

Jockey Club (Paris) 177–9

kitchen
  position within the home 46–8

Lady, The 143
Lasègue, Charles 38
leisure 11
  commercialisation of 2, 137,
      139
  eating as example of 3, 136
le Verrier, Lucille 75, 125
lighting 73, 74, 100, 135
Loftie, Mrs M. J. 50, 78–9, 100
L'Union (Paris) 177
Lyceum Club, The 196
Lyons & Co. 148
  corner houses 155, 212
  teahouses 154–5

maigreur
  see skinniness
manuscript cookbooks 44, 86
Marcé, Louis-Victor 38
meals of the day 74
  breakfast 74, 77
  déjeuner à la fourchette 78
  dinner
    courses of 107–8
  lunch 74, 77–8, 116
  petit déjeuner 78
  tea 74, 79, 115, 208
  supper 74, 76, 80, 177
mealtimes 73–80, 208
  in clubs 179
  in London restaurants 154–6
  in Paris restaurants 151–2
medical advice 25, 27, 28, 30, 32,
      44, 77
men
  as gourmets 165
  domestic role 81–2, 122–3
  knowledge of cookery 82, 89–90
  knowledge of wine 105, 107,
      111, 164
  looking after women at dinner
      33, 111
  see also restaurants and
      masculinity

menus 15, 102–4, 164–5, 209
    cards as souvenirs 82
    choosing of 81, 122–3, 139
    printed in restaurants 137
miasmic contagion 48
middle class
    boundary with working class 43
    gluttony of 31–2
    'rise' of 10
Mode de Paris, La 74
moderation 1, 13, 25, 31, 33
modernity 4, 6
    and loss of appetite 33
    and restaurants 142, 147, 150
    and speeding up of meals 6, 150
    bad diet as result of 32
Monselet, Charles 165–6
Montbourg, Emilie de 83
Montorgueil, George (pseud. of
        Octave Lebesque) 113–20,
        142

Newnham-Davies, Lieut.-Col N.
        156, 159, 164
nursing 40
    see also breastfeeding, wet
        nursing
nutritional advice 39

obesity 31, 34–6
occupation 39
    and nutritional needs 43
overeating 33, 37–8
    advice against 27
overindulgence 31

Pall Mall 7, 173
pastrycooks' shops 142, 157
performance 106, 136–7, 139–40,
        164, 172
political banquets 173, 188
portion size 152
Pot-au-feu, Le 41, 87, 103–4, 175
pregnancy 40, 82
prescriptive literature 12–13
    see also advice literature
Prince of Wales 135

privacy 46–7
prix fixe 135–6, 145, 152
punctuality 107, 114

Queen Victoria 78

Raymond, Mme Emmeline 107
recipes 83
Reform Club, The 175–6, 178,
        199
regimen 39, 45
remedies 83
respectability 26, 31, 34, 44, 69,
        74, 139–41, 172, 184
restaurants
    and masculinity 165–6
    foreign, in London 155
    invention of 136–7
    numbers of 154–6
    ordering food in 164–5
    separate tables in 137, 139, 164
    separation of space within 137
        see also cabinets particulier
    threat to domestic life 2, 62
    women in 137–8, 149, 157–61
ritual 61, 96, 99–100, 113
Ritz, Cesar 1, 4, 135
Ritz-Escoffier Partnership 2
Ritz Hotel 1
Rossetti, William Michael 65,
        120–1
Royal Family (British) 7, 80
    see also Prince of Wales; Queen
        Victoria

St James's (London) 7
Salle à Manger, La 6, 35, 68, 77,
        80, 81, 88, 157
Sandborn, Marion 101
Savoy Hotel 1, 135, 155, 159
self-control 29, 31, 34
separate spheres 10
servants 81, 83, 86–8, 95n93
    female cooks 87
    male chefs 87–9
Shaw, Donald ('One of the old
        Brigade') 144

siege of Paris 3
skinniness 37
social status 39, 142
sweet foods 81, 83, 157

table decorations 50–2
table d'hôte 145
taverns 142, 145, 149
thinness 34
timekeeping 13, 74–5, 87
Tortoni 7, 144
Tours, Constant de 144
Trocadero 148–9
  women as customers of
    160–1

undereating 33, 37–8

visiting 73–4

waiters and waitresses 154
Warren, Mrs Eliza 66–7, 68
Weiler, Amélie, 83, 212
West End 7, 174
wet nursing 41
Wey, Francis 76, 155

women
  advice against overeating 27, 80
  advice for keeping husbands
    happy 65–7
  and club membership 173–4,
    196–200
  and domestic work 81–2
  and shopping 143–4, 157, 174
  as nourishers 44, 81–2, 85
  as ornaments 111
  disgust towards when
    overweight 36–7
  food preferences of 157
  hosting dinner parties 50,
    60n146, 101, 130n51
  inability to appreciate fine food
    159
  knowledge of cookery 61–2,
    81–5, 116
  see also restaurants, women in

Yates, Edmund 69, 76, 123,
  142–3, 175, 183

Zola, Emile
  Au Bonheur des Dames 2